The Sword and the Rose

Tara Sufiana

Paperback: 978-1-966652-40-3
eBook: 978-1-966652-41-0
Library of Congress Control Number: 2025901742

Ordering Information:

Prime Seven Media
518 Landmann St.
Tomah City, WI 54660

Printed in the United States of America

This book is dedicated to the Sufis of Egypt, who shared their spiritual practices, their customs, their hearths and their hearts with me, revealing the beauty of universal Jove, which unites us all in the Great Heart.

MEDITERRANEAN
SEA
Alexandria
Tanta
CAIRO
Suez
SINAI
ISRAEL
Tel Aviv
Jerusalem
Dead
Sea
Rafah
Ein Hod
Beni Suef
al-Minya
Mallawi
el-Amarna
Bahariya
Farafra
Asyut
NILE
Western
Desert
Hurgada
Sefaga
Sohag
Luxor
RED
SEA
EGYPT
Aswan
High Dam

ONE

$\mathcal{M}$antled in thick powdery snow, the branches of the large fir trees rise and spread like white-feathered wings. The scene outside is a cold, beautiful, dark green and white alpine landscape—Such a contrast to the white-gold heat of Egypt, which have left a few weeks ago. Lying in a hospital in Samedan, Switzerland, a few kilometers from the chic wealth of St. Moritz, I hardly believe that I am here. My soul, still in Egypt, mesmerized by Sufi music and ecstatic celebrations, has not caught up with my body.

Several Swiss women share the room where I lie. Occasional words are exchanged in German. Although I understand a little, I do not make much of an effort to communicate. The other patients have visitors with which to chat. I am alone with my memories and feelings; my longing for El Arabi—my beloved, and the zealous path that I followed for five years in Egypt.

"Yella, Tahra!" I hear some dervish call me. ("Let's go, Tara.") This usually signaled moving on to another festival site or Sufi gathering, another vortex of fiery energy. My blood is accustomed to surging with excitement, my soul burning with passion for Allah, El Arabi and our family of dervishes.

I had forgotten the cold stillness of winter landscapes and quiet "civilized" people. Even the spectacular beauty of these Swiss Alps cannot wrench my heart and mind from the graveyards of Egypt, where my footsteps still echo on the tombs I have danced upon. Mystical experiences have been predominant in my life. Only the taste of salty tears sliding onto my lips and the stifled sobs restrained by my breath, remind me that my body is here.

The hospital is immaculate, the food nourishing, the doctors and nurses intelligent and caring; still they do not see who I am or begin to fathom the drama in which I was immersed for five years. They see a Swiss-American woman having her entire body checked out from head to toe, going from lab to lab for every sort of test, from one specialist to another. Scans reveal that the main problems lie in my intestines, ravaged by bilharzia and other microorganisms. A heavy bout of hepatitis did not help. In addition, one of my spinal discs dissolved along the way; my broken right elbow is not healing properly.

All these modern instruments and machines, amazing! So, this is the modern world! I feel like I have been propelled into a futuristic science fiction movie. Moreover, all this is happening only a three hour plane ride away from Cairo, where donkeys still pull wagons among the chaos of clogged traffic, and cripples propel themselves through the crowded streets of Cairo on sheets on cardboard.

My eyes have trouble adjusting to these fluorescent lights. Accustomed to rooms illuminated by one, or a few, lightbulbs, dark back alleys, and graveyards in Egypt, I never even thought to carry a flashlight. Within those dark spaces, I experienced so much light; not light produced by manufactured electricity, rather light that came from the hearts and souls of people focused on union with Allah.

The Swiss Social Services have already spent a month trying to awaken me to a more physical reality, such as the shopping trips, where djellabias were exchanged for sports clothes, and turbans for wool knit caps. A Swiss Swatch Watch was placed upon my wrist. I chose one with the type of numerals used in Egypt. To me they arc Arabic numerals, but actually, they are Indian. The numerals we use in the U.S.A. and Europe are Arabic.

The beautiful stone house where I live in Sils Maria is right next to a church. On top of the high steeple is a large clock that loudly chimes every fifteen minutes; on the hour it chimes the number of times of the hour, at fifteen minutes past the hour it chimes once, at half-past the hour it chimes twice, at forty-five minutes past the hour it chimes three times. The clock is just outside the upstairs living room window. If the chimes were not enough to remind me of time, all I have to do is glance through the window to see the large clock face staring at me. What a difference from the timeless space l experienced in Egypt. Damn that cockroach; no, damn the accident! The cockroach was innocent and lost its life when I slipped on it in the hallway of the Oxford Hotel in Cairo, falling on the hard marble floor and breaking my elbow.

Is the clock telling me it is time to get out and earn a living? All right. I will get out my guitar and sing as soon as my right elbow heals a bit more.

I sang on a street in St. Moritz one day. The snow was falling as I stood outside of a church on the main shopping street singing my heart out. Many people responded with smiles and money. But when l saw Madame Kurtzhoff, the social services secretary, darting from doorway to doorway of shops, as though she didn't want me to see her, I wondered if I was doing something socially unacceptable.

I later learned that it is not legal to play music for money on the streets in St. Moritz. The city officials feel that royalty, plus the richest people in the world, do not want to be reminded that some people have to put out much energy to earn a few francs. Perhaps they have forgotten that the troubadours were once the most respected of professionals, holding esteemed positions in European royal courts. Anyway, my right elbow began hurting me too much to continue. For now, I prefer to let my psyche remain in Egypt.

TWO

Alisa and I were sitting at her kitchen table in Ein Hod, an artist village twenty kilometers south of Haifa, Israel. The late April sun was streaming through the windows like the golden wildflower honey of the Carmel hills. I was gazing out at a small grove of olive trees, framed by the dry, rocky, shrubby hills that I so loved. The architecture of the homes of the artists in Ein Hod impressed me with its solidity; houses built of large light cream and yellow rocks nestled here and there in the hill town above the Mediterranean Sea. Most homes I visited had a view of the sparkling blue sea. From the Golan Heights to the Sinai desert many scenes remind me of old biblical paintings: shepherds herding their sheep across the arid landscape, turbaned men in long robes, cloaked women gathering water at a well, Bedouins on camels.

Israel was my home for a rich full year. I had come to visit a dear friend, whom I had known since the age of fourteen, an artist who had emigrated in the late sixties from the U.S. with her Jewish husband and children. My journeys were almost never short. This one would extend to twelve unplanned years.

From Vancouver, B.C., I had flown to Amsterdam, where I stayed a few weeks with friends on a houseboat on Prinsengracht Canal, while I earned some local currency singing at flower markets and churches. From there, I went to visit a doctor friend in Hanover, Germany, where I caught a share-ride to Greece through one of the efficient German share-ride agencies. The Greek driver, who lived and worked in Hanover, was going home to visit his family. He played Greek music on cassettes during the entire journey, while driving non-stop to Greece, except for a quick stop to eat in Yugoslavia.

In Piraeus, I caught a boat to Rhodes, where I planned to visit an American woman artist whom I had met on my way to Israel. Feeling refreshed by the sea air by the time we reached the port town of Rhodes, my spirits dropped when I discovered that all my travelers checks and cash were missing, except for five dollars in my pocket. Frantically, I went through my backpack and other bags repeatedly, finally surrendering to the fact that they had been stolen while on the ship. The five dollars paid for a room in a hotel for one night. Fortunately, my guitar and my voice remained with me. Exploring the historic town, where medieval knights had once gathered, I discovered some delightful cobblestone streets with fountains and charming old edifices as backdrops for singing. The troubadour in me was happy to express herself. The first evening I earned enough singing to buy a nourishing dinner; the next morning an early start brought in more survival drachmas.

It did not take long to find a lovely room in a pension in the old town, where smells of brilliant flowers, fruit trees, and food cooking, mingled with Greek music, awakened me to sun-filled mornings. It took me one month of singing and belly dancing in Greek tavernas to earn my boat fare to Haifa. At the same time, I had a wonderful month of swimming and sailing with some French people I met, and boating to Lindos and other ports on tourist boats, earning my trips plus tips singing. I spent a week on the unspoiled island of

Simi, northeast of Rhodes near Turkey, singing in restaurants and for an elaborate Greek wedding. Even without introductions that might have transpired with the woman artist who no longer lived on Rhodes, I enjoyed an active social life.

A boat ride took me across the Mediterranean Sea to the port of Haifa in Israel. From there, I caught a bus to Ein Hod Artist Village, twenty kilometers south of Haifa, where my friend Ruth lived. Through her, I met Alisa, another artist, who offered me sleeping quarters in a small cabin on her property. With a beautiful vista of the Mediterranean Sea, plus the creative friendships that flourished in Ein Hod, I thoroughly enjoyed the three months I spent there, before traveling around Israel and moving to Jerusalem.

In Israel I earned my living by singing in hotels, restaurants, night clubs, concerts, kibbutzim, festivals, on the streets of Jerusalem— my main home for eight months—and modeling for an art school in Jerusalem. I stayed at a Palestinian Hotel in the Old City of Jerusalem, close to the Jaffa Gate, where I loved to sing in front of large churches or near bazaars where Palestinian shop owners offered me tea and sometimes food. One shopkeeper dressed me in beautiful hand-embroidered Bedouin dresses, to model for him and send prospective clients to his shop.

Friendships flourished in Jerusalem. There were Jews from many other countries, as well as Israelis, English, Germans, Italians, Americans and the local Palestinians who kept me plied with tea during my rest periods.

During my first sojourn into the Old City of Jerusalem, I took out my guitar and began singing on the pedestrian street that led from the Jaffa Gate. When I finished singing a Sufi song I had composed, with devotional phrases in Arabic, a middle-aged man who had been listening introduced himself as the owner of the Petra Hotel. I happened to be singing in front of the hotel's portals, He was so moved by my song that he offered me a free room in his hotel. This kind Palestinian man invited me inside, and then took me upstairs to a pleasant room with curved arches at the comers of the ceiling. The room contained a double bed, night table, chest of drawers, closet and small bathroom; all I needed.

The Petra Hotel had a deteriorating old world charm, with high ceilinged rooms and small wrought iron balconies outside the rooms facing the pedestrian street. There were only a few guests staying there. A large English woman resided there semi-permanently. We later had a few fun evenings together talking and drinking. She was an alcoholic and liked to have company during her nighttime drinking bouts. One night we talked and laughed until early morning. Sitting on her little balcony, we watched the Old City awaken, a couple of boys sweeping the street and young men carrying trays of tea or coffee to shop owners. Giddy on brandy, we decided to lower a basket to the street from the balcony, with money in it for tea and croissants. "Sabah ilkhair," (good morning) we called to a tea server dashing about below. "Could you please bring us chai (tea) and croissants?" He smiled as we lowered the basket by the narrow rope we had tied on the handle; he took the money and returned in 5 minutes, placing a small tray with our cups of tea and pastry in the basket. We gingerly raised the basket, spilling nary a drop of tea, laughing.

The two young male Palestinian workers at the hotel enjoyed my presence, especially when I showed interest in learning Arabic words from them. Once I helped them clean rooms, discovering that instead of changing the sheets on the beds—if a guest had only stayed one or two nights—they simply shook the sheets out and put them back on the beds. Once, when an Israeli friend stopped by to ask for me, the workers expressed discomfort. They insinuated that I was a traitor, by hobnobbing with their persecutors.

After a couple of months at the Petra, I moved to the roof, where I could use two small cement rooms. The King David wall was so close that I sometimes saw tourists staring at me while I did yoga on the rooftop outside. I still sing a song that I wrote about the Petra Hotel:

> In the old city of Jerusalem, close to the Jaffa gate,
> you'll find the Petra Hotel.
> You can check in if it's not too late.
> The history of the Petra is a legend in the city of gold,
> It's felt so many footsteps of people both young and old.
>
> So if you're passing through Jerusalem,
> and you feel that you need a rest,
> Just check into the Petra,
> they'll give you the very best.
>
> Large high rooms with ceilings arched,
> elegance of days gone by.
> Lay your body between clean sheets,
> and heave a relieving sigh.
> You're at the Petra.
>
> In a cave of rooms like ancient tombs,
> they serve good wine and food.
> People are having a real good time
> to music of dumbeki and oud

You might see me dancing upon the tables,
when there's not much room on the floor;
and when I'm feeling really high,
I fly out the Petra door,
up to my room to sleep with the moon,
and stars and heaven above,
It's the grand old Petra Hotel, a place that I truly love,
in the old city of Jerusalem.

The last verse of the song describes a small restaurant in a basement below the hotel. Sometimes a group of musicians would play Middle Eastern music. I would belly dance for food and tips; we had fun parties there. I enjoyed the concentration of various religious faiths: the Coptic priests in their long robes and caps along Dolores Street, where pilgrims carried crosses on their backs in sympathy with the suffering of Jesus—the same street where he had supposedly carried his cross; the Jews gathering at the Wailing Wall to pray and stuff prayers scrawled on paper into the cracks of the wall; the beautiful Dome of the Rock—where Mohammed, the prophet of Islam, was said to have ascended to heaven on a winged horse— majestically presiding over the whole area.

Christmas Eve came on a weekend that year. I was singing at a vegetarian restaurant where I worked on weekends, a block off Ben Yehuda Street. Customers were eating fine vegetarian cuisine at candlelit tables on this holy night. Even though I considered myself more of a Buddhist and Sufi than a Christian, I was accustomed to celebrating Christmas.

That evening in Jerusalem I acknowledged the occasion by singing "The Cherry Tree Carol", about Mary asking Joseph to pick her some cherries ("for I am with child") as they walked through a cherry orchard, seemed an appropriate folk song. After singing a few verses, the usually pleasant owner of the restaurant came up to me, his face scowling. "That song is not appropriate in a Jewish restaurant," he admonished. I thought I was in a city where tolerance reigned for all faiths—obviously not!

As I walked down Ben Yehuda Street after my singing job, I ran into a Finnish girl I had met once before. She seemed to be at loose ends. "Would you like to go to a church service in the Old City," I asked her. She decided to come along.

As soon as we passed through the ancient portals of the Jaffa Gate, a couple of familiar Palestinians called out from a table on the sidewalk in front of a cafe, "Tara, come join us with your friend for tea." The Finnish girl reacted with hostility. "How can you associate with Arabs?" "Why shouldn't I?" "We're on our way to a church service that is about to begin," I told the Palestinians. "Another time."

We entered a very crowded well-lit church, close to the Jaffa Gate, and found seats near the back. The minister was speaking in English. The premise of his sermon was that Jesus was a Jew. The prepared speech that he read sounded more like that of a politician than a spiritual leader—mechanical, without feeling.

When the sermon and a closing song were finished, I realized it was time to go to Bethlehem, without the Finnish girl. I had been there before to visit the birthplace of Jesus, where the Church of the Nativity stands. It seemed to be the right place to go on Christmas Eve. I shared a sherut (group taxi) with a group of Palestinians. We arrived to join throngs of people, mostly Christians and Palestinians; Islam reveres Jesus as a Prophet.

Long lines formed to pass through metal detectors set up between barracks that Israeli soldiers operated. It saddened me to see the soldiers harassing young Palestinian men, forcing them to stand aside to be searched and questioned. In response to the humiliating treatment, which they so often encountered, the Palestinian men had sad dejected faces. I felt almost guilty as I, a white woman, was quickly ushered through the metal detectors to join the mass of people in the plaza next to the church. I joined a group that slowly swarmed into the church. Between the stuffy air and sweaty crowded bodies, the air inside the church was suffocating.

Gasping for air as I emerged, I found a seat in a cafe. While ordering tea and pastry, a group of young Palestinian men at the table next to mine struck up a conversation. Once they found a sympathetic ear and heart in me, they began to tell me their personal stories of suffering at the hands of the Israeli police. Israeli soldiers had bulldozed one man's family house. Another man told me that his family's land, which they had owned for many generations, had been confiscated in order to build an Israeli settlement there. One man peeled off his shirt to reveal terrible scars on his back, where he had been beaten in jail. Others shared their stories of torture and suffering. It was with a heavy heart that I returned to the Old City, longing for spiritual sharing with others before going to bed.

Someone told me about a midnight service at the Lutheran church near the Church of the Ascension, built on the spot where Jesus was supposedly resurrected after crucifixion, not far from where I lived. I entered a candlelit scene of glowing serenity accompanied by beatific music, including a resounding choir. Various laymen, as well as the minister, spoke in their individual native languages: English, Danish, German, French, Hebrew and Arabic. They voiced their beliefs about the unity of mankind, and love as the Christ spirit; intelligent kind voices represented by Christians, Arabs and Jews, united on this night of remembrance, interspersed with celestial music.

Walking back to the Petra Hotel, I felt uplifted and grateful to have ended my disconcerting evening with fellow human beings, love transcending the evils and confusion of the world. Reaching the rooftop of the hotel where I now lived, I meditated under a star-filled sky for peace on earth.

I attended many spiritual gatherings while living in Jerusalem. They were usually small groups of people who gathered for music, or classes in Tarot, Kabbalah and other esoteric studies. A young American man who resided at the Petra Hotel introduced me to some of these gatherings.

I had participated in several celebrations with Rabbi Schlomo Carlbach in northern California from 1969 to 1971. This charismatic Hassidic Rabbi sang spiritual songs in English and Hebrew, accompanying himself on guitar, while joyfully dancing up and down. No one in attendance could help but dance and sing along with him. I was pleased to discover that he was now living in Israel; I attended some of his upbeat celebrations.

Rabbi Schlomo Carlbach invited me to join a group of his followers for a Friday evening and Saturday celebration at a settlement outside of Jerusalem. It was a new settlement built on some dry barren hills. The houses were modem. Freshly planted trees, shrubs and gardens were beginning to add green and color. The high metal mesh fence around the settlement was disconcerting.

"It feels like a concentration camp to me," I told one of the participants. "Come with me," one of the settlers invited. I followed him to a fence about three hundred yards from the house. "See that village over there," he said, pointing to a little cluster of humble buildings. 'That's an Arab village. They do not like us to settle close to them. We need this fence and armed guards to protect us from possible attacks." I noticed a soldier with a large gun patrolling the fence-line. My guide failed to mention that this settlement was on land owned by Arabs who had lived there for centuries. The Israelis—in this case American settlers—were the illegal occupiers, bulldozing their way onto other people's territory. I rode in the first car to leave the settlement, feeling uncomfortable in spite of the beautiful celebration on Friday evening.

One afternoon while I was walking to the Jaffa Gate bus stop, with the purpose of going to central Jerusalem to sing on Ben Yehuda street, two Palestinian men hailed me to come to the tea shop where they were sitting outside at a small table. I joined them for fifteen minutes, practicing a few Arabic words while enjoying the glass of tea they offered. When I arrived at the bus stop I learned that the last bus—the one I probably would have been on if I had not accepted the invitation—had been bombed, killing a couple of passengers and wounding several. Saved again by hospitality and tea!

During the year I lived in Israel, the currency, the shekel, did not have much value, at least not when compared to the dollar. This meant that when I sang in the streets, coins that people placed in my open guitar case added up to an amount that was often heavy to carry to a bank, or back to my hotel room. I wrote a song called, "The Shekel Song":

> A shekel's not worth a nickel,
> not even a tenth of a dime.
> It's not worth a cent.
> How can you pay the rent?
> A peanut's worth more at this time.
> But the people keep throwing me shekels,
> as they pass through the streets of the city.
> While I'm singing my heart out to the people of Israel,
> to keep spirits high, so we won't feel self-pity.
> Give me flowers, incense, candles, or honey,
> a smile, a kiss, at least paper money.
> Because.... (back to beginning)

The reactions from listeners to this song varied. Some people thought it was funny, laughing and tossing me more money; others did not like to be reminded of such woes. "How can you sing about our money troubles when we are suffering." a grim-faced woman scolded me. In spite of such chastisements, I usually enjoyed singing in the streets, even when I had other jobs.

In spite of several unpleasant experiences, I loved that year in Israel. As I had been away from my mountain home in northern California for four years, I thought that I should be getting back soon. Yet, how could I leave this area of the world without visiting Egypt? I remembered, while eating a felafel in a restaurant in San Francisco, four years earlier, the Egyptian restaurateur told me that I would love Egypt. "Try to visit my wonderful homeland," he had said, I had felt attracted to Middle Eastern countries ever since enjoying Morocco for four months—interspersed into my Flamenco period in Spain— twenty years earlier. Now, I realized how close Egypt was by bus, from talking with travelers who had gone there and back.

"I think I'll go to Egypt for a few weeks before going home," I told Alisa while we drank tea in her kitchen. "I' II return here for my things, then fly to San Francisco from Tel Aviv. I have already paid for an EST training course in Jerusalem, scheduled in three weeks. Perhaps it will help me attune to financial abundance." I always earned enough money for food and a place to stay, but rarely had much extra since leaving Europe. "You mean you're actually going to be a tourist for once in your life, Tara?" Alisa grinned. She knew about my extended traveling adventures. "Well, don't forget to dance on top of the pyramid, as Yosi and Aron suggested at the party last week." Alisa was referring to a conversation with two young Israeli men who had returned from a short visit to Egypt. They had enjoyed my dancing at the party. "I can just see you dancing on top of the pyramid during the Sound and Light Show," one of them teased. "The show could use some real live action, besides just a film and talking," The image stuck in my mind.

I loved Ein Hod and my friends there, the charming village, the interesting artists, the great parties at the restaurant and in homes. Accompanied by eight enthusiastic Israeli musicians, I had produced a show of my songs and a 'Divine Mother' dance in the Ein Hod amphitheater. It had been a magical experience—the weeks of rehearsal and performance under a full moon. It was always difficult for me to wrench myself away from a place where I had lived, expressed myself, and made friends. However, once I moved on, new adventures absorbed my attention, leaving little space in my mind for nostalgia, except when I fell in love.

Returning by bus to Jerusalem, I packed up my things for storage at the hotel. The next day, after I picked up my sleeping bag, guitar and small backpack, I took a bus to Ein Gedi on the Dead Sea. My plan was to enjoy a leisurely trip to Elat, cross the Egyptian border through the Sinai that I so loved, and swim and sleep at the Red Sea on my way to Cairo. Instead of taking the usual route by bus from Tel Aviv to Cairo, via Rafah., I felt that the sun and sea would be relaxing and healing after the intensity of Jerusalem. It felt like a path of Light.

THREE

*W*hile I was soaking up sun, mud and salt water at the Dead Sea in Ein Gedi, a group of Palestinian families came dancing and singing along the beach, playing tambourines and drums. Without waiting for an invitation, I joined in with an impromptu belly dance. They were celebrating an Islamic holiday. A tall, dark-haired young man arose from sleep nearby on the beach. By this time, I was singing and playing my guitar, including Arabic phrases in the song, to the delight of the Palestinians. The young man brought out his guitar to accompany me.

After the group dispersed, Ron introduced himself as an American who played music on the streets in Tel Aviv, where he lived. During our conversation, I told him I was on my way to Egypt. He said he also wanted to visit Egypt, but did not want to travel alone. "Could we travel together," he asked. I was not sure. Magic usually occurred when I traveled alone. The following morning we decided to visit Massada, the famous mountain fortress where in A.O. 73 some 960 Jews of the Zealot sect committed mass suicide rather than surrender to Roman soldiers.

Instead of taking the funicular, we walked up the mountain. It was not easy; carrying my backpack, guitar, some fruit and a gallon jug of water. Ron was physically out of shape. Although he only carried a small daypack, he begged me to stop and rest about halfway up. He lay prostrate on the rocky ledge while I surveyed the vast desert vista extending to the Dead Sea. Ron could barely make it up the last leg of the journey. The wind was getting stronger as we ascended, howling and blowing sand and dust into our eyes as we neared the top. Soldiers emerged from a small cement building, informing us that a fierce storm was brewing. The funicular would not be operating until the storm was over. All the other tourists had left. We were stranded on top of Massada.

"Come out of the wind and drink a cup of tea," one of the soldiers offered. It was a relief to find shelter from the wind and sand. Ron and I sat on a little cot, the only available seating. Other soldiers were bringing out food—bread and feta cheese, olives, canned corned beef and leftover boiled potatoes. They urged us to share their supper. It was almost dark. I felt claustrophobic in the small square cement room with a light bulb dangling from the ceiling. Shadows danced on the walls. "I'm going outside to get some fresh air and look around a little," I said. "Be careful out there in that storm," replied a soldier. "You both can sleep in here on extra bunks."

Wandering around outside, I found a place protected from the wind by the crumbling ruins of an old fortress. There was no roof, only uneven four-foot high remains of walls. Returning to the hut for my sleeping bag and pack, I was relieved to see that Ron had accepted the soldiers' invitation to sleep there. They all found it strange that I wanted to stay alone outdoors. "We can't be responsible for you out there. You'd be a lot safer in here, and a lot warmer too." "Thanks, anyway," I bid goodnight and went back to my fortress. After laying my sleeping bag on the stone and sand ground, I meditated for a little while. Listening to the wind whistling over my head, I felt lost in an ancient period, haunted by ghosts of the past. I was soon fast asleep.

For the next couple of days, although the storm persisted, I was able to walk around the entire Massada area. I visited the various sites: an abandoned mining operation, the remains of ancient buildings once designated as homes of officials and of laborers who worked the mines. A few times, I shared meals and conversations in the hut with the soldiers and Ron. They did not venture out much. I would return to my private spot to read and sleep.

We left Massada two and a half days later, taking the funicular, rather than walking back down the mountain. Hordes of tourists were at the bottom waiting to board the funicular. I took out my guitar and began singing. The shekels poured in, money for my journey to Egypt. By now I realized that Ron was a six-foot-three-inch softie, yet I let him persuade me to return to Tel Aviv with him to sing for a large festival, so that we could continue on to Egypt together. Before dusk, we boarded a bus to Jerusalem, where we would need to change buses for Tel Aviv.

Already dark when we reached Jerusalem, Ron expressed a desire to stop at the Wailing Wall to pay homage to his Jewish ancestry. An American Rabbi that Ron had met previously was there, urging us to come to his house nearby for dinner. Ron loved to eat. The Rabbi also invited us to sleep there that night. I agreed.

The house was a charming Israeli-designed white stone house in the Jewish Quarter of the Old City. During their early settlement years, Israelis forcibly removed the Palestinians who lived there, as they did in many other places also. Two thousand Palestinians had been displaced; many still lived in refugee camps in large tents, which one could see on the outskirts of Jerusalem, as well as places in the desert. As much as I liked the architecture of the Jewish Quarter, the knowledge of this injustice saddened me.

We dined by candlelight around a long, beautifully polished wooden table with the Rabbi's quiet wife and two young children. While the Rabbi monopolized the conversation, it became obvious that he hoped to recruit Ron for a yeshiva. He seemed irritated that I was not Jewish. When it came time to sleep, our host took me to a rocky little plot outside. "A Christian hostel once stood on this spot," he informed me. "You can sleep here." Ron had already been tucked into a soft double bed in a lovely guestroom. Had my host assumed that I was Christian? I patiently cleared away enough rocks to lie flat. Lying there in my sleeping bag, still trying to remove stones from beneath me, I wondered if I should have told my host about the refuge my mother had given to Jews in Switzerland during the Second World War. She had taken Jewish refugees who were escaping Nazi Germany into our tiny apartment in Bern before I was even born.

Rummaging through my pack looking for my toothbrush, I discovered that my wallet, with all my money, was missing. It must have been stolen at the Wailing Wall when I lay my things down beside me. It was hard to believe that someone could have entered my bags while I was near them. However, I did not think that this prosperous Jewish family would have taken money from me. I finally fell into an exhausted sleep.

The next morning when I went to the house to find Ron, our host informed me that Ron had been taken to a yeshiva. When I explained that Ron had asked me to accompany him to Tel Aviv and Egypt, the

Rabbi screamed: "You are trying to take this Jewish boy away from the yeshiva, away from his roots." He kicked my backpack out the door, smashing it into my leg and toppling me over. Trying to regain my balance, while falling, I followed my backpack as it tumbled down the steep stairs. With bruised knees, sore arms and legs, barely able to walk, I went to sing for a while near the Jaffa Gate to earn bus fare to Tel Aviv. That afternoon I left.

In Tel Aviv, I visited a woman artist I knew slightly. She invited me to sleep on her couch in the living room. The next morning I contacted the festival officials and auditioned for them. They assigned various stages for me to sing on during the three-day festival. On the third afternoon, Ron walked up. He waited until I was through singing, gesticulating madly to talk to him. "Tara, I'm so sorry about what happened. I was brainwashed into staying at the yeshiva, seduced by good food. Please come and stay at my apartment. You can have your own room."

His apartment was filthy. I cleaned it and cooked meals for numerous 'hang-our guests who came and left constantly. Again, I let him talk me into accompanying him to Egypt. We got our visas and left by bus. The ticket included two nights in a hotel in Cairo. Although I had only $40 besides my ticket, I decided to trust in Allah.

At the border of Egypt, in Rafah, I brought out my guitar and sang a few songs while waiting in the terminal. The tourists sat in vinyl chairs smiling, not offering even a penny to my open gold-lined guitar case. Nevertheless, the Egyptian custom officials enjoyed my music, especially my self-composed Sufi song with Arabic phrases.

When I went to the window to pay the border tax, the man behind it beamed at me: "How much do you want for one of your cassettes," he asked. I guess he had seen the box of cassettes near me. "Well, I usually get ten dollars for a cassette." He smiled apologetically. "In Egypt a cassette usually costs about 1.70 L.E. (Egyptian pounds). I never pay more than two pounds for a cassette. I earn only eighty pounds (the equivalent of $40 at that time) per month." He paused. "I love your voice. Is that Arabic song on it?" He was still beaming. We finally settled on five pounds, which would pay for my border tax.

The hotel in Dokki—an area west of central Cairo, across the Nile on the way to the pyramids—was pleasant. I scurried around Cairo for a couple of days, looking at a few historical sites, the pyramids, and absorbing the smells and atmosphere. I realized that I wanted to travel alone, to honor my need for my own psychic space, to follow a more intuitive, free flowing path.

On my third day in Egypt, I boarded an early morning train to Luxor. The third class train ride included the company of peasants— who kindly shared their food with me—goats, chickens, large bundles of vegetables, and tambourine-playing male singers. We stopped at every tiny village, even places where there appeared to be nothing but fields and the Nile River. When we arrived in Luxor at one a.m., I was surprised to hear music and find brightly lit streets crowded with people. As I walked through the streets, I saw groups of men dancing inside open-faced tents to hypnotic music played by small ensembles of musicians. Throughout the streets and in tents, women cooked food over small kerosene stoves. Someone told me that it was the final night of a religious festival. I danced and wandered around for a couple of hours before a young Egyptian boy led me to a small hotel to sleep. I was unaware that I had been among Sufis.

A series of invitations from young Egyptian men began. For the next two weeks, young Egyptian men escorted me on donkey rides to the Valley of the Kings and Queens, felucca sailing on the Nile, tours of tombs, plus visits to different homes. I was introduced to an affable man who owned a pleasant hotel in the village of Gurneh on the west bank. Built like a villa, with a roof terrace overlooking the Valley of the Kings and Queens, and a desert landscape intermingled with stucco houses of villagers and some trees, I decided to reside there for a week. Fathi, the owner, invited me to several sumptuous feasts, which we enjoyed on the roof, as servants came back and forth with a variety of dishes. Fathi liked my singing so much that he would not accept money for his hospitality.

I would sing for his guests when appropriate. When I walked out of the building in the morning onto the narrow dirt street, I would see the artisans sitting against the walls of the hotel and other buildings for shade, crafting beautiful objects—urns, vases, animalistic figurines, small boxes with lids—out of the local alabaster. The translucent gypsum varied somewhat; shades of rosy beige threaded through the clearer white. Other people along the street were potting water jugs out of clay or making souvenir items to sell to tourists. I sometimes wondered if the long dress-like djellabia worn by the fellahin (fanners) was practical for such manual labor. Apparently, it suited them just fine; their fields of vegetables, melons and grains looked well tended. Some days I swam in the Nile River—crocodiles often nearby—and dozed on the banks. Narrow canals of water threaded throughout farm fields for irrigation. One day I watched a farmer on the bank of the Nile lifting water from the river into a canal by means of a long wooden pole with a large wooden scoop on one end. He would press down on the narrow pole end so that the scoop in the river would rise up in the air filled with water and dump the water into the canal. It looked like backbreaking work. This workout watered his fields, which seems more productive than lifting barbells in a gymnasium.

A tour guide friend often took me to Egyptian weddings in the countryside, which lasted all night long, sometimes for a few nights in a row. I participated by dancing to the folkloric ghawazee (wedding) music. Men in long djellabias and white turbans played haunting music on the "mizmar '. a type of oboe; the 'rebab', a two string pike fiddle with a coconut shell body and a parchment head on which the bridge rests; the 'tabla beladi', a two-headed cylindrical drum, with goatskin heads mounted on hoops secured with cords; the 'arghool', an ancient Egyptian instrument composed of two reed pipes tied together with string; the 'salameya', a short high-pitched end-blown flute of the 'ney' family; the 'darbukka' (dumbek) drum; and the 'tar', a cylindrical hand drum. While listening and watching the Benat Maazin dancers, an ancient memory stirred me. Having worked for several years as a professional belly dancer, I often joined the dancers or danced solo. Soon I was invited to dance at almost every celebration happening in Thebes. Grateful hosts bestowed gifts of djellabias and dance skirts upon me.

One night I danced at the wedding of an American couple that had met in Luxor a year earlier while on holiday. They had decided to return to get married at the Karnak Temple, that they so loved. The ceremony took place on a full moon night, replete with mystical energy. Local musicians played rababa, flute, violin and tablas. In a flowing green djellabia that a stick-dancer had presented to me, I danced among the ancient sphinxes and columns of the temple, feeling more Egyptian than American or Swiss.

The renowned stick-dancer taught me the rhythmic and graceful stick dance, usually performed by males as gentle mock combat. Folkloric events charmed me. I continued to participate in many wedding celebrations, often being hired by the wedding party. Folkloric musicians accompanied me when I danced on cruise ships, but the atmosphere was more commercial, with tourists as audience. The local weddings were joyful affairs that often lasted for two or three days. Summertime was the most popular season for weddings. One festivity followed another. Egyptian friends, who knew the hosts of the parties, would take me into the countryside to partake in these all-night ancient ceremonies. The spontaneous enthusiasm of the fellahin (peasants) who participated in the dancing, singing and sharing of food and tea was contagious.

Drinking in the soft Nile breezes under a vast canopy of stars and moon., I felt a shedding of burdens and complexities, which often accompany modem materialistic society. The slower pace of Upper Egypt and the relaxed warmth of the Egyptian people erased any last traces of stress. Life flowed like the river, in which I was already swimming daily.

On top of all this magic, I found a job singing at a Swiss hotel on Crocodile Island, a twenty-minute horse and buggy trot away from the center of Luxor. Six nights a week I sang in several languages for tourists from all over the world, accompanied by my guitar and ankle bells. After finishing singing at ten or eleven p.m., I would be whisked off to belly dance for a wedding, a party on a cruise ship, or a show at one of the first class hotels. The Egyptians were surprised and enthusiastic. "You dance like an Egyptian," admirers would exclaim. Dancing to Egyptian orchestras along the Nile felt like a fairy-tale. My cup of life seemed to be in the correct position for filling, like the crescent moon that hung in the sky like a slender bowl, angled to be filled from above.

One afternoon, while basking near the Swiss hotel swimming pool, a local Egyptian businessman, who often came to hear me sing, asked me if I would let him read my palm. I agreed, surprised that this man was into palm reading. After telling me some information about my life—some of it already past and true, he said, "You will stay in Egypt a long time because you will want to stay."

This was hard to believe. Although I had already been in Egypt for five months, I had unfinished projects in Israel, plus I had been away from my home in California for five years. Yet, I had to admit that I was having a wonderful time in the Land of the Pharaohs.

One evening, when I finished singing at the hotel, a famous Egyptian entertainer came up to me. "I'm enjoying your music," she said. "You have such a beautiful voice. I think you would be appreciated on Egyptian television. Go to the TV station in Cairo."

I might as well, I thought. It is on my way to the international airport. After bidding my friends and jobs good-bye, I boarded a train to Cairo.

FOUR

*C*airo's intense energy was exhilarating even though the weather was still hot in October. The dirty streets, crowds, and noisy traffic did not bother me; after five months in Luxor, I was relaxed and refreshed. A few days later, I walked to the television station. Arriving at the large modem building on the east bank of the Nile, I made a few inquiries, and was soon ushered upstairs to the office of a TV producer. After listening to me sing, and liking what she heard, she suggested that I contact Hamdiya Hamdi, the host of a TV show called "The World Sings." I telephoned her the next afternoon from a busy shop in the Babalouk area "Would you like me to sing a song over the telephone," I asked, from the crowded noisy street, where I stood at a counter that divided a small shop from the sidewalk "Yes, if you can," she replied, sounding amused by this unorthodox audition.

I sang a favorite song from my self-composed repertoire, "Nature Is Endless", accompanied by honking car horns, shouting Egyptians, and horrendous traffic noises. The owners smiled from the other side of the counter. "That's wonderful," exclaimed Hamdiya Hamdi, when I finished my lengthy three-verse song. "I'd love to have you on my television show. Can you be here two weeks from Saturday with your guitar, to sing live on the show?" I agreed. "Better be here by six-thirty p.m. in order to have make-up and hair done before the eight p.m. show." "Okay, see you then."

I arrived at the TV station on the scheduled evening, drank a 7UP while the hairdresser ironed classic silky curls into my long hair, and the show began. My hostess and I sat in simple modem chairs on either side of a small table bedecked with flowers, facing the camera in our fresh over-perfect hairdos. Hamdiya Hamdi interviewed me, asking about my origins and music career. The interview continued during pauses between taped videos of American rock stars. Toward the end of the show, I sang my lofty spirit and nature song under blinding lights.

My mood was buoyant when Hamdiya Hamdi let me out of her car in front of the cafeteria next to the Oxford Hotel, where I was staying, I went into the cafeteria to enjoy a snack. At a counter wrapped around a mirrored pillar, a young foreign woman approached me. Speaking with an Australian accent, she told me that she had just seen me singing on television; she loved the performance. At home in Sydney, Australia, she worked in a theater company—acting, dancing, directing. Now she was visiting Egypt with her boyfriend. We discussed the performing arts for several minutes, and then returned to our respective hotels with the intent to meet again.

Occasionally, I sang at Khan al-Khalili bazaar. Street singing is an excellent way to make contact with the people of a country. While sharing my heart and art, participating in the life around me, I could earn local currency by selling my cassettes and from offerings of appreciation, Sometimes I was invited by restaurant or club owners to perform in their establishments for an evening, a week, a month, or even longer.

One late afternoon, a week after the *TV* show, I went to Khan al Khalili bazaar to sing, A young man watched me for a few minutes, and then introduced himself as the boyfriend of the Australian girl, Alison. "I recognized you from Alison's description," the amiable Larry said, as he shook my hand. "An Egyptian doctor friend is going to take us to a festival tonight. Perhaps you would like to join us. If so, come to our hotel nearby, at eight p.m., room 240 at the Hotel Hussein on Sayyidna al-Hussein Square." "That sounds like fun," I replied. "I'd like to see Alison again" When I knocked on their door at the appointed hour, the Egyptian doctor, Kamal, was with them. We chatted amiably for more than an hour on the balcony overlooking the square.

The Sayyidna al-Hussein mosque is an Islamic center for the entire Muslim world, as well as a bustling meeting place for Cairenes. Having been beheaded near Baghdad during a holy war, Sayyidna al-Hussein—the grandson of Mohammed, the Prophet—is considered a martyred saint in the cause of Islam. I was told that his sister brought his head to Cairo, which is now supposedly buried within the macam (sanctuary) of the mosque, a holy shrine hosting many pilgrims who come to pay homage. It was from this spot that I would begin my initiation into the world of Egyptian dervishes and thereby lose my head too, by western standards.

Alison, Larry and I left the hotel at ten p.m. Kamal, the doctor, said that he would come an hour later when the festivities were warmed up. He had guided Larry and Alison the previous night, so they knew how to get to the festival. Larry carried my guitar, slung over one shoulder by a strap, as we wandered through a maze of rough dirt and narrow streets in a nearby old section of Cairo. Such hidden medinas can remain unseen by foreign eyes.

The farther we walked the more crowded the streets became, until we arrived at a vortex of energy at the mosque of a female saint,

Sitta Fatima Nebowiya. Brightly colored lights, strung across the mosque, zapped psychedelically, music blared from loud speakers on either side of a small, low wooden stage, where a group of six musicians played, while people danced on the ground in front of them. Lining the rough streets were women serving tea and food from small kerosene stoves, sitting on mats of straw or cardboard, or inside the openings of buildings or tents. It was difficult to get through the throngs of people. Excitement was contagious.

Alison and Larry wanted to take me to visit a sheikh that they had met the night before. Passing a small house where a circle of Sufis sat inside the open door, one man in the cluster hailed us, inviting us inside to eat. "Join them if you wish," Alison said. "We'll be across the street in that building—she pointed—with Sheikh Mohammed. Come over afterwards."

Seated on an earthen floor, in a dark room with a small circle of quiet Egyptians, I felt the inner peace of a sanctum in the midst of chaos. We ate together out of one large aluminum bowl, filled with stewed potatoes in tomato sauce. and some green chicory leaves on the side. We used crusts of coarse farmer's bread as utensils, dipping our individual chunks of bread into the bowl, bringing the dripping pieces to our mouths. At one point, I thought about how a spoon might make the process easier. A man looked at me and handed me a large soupspoon. It was comforting that someone would respond to a thought in this way; no need for words in this communion of hearts, an inner language that we seemed to share.

Crossing the street, I saw my friends through the large open entrance sitting on cushions with a dignified large turbaned man, amidst a roomful of people. The walls of the large space—perhaps a converted garage—were covered with hand-sewn, appliqued, cotton cloth designs in bright colors of red, green, black and white, called 'arabesque'. The room was ablaze with lights and buzzing energy.

This was the hidema of Sheikh Mohammed. I later learned that a hidema is a temporary site of hospitality during a festival, where a sheikh or sheikha of a particular Sufi tarika (path) and his/her entourage serve food, tea, and water pipes at a mulid (religious festival). Troubadours who make their rounds at such festivals often provide music.

Sheikh Mohammed was a very tall, handsome man, with a noble bearing. Alison and Larry hailed me as I entered the room. The sheikh gestured for me to sit on a bolster near him. A woman carried dates and tea on a round aluminum tray across the room and placed them before me. Basking in the ecstatic spiritual energy, smiling to various warm faces across the room, which seemed to relish my presence as much as I did theirs, I felt a sense of peaceful wholeness. Doctor Kamal entered and joined us.

A group of musicians came in with their instruments, which they quickly attached to an amplifier and speakers. The singer took the microphone in his hands, swaying it rhythmically on its cord. As soon as the musicians tuned up, the singer began alone, without accompaniment—a haunting call in a plaintive voice, stretching the notes into a far-reaching place. I felt that he was calling God and making a connection. The invocation resounded through the room, throughout the universe. After about five minutes, the musicians joined in. The music was so beautiful that I almost cried. Gradually men rose from their cushions and formed two lines facing each other. They began slowly bowing and raising their torsos in time to the music and the clap of the leader's hands, chanting "Allah Hay! Allah Hay!" As the music increased in speed, they started to tum their torsos from side to side in rhythm to the music and chanting.

Unable to resist my impulse, I joined the lines. As the music grew in intensity and speed, the movements became less structured, each person dancing from an inner state of awareness, yet still in unison. I found myself flowing into a freer form of interpretation, while staying in harmony with the group of men. No one seemed to mind that I was the only woman dancing.

After an hour of this group zikr, an Egyptian woman came into the space between the two lines, dancing in her own style until she seemed to be in a trance. She ended up whirling and reeling, then screamed and fell to the floor. This seemed to be part of the spiritual entertainment for those who sat along the walls, smoking water pipes and drinking tea. Kamal explained that this was a well-known sheikha, noted for her dancing. Sheikha Dunya and I were to become friends, with her promoting my own talents as inspiration and entertainment for their hidema, which she co-hosted with Sheikh Mohammed.

When the music finished and the excitement subsided, Sheikh Mohammed, having noticed my guitar, asked me to sing. I sang a Sufi song that I had composed in California.

Having attended Sufi meetings and camps in northern California fora few years, I was initiated as a Sufi in 1971 by Pir Vilayat Khan, in a beautiful ceremony in the coastal range mountains of Mendocino County. After the Sufi Camp, I was guided to my own 40 acres of land on a nearby mountain.

Now, among these Egyptian Sufis, the sacred Arabic words that I chanted struck a familiar chord the hearts of the attendees. After their initial surprise to hear a foreign woman chanting, "Supon Allah, Alhamdulilah, Allah Ho Akbar," they joined in. The song seemed to have no end as they continued on and on, chanting enthusiastically and encouraging me to continue strumming, until I felt as if my right arm would full off. A drum joined in to accompany the rhythmic guitar sweeps. Soon the people were up and dancing. When I would try to stop, Sheikh Mohammed would urge me to continue, also chanting in his strong deep voice, "Hu Allah, Hu Allah, Hu Allah!"

When I finally managed to end the music after forty minutes or more, I sensed that I was accepted into the dervish fold. We experienced a kinship that existed before I ever played upon their stage before nationalities were even formed. "Enti dervish! Enti Madad," ("You are a dervish, you are a spiritual channel"), Sheikh Mohammed exclaimed, while others acknowledged their delight, drawing closer to stare. shake my hand, or embrace me, offering fruits and candies and nuts. One elderly sheikh presented me with a silver open-front flaring robe, which tied at the waist with fine silver cords.

I learned that madad means server, denoting someone who channels energy and light, bringing others closer to Allah. When a munshid (a singer of sacred music) is singing beautifully from source, listeners will exclaim, "madad". This title can include healers, dancers, poets, singers and saints; any channel of spiritual energy.

Coincidentally, my middle name is Tara, an alternate name of a favorite female saint in Egypt, Sayiddah Zaynab, the great granddaughter of the prophet, Mohammed. Tahra, in Arabic, means purity. "Now it's time for you to dance alone, Tahra," directed Sheikh Mohammed as the musicians commenced another set of music. Even when I performed in nightclubs, I created rituals of devotion. My talent and power came from the source of creation; I acknowledged such energy with reverence, opening myself to the fount of creativity, while allowing my ego to be absorbed into divine will.

For Sheikh Mohammed's hidema, I incorporated several of the movements that the dervishes had executed during the previous set, and some oriental dance movements that emerged spontaneously. I felt as if I had been dancing on such dervish stages since time began. The music did not seem strange or new to me. It felt as if it were an aspect of my soul, which my spirit had been homesick for; I had found a missing piece of myself. Perhaps in the minds of the audience, concepts of agnebia (foreigner) were also joggled.

Realities need to be shaken up sometimes in order to enlarge our scope of understanding and broaden our horizons. The more clearly we can see our interconnectedness and break down barriers of separation, the greater the chances there are for peace on earth. A role of the sheikh or sheikha is to shake up the minds of people, especially their preconceived realities.

A Sufi recognizes religions, countries, and physical forms as merely shells. A Sufi can recognize Sufi consciousness in any form, in any country. This is not because all Sufis have a similar expression or personality, or even the same belief systems. Each Sufi expresses his/her own unique individuality, yet the essence is the same. If one bakes a loaf of bread and breaks it into pieces, each piece will have a different shape, all the more delightful in the variations.

When I finished dancing, others came forward to join in the all night celebration. The energy of the festival was growing as the night progressed, buzzing with excitement. The Australians and I wandered off to the main square outside of the mosque, where the largest zikr dance took place. Dancing in this arena, my eyes became transfixed upon the twinkling colored lights that decorated the roof and entrance of the mosque. I sensed an eternal pulsation, existing during millenniums gone by, and continuing now, even with the modem touches of electric lighting, amplifiers, microphone and speakers. The ancient music emerged from the depths of soul. nature and spirit.

I was delighted to learn that the festival would last three more days. Each evening I returned to dance, sing and enjoy the ambiance of my newly found Sufi family, which kept growing as I met various sheikhs with their groups. and became acquainted with individual Sufis. It felt like a family that had always been there for me, and always will be. Inshallah! From their perspective, I was a long lost sister who had finally found her way home.

Just when I was feeling sad to see the mu lid end on the final night, l was informed that there would be another one, much larger, at Sayyidna al-Hussein, officially beginning in a week. Many of the dervishes—especially those who traveled from one mulid to another, camping out in various places, without a permanent home—were going to move directly to the Sayyidna al-Hussein area. They would set up their tent, carpet, or cardboard space, and continue cooking and sleeping on the ground or sidewalk at the next festival. Sheikhs and dervishes scrawled Arabic words on scraps of paper and pressed them into my palm. These were names and addresses of hidema sites, especially the larger ones that had a building or large tent for an address. "Don't forget to bring your guitar and sing," the sheikhs implored. "You can work to earn money as the other munshidin do." At large festivals, munshidin usually wander from one hidema to another—often with a group of musicians—to perform for the patrons and guests. While the munshid is performing, members of the audience walk up to the artist and place money in a free hand. In my case, they placed money in my lap because my hands were occupied with the guitar. At the end of a mulid, the presiding sheikhs would sometimes pay the munshidin from their own pockets, or collect money from the audience for the performers. Sheikha Dunya sometimes collected money for me while I was dancing or singing.

There was a hierarchy among the munshidin, according to talent and channeling ability, plus presentation. It could be helpful to be introduced to respected and wealthy sheikhs, whose hidemas tend to attract a wealthier clientele. However, I observed that many munshidin—including myself—sang for hidemas of varied social strata, attracted more by the light of the people than the money. Sheikh Mohammed was one of the most influential Sufi sheikhs in the arena upon which the dervishes played their endless devotions to Allah.

From the very first mulid that I attended, the dervishes began teaching me their songs in Arabic. Usually more than one person tried to instruct me at the same time. They would say the words too fast to write down, though little by little I wrote down snatches of what I was being taught until I could put the pieces together. At least two or three instructors would shout words so loud that I could not hear any of them clearly. At the same time, they talked to each other. Often a young dervish was too impatient to finish a song, did not know all the words, or was rapturizing about the beauty of my eyes. The tune was rarely clear. Invariably, once I felt that I had a beautiful song and the Egyptians responded enthusiastically when I sang, someone else, at another time, told me that my words were not right, or that my accent needed correcting. Sometimes I was whisked off to a professor of the Koran, or an accomplished munshid, who would re-instruct me. The next time I sang the relearned song for a sheikh whose opinion I respected, he might change it back to what I had originally learned This was exasperating. Yet, somehow, I was inspired to create about twelve Sufi songs in Arabic—some of them rather lengthy dramas—over the course of a few years.

Thus, I became a munshid, gaining the respect of other munshidin who also helped me with songs sometimes. They were delighted that I did them in my own way, with guitar and ankle bells. We often ate together at hidemas, joked, talked and basked in each other's creative energy. My days had become nights; I slept through most of the daytime commotion of everyday life in Cairo.

Nightclub jobs were sometimes offered to me. Occasionally, I did sing or dance for weddings or folkloric concerts. Yet, my spirit kept guiding me to the mulids (religious festivals), more fascinating to me than the other forms of celebrations and entertainment. Gradually, I began to learn new words and phrases in Arabic, many of them religious expressions that touched a deep chord in the hearts of Egyptians. During my third year in Egypt, just when I began to despair of ever learning Arabic, I found myself able to converse in broken Arabic.

Familiar faces and personalities began to etch their way into my heart. I felt a close bonding with many Sufis. I dressed in long Egyptian dresses and djellabias, not unlike the style of clothes that

I had favored most of my life. Lovely scarves covered my hair and head; therefore, orthodox Muslims, who might consider it haram (forbidden) for a woman to show her hair, could also accept my appearance. Most modem Egyptian women do not cover their heads, even if they are devout Muslims. I was part of the Sufi life in Egypt; their culture, their customs, their society; most of all, I was immersed in their mystical practices and faith.

FIVE

book could be written about the Oxford Pension-Hotel in Cairo, where I often lived during my five years in Egypt. During my first week in Cairo, after leaving Luxor, I met a young American and his girlfriend in a coffee shop near Talaat Harb Square. He also played guitar and had performed on streets in Europe and Israel. He remembered seeing me sing in the Old City of Jerusalem. "Why don't you come and visit us at the Oxford Pension, where we stay," he suggested. "It is an interesting place, with all kinds of travelers coming and going; the only place I would stay in Cairo. We will be leaving in two days. You could have our room."

Curiosity prompted me to go there the next day to see what was so great about the Oxford. The rather colorless pension, where I stayed during my first week in Cairo, was in the same area as the Oxford, according to Jerry, "about a five minute walk." It took me seven hours to find the Oxford. Every time I asked an Egyptian where Sulliman Pasha was, several people blurted out contradictory directions. I was walking in circles, stumbling over stones and rutted streets, through endless masses of jammed-up automobiles, nerve wracked by car horns, and asphyxiated by exhaust fumes.

When I finally arrived at a large old building on a continuation of the street that I had started on—Sulliman Pasha is another name for Talat Harb Street—I was exhausted, hot and grimy. Looking up at the perpendicular row of signs next to the doorway, I saw a small sign, Oxford Pension. The name was later changed to Oxford Hotel, when the manager—the brother of the hotel owner—listened to a song I wrote with that title. A creaky, ancient elevator—with a brass accordion-style door—took me up five floors. Besides flats where families lived, I saw signs for doctors' offices, tailors, a film distributing company, a dentist office, and various other businesses.

The fifth floor harbored the Oxford Pension, plus one other flat. High ceilings, large rooms, latticed window shutters in the foyer, some large mirrors here and there, solid old wooden furniture—handsome, yet showing the ravages of time, such as large oak chests with knobs missing and scratched or flaking splinters and worn upholstery— all contributed to an atmosphere of musty elegance of days gone by. Obviously, foreigners—probably British and French, during their respective occupations of Egypt—and wealthy Egyptians, had occupied such spacious flats in the past. The building was situated right in the heart of central Cairo, between a popular cafeteria and a fresh juice stand, which served mango, guava, pomegranate, orange, strawberry, grapefruit, coconut and carrot juices.

The lounge of the Oxford was cool compared to the hot streets. rested in an over-stuffed, red leather armchair, while my friends were summoned from their room. Jerry and his girlfriend emerged with broad smiles, inviting me to their tiny back room. By then, it was early evening. They brought in bottles of cold Stella beer to refresh us while we chatted and played music together. Occasionally another hotel inhabitant stopped in. This inexpensive pension was a friendly, sociable place. My friends told the manager, Pateros, that I would be moving in the next day after they departed. He was pleased to have the vacancy already filled.

During the next few days, the TV show was arranged. Soon after, I was immersed in the dervish scene. so I became one of the Oxford residents, even adapting to sharing my space with numerous cockroaches.

Painted on the wall next to the bed was a grotesque drawing of a suffering-faced Jesus, complete with thorns on his head. The manager agreed to let me paint my room. I brightened the dark little nest with various shades of red; a blood-red paint covered the thorned Jesus wall. Painting the furniture, woodwork and door trim black created an oriental mode. After building a canopy frame over the bed, I draped some gauzy, glittery material that doubled as mosquito netting. Later, when I had left the Oxford, I heard that travelers had nightmares in that red, red room, so the walls were repainted.

I thought that this small inside room would be quieter than the larger rooms facing heavily trafficked streets. The noise of the elevator outside my alley-faced window did not bother me much in the beginning. I was usually at festivals during the noisy evening hours. Many people who stayed there were night people. Often, when I returned in the wee hours of the morning, a party was going on in one, or more, of the rooms. Occasionally I joined a party for a little while.

It was relaxing to communicate in English, or sometimes in Spanish or French. I even managed a few words in Italian or German. I enjoyed meeting people from different parts of the world. Addresses were exchanged, as well as information, tips and advice. Some of these encounters led to life-long friendships, at least through mail and fond memories.

The Oxford had a homey quality. Travelers returned on their way to other destinations in Africa or India, enjoying the freedom of being able to come and go at any time of day or night, plus inviting friends into private rooms for conversation or parties. For residents who stayed for lengths of time, it was a little community of foreigners—mostly English and Germans. but also Israelis, Italians and an occasional American.

Mustafa, the tea and coffee server, was a beloved character at the Oxford. "Aiwa, chai," he would call out as he shuffled stoop shouldered into a room, balancing the ordered refreshments on a small tray, his large eyeballs as white as the djellabia that he wore, in a warm brown Nubian face. He was from Aswan. He had been working at the Oxford for thirty or more of his sixty-seven years. He worked long hours—sometimes from seven or eight a.m. until eleven or twelve at night, but usually no more than ten hours a day—for thirty L.E. (Egyptian pounds) per month. That is about fifteen dollars. Later, I was told that he earned sixty L.E. per month, including tips. Perhaps. He was often over-tired, yet he enjoyed the congenial atmosphere and the affection of the travelers.

A few of the residents were teaching English to Egyptians at schools in Cairo or outlying regions. Others were studying Arabic. There was the occasional foreigner who exported papyrus. belly dance costumes, jewelry, or leather goods to their respective western countries. One young German man imported pornographic magazines to Egyptians, which I felt was a sleazy exploitation of sexually frustrated Egyptian men, certainly not a wholesome way to introduce Egyptians to foreign women. Such magazines and videos only reinforced the idea that foreign women were sexually available.

There was only cold running water at the Oxford. Most of the inhabitants managed with cold water, until the manager put in a propane water heater. For 50 ersh (25 cents), a resident could take a hot shower. If too many people took showers in one day there would be no hot water left, and one had to wait at least half an hour for the heater to heat the water. I found cold showers refreshing until January, when the weather was cool and rainy.

An Egyptian travel agent, Farouk, lived at the hotel, claiming that he preferred to live in his large room. which was cleaned daily for him, rather than take care of an apartment. At the time, he was the only Egyptian allowed to stay there.

Farouk lived right across the hall from me. He stayed up late, especially during Ramadan, when we had some interesting chats in his room over a bowl of creamy rice pudding that he brought from a little shop nearby. During Ramadan, when there were few mulids or hadras, Farouk taught me the first sura (verse) of the Koran. We encouraged one another to fast (summe) during the day, and eat only a little during the night. Looking forward to the rich pudding helped.

A frail-looking woman with long gray-blond, stringy hair, framing a haggard face, appeared at the Oxford one day. She seemed to be in her own world, non-communicative with other guests. She would push around an old shopping cart—the kind one finds in supermarkets, rolling it through the hallways, filled with her piles of things. She even took it onto the elevator and into the streets when she went out. Maybe she did not trust leaving her few belongings in her room.

This woman looked so sad and lonely. One day I struck up a conversation with her in the foyer. She immediately responded with long stories about her life in Lebanon. Her husband was still there. "I had to leave", she told me. "The war with Israel has destroyed Lebanon. It used to be such a beautiful country, with forests and mountains. The bombing has destroyed much of the nature, as well as Beirut and other cities and towns. I got so depressed. I miss Lebanon, but don't want to return to such devastation." She had obviously been a strikingly attractive woman, but now looked wan and dejected, even a bit crazed.

Romances flourished at the Oxford. Some of these alliances survived the first romantic encounters. A lovely German girl and young Englishman married, and taught English at schools in Cairo for several years, before returning to England and further travels. An Italian couple met there and married in Italy, returning every year to Cairo, en route to southern parts of Africa. They used to fight a lot; sometimes emerging from their room with bruises and tears. Yet, they always made up and declared undying love.

The building that harbored the Oxford Hotel was on a corner, so two sides of the hotel faced busy streets. My room faced a dark dirty fire escape enclosure, from which one could hear Egyptian families below—sounds of cooking, voices of women chattering, and sometimes a man or child's voice. The most irritating noise was the rattling and clanking of the old elevator.

On the roof were a cluster of cement rooms that housed the porter of the building and his family. His sons were young men, already working at jobs. Mustafa had a room up there also. When I felt a need for some quieter space, I would sometimes go up to the roof to meditate and do yoga. The air was breezier there and I could see across the rooftops of Cairo. Many rooftops were fixed up and inhabited. One family had created a villa with large potted plants, bamboo screening and freshly painted stucco walls.

When I first went to the roof, the porter's family seemed a bit disconcerted. Sensing that they wanted their privacy, I stayed on the other side of the roof, under the laundry hanging on the clothesline. When there was a breeze, the large white sheets would wind themselves around my head, or flap against my face and body, enshrouding me like a mummy. One day Mustafa introduced me to the family. When they heard that I could speak Arabic, they were delighted, inviting me to eat with them several times on their straw mats under a straw-mat canopy. The outside rooms of the Oxford had narrow balconies with wrought iron railings. When I was visiting another guest, we would often sit on the balcony, looking across Cairo. The scenes before us were fascinating; crumbling buildings stuffed full of vibrant life radiating out in all directions. The roofs were the most visible, revealing the daily lives of Egyptians. Alternatively, we would watch the people and cars on the street below. Sometimes I did yoga on a balcony in the sun. On the backside of the Oxford building, was a lovely garden with a stately colonial mansion in the center. This housed the Consulate of Switzerland, which I visited occasionally to keep my papers in order. My American passport had been stolen at the Wailing Wall in Jerusalem, when my money was taken, so I was using my Swiss passport. The Swiss community had a clubhouse in a pleasant part of Cairo, set in a natural setting of trees. The Consulate invited me to the August First, Swiss Independence Day celebration one year.

I asked Rick, a gay Oxford resident who taught English full time, if he would like to escort me. He was delighted. He adored women with style, and for this occasion, I discarded my djellabias, wearing instead a modem, elegant dress. Rick turned out to be a great dancer. He bought a bottle of wine, Swiss sausages, potato salad and other fine dishes for us to eat. This event was a refreshing change after three years among Egyptians; to laugh, talk and eat with Europeans— mostly Swiss—and ballroom dance to music of an orchestra, playing everything from waltzes to rumbas, in a charming lantern-lit garden.

Back at the Oxford, I came and went in my own twilight reality. The residents could see my sparkling happiness when I returned from a mulid or hadra. I shared tales of my adventures, of journeying from one festival to another, or staying at homes of Sufi sheikhs in the Delta and elsewhere.

Occasionally travelers asked me to take them to a mulid When I acquiesced, I rarely enjoyed it as much as when alone. Taxi drivers tried to charge tourist prices rather than the normal Egyptian fare that I paid. When I was alone, they did not usually hassle me for money, especially when they took me to mosques. Besides, taxi rides, for me, were a time of preparation and centering, even meditating.

With foreigners, I began to feel like a foreigner; even my Egyptian friends seemed to see me as a foreigner amidst the others. When alone, I was part of Egyptian society, especially among the dervishes. Foreigners were pleased by the adventure, but they also seemed relieved to return to familiar surroundings and culture. They would usually return to the hotel much earlier than I did. to speak their mother tongue, with beer in hand.

One morning while I was resting after a mulid, a knock on the door awoke me. As I opened the door, a pleasant looking young man introduced himself as Harry, an English photographer and filmmaker. "One of the residents said that you spend a lot of time with the Sufis. I would like to make a documentary film about them, as well as take photographs for a magazine article," he immediately explained. "Come in," I groggily replied, and sat him on the only chair, while I sat on the edge of my bed.

Harry spoke more about his interest in the Sufis. "Could you guide me to some of the festivals? In exchange I will make a video of you dancing and singing with the Sufis, plus some good still shots and a good quality recording of your songs, which I hear you sing for the festivals."

Hesitating, because I preferred to go alone, and feeling protective of my dervish family, I told him I was not sure it was a good idea to publicize them. Harry assured me that he would follow the flow quietly, do the film and article in such a way that would be of interest to people, but not bring in hordes of tourists. Realizing that what fascinated me, would not necessarily hold the attention of most people, I agreed to take him to a mulid that evening.

Although Harry was a sensitive person. the modesty that he tried to convey did not carry throughout the many occasions that he accompanied me. I had requested that he not take pictures when people did not want him to. This was not usually a problem, as most Egyptians seem to enjoy having their picture taken. However, a few times he took pictures when the subjects turned their heads and indicated 'no'. Harry was high strung and would get over-excited at mulids while filming, sometimes filled with self-importance, which the sensitive Sufis could feel.

Even the sheikhs who loved me protested his presence at one hadra. Hany became angry. I could not take him with me anymore. He had not kept his promises. However, we did have some nice times together. Harry vas amazed by the dervish scene, sometimes overwhelmed. "I don't see how you can handle this strange reality for such long periods of time," he once exclaimed. Sometimes he would get so freaked out that he would rush back to whatever hotel we were staying in at the time, pop a valium, chased with a couple of beers, trying to re establish his identity in a more western environment. Harry's approach was different from mine.

The experience with Harry clarified the difference between an objective observation and a subjective experience. With no preconceived ideas about the Sufis in Egypt, my involvement was organic, perhaps pre-destined. The dervish within was unveiled and nurtured.

This may be true of all archetypes. They surface when the individual is ready for that particular expression. Various archetypes can overlap one another, and even dwell harmoniously within. This takes what the Buddhists call, "a Big Mind and a Full Heart." It may be that the seeds of all forms of consciousness lie within us. When well nourished, these seeds sprout, flower and fruit. Each flower has its own special impregnation, germination and growth period.

Trying to copy someone else takes us further from our true nature. We can learn from one another; yet, we need to be true to our inner nature. This is not a mental concept, but a deep well within the psyche. When tapped, a fountain of joy and peace flows forth to quench the thirst of seekers along the way.

Sometimes I questioned why I preferred to be in the presence of dervishes, with whom I could barely communicate verbally, rather than with westerners with whom I could converse. One reason may be the difference between right and left-brain activity. The Sufis, like most mystics, tend to be right brain oriented—at least during their spiritual practices: intuitive, spontaneous, and motivated by feelings, emotions and the subconscious. The path of music and dance—as for all arts—is predominated by the right brain hemisphere. Westerners tend to emphasize the left-brain, which fosters logic, rationality, practicality and materialism. I tend to gravitate toward spiritual-mystical experiences, with music and dance as major threads in this colorful tapestry.

Bhagavan Rajneesh once said, "The only thing we have to lose is our mind." I could lose my mind with the Sufis, especially while zikr. dancing or singing. Like waves washing over me, Sufi music clears away physical, mental and psychic rubbish. This is the path of a Sufi, or any mystic—a search for purity and power to transcend limitations—those particles that turn into dust. To sense our immortality is the homecoming we long for.

Western society, including westernized segments of third world countries—usually the rich—respects success, wealth, and cleverness, which may even lead to corruption. Perhaps Jesus said "the meek shall inherit the earth," because he saw that wealthy people tend to become greedy, even destroy nature, diminishing the spirit within life. It has been said that Sufism is the mystic path, branch or flower of Islam. My research indicates that Sufism existed before Islam. While browsing in the American University library in Cairo, I read that the Prophet Mohammed took some of his guidelines from the Sufis. It appears that Mohammed had spent some time with the

Sufis before founding Islam. After Mohammed died, Islam spread from Saudi Arabia to Egypt, Turkey, India, Iraq, Iran, Afghanistan, Pakistan, Syria, Lebanon, southern Spain, Sicily, Asia and Africa. The Sufis were absorbed into Islam, continuing their mystical practices, sometimes in secrecy. It really does not matter which came first. The original basic principles are the same. Those who are so caught up in form that they forget—or never understood—the essence, tend to distort truth within all religions. Without direct mystical experience, religion is hearsay. According to Idries Shaw, in his book, The Sufis, "formal religion is for the Sufi merely a shell, though a genuine one, which fulfills a function. When the human consciousness has penetrated beyond this social framework, the Sufi understands the real meaning of religion. The Sufi sees and contacts the Sufic stream in every culture, as a bee will suck from many flowers, without becoming a flower."

Most Sufis today are devout Muslims. Islam is a workable shell for such mysticism. Terminology concerning the divine is in Arabic, full of power. Devotion to Allah, and the inner connection that such **devotion fosters, is the essence of Sufism, no matter what the name** and trappings of an orthodox religion might encompass. The practices of Sufism are transmitted from one heart to another.

Mysticism has always been a part of human experience. Only veils of narrow egohood can blind us to our yearning for union with the Beloved. Differences between Sufism and orthodox Islam can be found in the differences between all mystic paths and orthodox religions, all over the world. Orthodox religions tend to foster a belief in a God that is separate from self, nature and all life forms. God is an all-powerful judgmental ruler, awesome and fearsome. Heaven and hell are places rather than states of consciousness. Mystics experience

God as the essence and source within all of life. God is the spirit within humans, plants, animals, water, earth, fire, air, rocks, and even witnessed in inanimate objects. The orthodox Christian separates spirit from nature; the Essene path that Jesus followed embraces both spirit and nature. The orthodox Jew is strict and obedient to a mighty God; the Hassidic dances, sings, and rejoices in God's love.

All esoteric religions embrace the feminine principle. This includes the subconscious, spontaneity, feelings, and our dark and wild aspects—nature in all her manifestations. The dervish gives expression to this through dancing, chanting, grunting, moaning—expressing the child and the animal within, in a harmless, cleansing way that fosters transformation. In contrast, a caged and stifled animal within becomes neurotic, dangerous and revengeful. We can observe our own western societies becoming more violent as our modem life style creates alienation from nature. Unable to confront his/her dark side, the over-tamed, leashed conformist claims free-spirited individuals as scapegoats, transferring guilt and frustration to whoever is 'different'.

Like Native Americans and other indigenous people, dervishes sit on the ground in a circle, sharing the sacred pipe—in this case a water pipe, celebrating the Great Spirit, Allah, and ritualizing music and dance. Clan and tribal formations are integral to all natural societies. Races remind me of grains. I see the American Indian as com, the European as wheat, the Far Easterner as rice, the Tibetan as barley, and the Middle Easterner as millet (couscous). Modern white man is like refined bleached flour.

Mystical practices are an integral part of the life style of root races. With the Oriental comes Buddhism; the Tibetans have a more colorful and rigorous form of Buddhism. The Europeans have Druidic and Celtic practices. The Africans and Native Americans have their rhythmic rituals and the Middle East has Sufism, Hassidism, Zoroastrianism and other mystic religious sect. In Egypt, the frequently practiced Sufi ritual is called a 'hadra'

SIX
THE HADRA

Dance, dervish dance!
Bring the Face of God before you.
Only love can lift the heart up so high
that it's true color is restored by the Sun!
See Him near and clapping, that perfect
One who fathers Divine Rhythm.

O dance, dervish dance,
and know you bring your Master happiness
whenever you smile.
Last night, my tears took flight because of Joy.
The sky got crowded and complained
when I discovered God hiding again in my heart,
and I could not cease to celebrate.
O dance Hafiz, dance!

Write a thousand luminous secrets
upon the wall of existence
so that even a blind man will know where we are,
and join us in this love

Dance, dervish dance,
O bring the face of your Beloved before you!

(Hafiz)*

"Allah Hay! Allah Hay! Allah Hay! Allah Hay!" The sonorous, hypnotic voices of men chanting in rhythm to zikr music draw me onto the long straw mat to join the wave of swaying movement. Invisible energies carry me from an ordinary physical reality into a deep place of unity with the universe. I feel it from above as cosmic energy, from below as earth energy, and from those around me who are immersed in this group consciousness. Closing my eyes, I see and feel it all within myself.

If I would choose one predominating experience out of the numerous ones during the five years of practicing with the Egyptian Sufis, I would say it is the ability to go within; inside my body, inside my being. As soon as the zikr music begins—even from a cassette or in a roomful of noisy people and distractions—I feel myself flowing into an inner space where I feel subtle energies. Using the special movements that I have learned from the Egyptian Sufis, I begin to nod my head or turn it slowly from side to side, tilting it in a way that releases tensions in my neck, facilitating a state of greater sensitivity and responsiveness. I begin to move my shoulders, releasing blocks and freeing my wings. My hands move circles of light around and through the universe. Pulling threads of energy from above, I can send, or even throw the energy, to others nearby. Just sitting with other dervishes who are also sensitive to subtle energies, even without music, I am drawn into that psychic space.

'Gowa' is the Arabic word for 'inside'. I use this expression when I want to turn away from external annoyances; especially the continual questions that the average Egyptian seems to feel compelled to ask foreigners. "What's your name? What is your country? Are you married? Do you have children?" If a woman does not have children, Egyptian men wonder what in the world she is doing. Isn't motherhood the main role of women? Moreover, one child—I have one son—is hardly enough. My only relief from this rusty old record is to tum inside.

The back seat of a taxi is often the easiest place for me to meditate, outside of my own room, especially if I am on the way to a dervish gathering. Sitting cross-legged, I practice Sufi mantras mixed with yoga and dervish practices. Rolling my head slowly, I softly chant, "Ley Illy Hey II Allah (American Sufis pronounce this "La Illah Ha I l Allah"), Mohammed Rasoulila." A favorite practice of mine is 'shakti kriya' with psychic breath, a practice that I learned from Swami Janakananda in Denmark. Inhaling deeply and pressing forward with both hands—arms straight—on the thighs, retaining the breath while contracting the sphincter muscles, I pull the energy up the spine, and then return to an upright position just before exhaling and releasing. It feels good to exclaim, "Allah," as I exhale.

The inevitable questions from the taxi driver begin: "What's your name?..." My eyes are still closed as I continue breathing, mumbling a simple interjection, "Ana ma Allah min gowa." ("I'm inside with Allah.") This usually silences a devout Muslim for at least a few minutes. Occasionally a taxi driver will refuse the taxi fare, saying something like, "Give it to Sayyidah Nafisah," or to whichever saint whose mosque I am going to.

Having arrived at my destination—either a mulid, a religious festival commemorating a saint's birthday, or a smaller Sufi music zikr gathering called a 'hadra'—I am almost always greeted. or embraced, by one or more Sufis who know me. 'Hadra' literally means 'presence', or as one interpreter expressed it, "Who's coming?" This implies that the Prophet Mohammed and other departed saints are present at such gatherings. It is not difficult to see why the spirits of saints would be attracted; such music of devotion is meant to invoke higher spiritual energies. Not unlike ceremonies of Native American and African tribes, ancestors are honored through chanting, music and dance. In this case, the Prophet, saints, and respected sheikhs are the ancestors. Muslims like to claim a family relation that can be traced back to the Prophet Mohammed. If there is no family tree relationship, a spiritual connection to the origins of Islam is considered lineage. A sheikh or sheikha and his/her clan, or perhaps the combined efforts of several sheikhs, organize a hadra. Sometimes a hadra will become a weekly, or yearly, event. Annual mulids are scheduled by the Islamic moon-cycle calendar rather than the modem western calendar. The hadra takes place at the tomb of a favorite saint or sheikh. If it is a yearly event, it is called a 'mulid'—celebrating the departed person's birthday—even if there is only one hidema, presided over by the dead sheikh's son, daughter, or other family members. One of these, sometimes a son, is the new sheikh for that village or group. It is similar to any tribal situation in the world where religious practices are considered of prime importance. Social structures are interconnected with religion. Since all is Allah, and there is nothing but Allah, then Allah is the center of focus. It is up to the presiding sheikh and all devotees to surrender their will to the will of Allah—self-effacement of the ego. Islam means surrender.

From the main entrance to the hadra, the musicians are grouped at the far end of the tent or other space provided for the gathering—sometimes a long straw mat on the ground outdoors. The men line up in rows on each side of the mat. The women, fewer in number, are gathered closer to the entrance and along the sides. Most of them sit on the ground in groups, preparing tea and food, or watching.

Sometimes women zikr-dance among the men. This religious form of zikr-dance is not called dancing; it is called "zikr", which is the word for mantric chanting, repeating the names of Allah. Yet, movements often accompany the chanting, even while sitting down. Orthodox Muslims told me that dancing is haram (forbidden). If a foreigner calls zikr "dancing", strict practitioners of Islam will correct the foreigner. However, westerners would probably tend to call such movements, "dance".

Among some groups of Sufis, women are prohibited from joining the zikr. Perhaps, a husband or other relation forbids a woman to join in. Once I saw a husband beat his wife out of a zikr set with his long cane stick. No one raised a hand to help her. Her joyful abandonment changed into frightened docility. However, this is rare. Women often have the freedom to join the zikr.

Concentration on the dance is usually stronger among the men, who move in unison, so I prefer to dance with the men. This cohesiveness may be due to their more frequent attendance and training; it is more socially acceptable for them to be out of the home than for a woman. The women are kept busy with household chores, caring for their families, and cooking; even while attending mulids and hadras, women cook, serve food and tea. One hears the phrase, "a woman's place is in the home", echoed often in Egypt. Occasionally I was reprimanded for being footloose and fancy-free.

The singer holds the microphone near his mouth and begins 'a cappella'. If his musically spoken invocation to Allah is sincere, it seems as if the very first sound he utters comes from source. This timeless space feels like my true home, a place from where I have come from and shall return to. Even if the energy preceding the invocation has been dispersed or is chaotic, there is an instant unification when the singer begins, a sense of harmony. This is the time to center oneself, tune in, and feel one with God, with those sharing the space, and with all of life. Gradually the flute joins in; ethereal waves of light vibrating through the singer's voice, caressing it, accentuating, and sometimes flying like a bird. Then the drum, called a tabla or dumbek, resounds into the heart of Mother Earth, pulling consciousness deep into her ever-present womb of birth death-rebirth. Sometimes there is a leader at the top of the two lines of men, who beats out the rhythm on a cylindrical hand drum that he holds in the air with one hand, called a 'tar'; it is similar to a 'bodrum'. The deep breathing and droning pulls me deeper and deeper inside, "Ah, Mother, you're darkness, and Mother, you're light. Mother, you're where we all come from tonight." I forget the tedious motions of mundane existence. I want to stay engulfed in this hypnotic spell; a rapture of cascading music that caresses me back to my true nature. As though sleepwalking, I rise from my seat and glide toward the music, toward the lines of swaying bodies, toward an eternal sea of rhythm. I slip into the sea and swim. Arms and shoulders pressed close together, our lines sway in unison, bending forward and back, leaning toward those opposite, rising back up toward the cosmos. Gradually we begin turning side-to-side, soaring on waves of energy. Now an oud joins in; the strings plucking the fiber of my being, picking notes from the nether spheres. A violin bow trembles lightly across the strings of the violin, creating a sensation of swimming below the surface of water. Shrill trills of women occasionally punctuate the music. As the music picks up speed, the violin reminds me of the quickening of country western fiddling.

Now the musicians form a semi-circle—playing flute, drums, tambourine, large finger cymbals, oud and violin. With the rise in the energy of the dancers and onlookers, excitement builds collectively. My body becomes liquid fire, grace and passion. Without any rhythmic interruption, the dancers gradually space themselves so that there is room for arms to swing. As I spread my arms, I begin to fly. "Oh please let there be enough space, so that I can soar freely on this magic carpet. I am tired of being a chicken with wings closed in. An eagle needs space. The flute takes off again; the flutist is a snake charmer. If this is hypnotism then let me be hypnotized in such ecstasy until my bones are ashes upon the altar of mother earth. "Allah Ho Akbar!" God is great! As I turn from side-to-side, my feet are farther apart. The movement is stronger, more assertive. One loosely clenched hand grabs an invisible rod of energy as I reach skyward at a forty-five degree angle. Pulling the energy toward me, I turn, my other hand reaching to pull a shaft of energy from the other side. Stomping one foot on the ground to the beat, I slowly dance in a circle around the stable foot. Soon my pelvis is swaying back and forward while my arms move in harmonious counter-balance. By repeating certain movements—sometimes enlarging them or allowing new movements to emerge from that inner space where music and dance are one. Perhaps my shoulders, wrists, or feet need to release energy; I find ways to free them while keeping the rhythm. As I draw energy from the earth, or light from above. I can pass them on to those around me: perhaps a cripple dancing on his stumps near my feet, or a woman who has just passed out, lying prostrate on the ground in swaths of black nylon, or to a foaming-mouthed male possessed by malevolent spirits.

Is this a dream? It feels more real than what is normally called reality. I feel compassion for the deformed, for the possessed, for all our sufferings. Yet, there is nothing repulsive. I am simply keeping time to music that draws me on and on.

Sometimes eyes meet and twinkle, "Hello, happy to see you, to feel your presence," or something even deeper; that special feeling that we are all swimming in the same super conscious sea. In addition, is not love 'sharing the same universe'?

Strong male energy is grounding and yangizing. Some women twinkle and flirt, share gentleness, love and compassion. Some women's faces contort in grimaces; angels and demons, light and darkness play across their facial expressions. Beauty and ugliness are equally exquisite in their honesty, no posing or superficial smiles. Fire and water is felt in the eyes, limbs, belly and womb. Breath carries oxygen to all parts of the body, clearing the mind. A woman gasps, then screams, gyrating and whirling to the ground. Someone attends to her, removing her body from the other dancers.

The music intensifies and quickens. I am flying, soaring into limitless spheres. The rhythms of my being are united with the rhythms of the music. We cascade into a finale. Light rains down upon us.

We feel our deep Sufi connection when our hearts fly in unity. A heavy heart is like a weighted body drowning in the sea of delusion. A heart dancing in light, nur, is the expression of Allah, of the Christ spirit of love, of the peace of Buddha. Truth does not have religious divisions. "Ya Hay, Ya Huq' Ya Hay, Ya Huq'" ("O life, O truth!") Along with these highs and ecstasies, negativity can also emerge. Increased psychic sensitivity reveals pain within—disappointments, fears, anger, loneliness, jealousy, impatience, despair, and other deep feelings that may have lain dormant or buried. The purpose is to transform and exorcise the negativity. More often than not, positive emotions are experienced. "Jinn" is the Arabic tern, used to connote invisible entities that live in fire and can sometimes possess people. Jinn are not always negative; they can be helpful spirits. However, the word Jinn, usually refers to what westerners would call 'demons'.

My experience is that fiery energy is often increased by the music and energy of such gatherings. If dancing and other expressions flow well, the fire energy is grounded or released and channeled beneficially. Love is the best transformer of such energy, especially when in touch with a tantric partner. Holding a beloved's hand, looking into each other's eyes, or just feeling love flow, can serve like water to soften and facilitate streaming, rather than holding, pain.

One evening when I was feeling intensely emotional, I could actually feel my heart crying. The image of blood accompanied a sensation of moisture-fluid discharging from my heart. There was pain from pressure against my chest and ribs. I had to cry externally to release the pressure. Then I felt exhausted. This may have manifested from painful past experiences, or perhaps collective psychic experiences that needed to be released. After a twenty minute rest, I felt renewed.

Even in my hotel room—while cleaning, sewing, reading or writing I would often listen to Sufi music on a small cassette recorder that I had purchased at the bazaar. Listening to the music, I could remember all those wonderful faces; the men's turbaned heads above their djellabias, the women swathed in black nylon or brightly colored long-sleeved floor-length floral print dresses. I would recall the comforting bosoms of large-breasted women, nurturing my child within. I could forgive the accidental, or purposeful, stick whacks; the rare fights; the teenagers who once ran off with my guitar; the crazed woman who dragged me to the ground with her shawl, strangling my neck. I have trudged and stumbled through so much mud, trash, garbage, dust, rubble and rock to get to a hadra or mulid. Was it worth it? In my higher moments, I would tell myself that even the wonderful music events that I had attended in Northern California did not hold a candle to these Sufi gatherings in Egypt. Perhaps the Grateful Dead concerts, the San Francisco Sufi Choir, or the wonderful Middle Eastern music I so often belly danced to, came closest to this dervish 'tour de force'. In Egypt, the hadras are held in gratitude for the dead, and the dead—grateful or not—are envisioned as participating in such festivities.

SEVEN

The large mulids evolve into endless labyrinths, winding through graveyards, following dirt or paved roads, or alleys; all are occupied by hidemas—in tents, on roofs, in basements, warehouses, unfinished buildings, or simple mats lining the ground in any nook or cranny where people can find space. All these camps are centered around the tomb of whichever saint or sheikh(a) is being celebrated. Sometimes the mulids are so large—with, literally, millions of people attending—that some of the hidema sites are halfway across the town or city. Thousands of colored lights twinkle brightly on wires hung from buildings. The mosque, or tomb, will be the most plentifully decorated, attracting all toward it.

Large mulids might include carnival-type amusements; sideshows, rides for children and even a tent with low-class belly dancing—more gyration than art. Apparently, these belly dancers double as prostitutes between shows, capitalizing on sexual energy, which might be heightened at such high-energy events; people choose various ways to channel abundant energy. These sideshows struck me as rather sleazy and inappropriate for a religious festival. Profit rather than spiritual elation was the motivation. Not that belly dancing and sex cannot be sacred participants; if such expressions create union with the divine, then this is part of the holy sacrament.

Trying to get through the hordes of people on leila kebir (the big night) can be a frustrating activity. Sometimes a man will use the crowd as an opportunity to pinch or grab a foreign woman, if there are any. Due to the influence of western films and television shows such as Dynasty, and false information, foreign women are considered—in the minds of some people—sexually promiscuous. Unfortunately, American film companies earn fortunes exporting trashy films to third world countries. Almost naked women, engaged in sexual intrigues with male stars, are presented to naive poor people who understand sex as a procreative union for married couples. The enormous wealth depicted in these movies is, to these simple people, a remote fantasy.

When alone, or among other Egyptians, people thought of me as one of them. However, when I was with a foreign girl, both of us became prey for hungry hands. More than once, I rammed my elbow or a fist into an Egyptian man who grabbed me licentiously. One night I knocked a tall young man down in the square of Sayyidna al Hussein. The crowd cheered as the police cleared a pathway to the mosque for a German girlfriend and me.

Sex is considered taboo unless lovers are married in Egypt. Extramarital sex seems to be rare except among rich or westernized Egyptians. However, the hypocrisy and sneakiness of sexually frustrated men was infuriating. In one instance on a crowded bus, I scolded and slapped a man who had pinched me. Red-faced and confused, he scrambled out the back door of the bus at the next stop, so embarrassed that I was sure he would never touch a foreign woman again.

Although my Arabic was negligible during the first few months in Egypt, the psychic communion I shared with the dervishes facilitated communication that manifested in practical actions, such as when the spoon was handed to me when I thought I needed one.

Twenty years earlier, I was told by a psychic in southern California that I have an invisible Arabic guide on the spiritual plane. It had not occurred to me, at that time, that I would ever go to an Arabic country. Only in Egypt did I remember the clairvoyant's psychic reading. Stranger yet, is a connection between a mirror I have and a picture I saw on a wall in Tania, Egypt. For many years, I have kept a small mirror with a picture of an Arabic man imprinted on it. I had no idea who the picture portrayed or why I liked to look at it frequently. One day in Tanta, I saw the exact same picture hanging on the wall of a Sufi sheikh's house. He told me that the man is a well-known and loved Sufi master from the thirteenth century, who had come to Egypt from Morocco.

What amazed and delighted me most about the mystic communication I experienced with the Egyptian Sufis, was not so much having my thoughts responded to, but that a timeless space reached beyond our personal limitations. wherein our souls seemed to know one another. Having already learned some sacred Islamic words as a Sufi in California, new words and expressions reinforced my awareness of their power.

ALLAH (God) is in itself a mantra. Such a sound can open the heart chakra, as well as other energy centers in the body. Some Egyptian Sufis told me that scientists have discovered that the heart beats, "Allah, Allah!" ALHAMDULILLAH (Praise be to God) is used frequently in Egypt. When a person inquires about the health of another, the answer is usually, "Alhamdulillah!" Even when the person is ill or suffering—even missing an arm or a leg—a devout believer will thank God; partly because things could be worse and mainly because the believer feels that Allah knows best, that all comes from Allah. People do not want to hear about another's ills in any culture. When I exclaimed, Alhamdulillah, even when I felt terrible, it reminded me of the good fortune that I did have, a gratitude which I could share with others. ALLAH KARIM (Allah is most generous) is another widely used expression among Sufis, most frequently among the poor. Generosity from Allah is praised even when one has no money. Any gesture or manifestation of the bounty of the universe can trigger such an exclamation as, "Allah Karim!" ALEIKRAMAK (ALEIKRAMIK for a woman) means "God bless you." When we bestow blessings upon another person, it reminds us of the value of a human being. INSHALLAH (if God wills) is expressed whenever planning for something in the future, even if it is just a meeting for the next day. "I will see you tomorrow, inshallah!"

For five years, most of my meals were shared with the Sufis. Surrounding almost any mosque in Egypt, small clusters of Sufis sit on straw or cardboard mats, serving tea and food. It is almost **impossible to avoid numerous invitations to join one group or** another—or even an occasional single person. If! said I was in a hurry, the hopeful hosts looked hurt or disappointed. It was enjoyable to sit on these mats with Sufi acquaintances stopping by to say hello, sometimes joining the rest of us for tea or food.

Frequently the meals consist of mulahiya, a dark green slimy leaf vegetable, chopped up finely and cooked into a soupy mixture with olive oil and garlic. Overcooked potatoes in tomato sauce are also common. Okra stewed in tomato sauce might replace the mulahiya. Brown farm bread or pita serves as a utensil to dip into the soupy vegetables. Salad usually consists of tomatoes, onion and vinegar, with too much salt for my palate. In homes, food is served on a large round metal tray or a low, round, carved wooden table, or on the floor, in the middle of the circle of people. Even in wealthier homes, the ground floor is often packed earth. Sometimes a large carpet covers the earthen floor. It is swept with a small hand broom after each meal. There was never much time between mulids and hadras. They could be continuous if I wanted to travel from region to region.

During my last two years in Egypt I gave up my little room at the Oxford and roamed from one festival to another with the dervishes, visiting various Sufi homes in the countryside to rest in between festivals. Sleeping in bare rooms, on roofs, on the floor of prayer rooms or mosques, beside tombs in graveyards, in mangers of straw amidst goats and donkeys and chickens, or in the homes of wealthy sheikhs, where servants waited upon me, I followed the dervish path.

More often than not, I was wrapped in a grubby rough wool blanket. It was a rare occasion when there were no bugs eating me during the night or day. This may seem strange since I could have been sleeping in posh surroundings in wealthy homes or in an inexpensive hotel. Tending to gravitate toward the Sufis who radiated the most love, I often found myself amongst the poor; they make up the greatest portion of the population of Egypt. At festivals, I usually slept in a tent or hidema room. Both men and women snored heavily; many men coughed from incessant smoking of water pipes. Babies cried. Music from a nearby hidema—sometimes a loud tape recorder—blasted into the wee hours of the morning. Just as one noise source quieted down, another would begin. At daybreak, the amplified calling of the mussein at a nearby mosque—when distorted by a raspy sound system—was yet another irritation. Questioning why I put myself through such agonies, I can only answer that I could not resist the magic. Sometimes I was so tired that I could not leave the arena of action to find peace, particularly when I did not know where I might find some. Even in small villages, with numerous relatives dropping in to see the agnebia (foreigner), I might not find any solitude. I never ceased to be amazed by the ability of Egyptian5 to sleep through so much noise, including blasting television

Occasionally, I had the good fortune to visit a quiet house. In the villages, there was usually a festival—a wedding, a Sufi hadra, or a holiday—that charmed and refreshed my spirit, regardless of sleep. There were always new groups who wished to hear me sing. However, sometimes I was desperate for silence.

A Moroccan Sufi master, Jabrane, once told me, "A Sufi must learn to die before dying." Such training took place spontaneously in the graveyards of Egypt. Each time I came back from the dead I felt closer to life. Familiar faces, lights, music and laughter were never so beautiful as after a near death experience. I sometimes wondered if there were spirits in the graveyards who wished to possess me and carry me into the underworld with them.

One night during an intense mulid in the graveyards of Sidi Ali Zayn al-Abidin, I was overcome with a feeling that I was dying. Stretching out on a tomb where a group of dervishes had gathered, fear overcame me as I felt my life force slipping away. One of the men, sensing that I needed vitamin C, rushed off to get some oranges. A woman I did not know cradled my head in her lap, almost smothering me in her sticky black nylon dress. When the man returned, he began peeling oranges rapidly, shoving the segments into my mouth. It helped. Miraculously, I was up and about again, even going to visit other hidemas before returning to the Oxford Hotel.

There were moments of pain and tears, both physical and emotional; much of this was a result of physical exhaustion and over-input, taxing my nervous system. Charmed by the music, bright lights and the participants who would press me to stay, I was too tired to decisively leave. The endless smiles and cups of tea seduced me into the vortex of the celebration until I could no longer feel physical limitations, until it was too late.

A few Sufis would die during or after festivals. One respected sheikh, in his sixties, died at the train station in Cairo as he was leaving a large mulid. This lovable man probably died in a happy—even if exhausted—state of mind.

One night at a mulid-hadra at the small mosque of Sidi Yunis, in a graveyard high on a hill overlooking Cairo, I zikr-danced for six hours, with only two fifteen-minute semi-rests, sitting with a cup of tea in my hands, still moving to the music. It was an amazing six hours, sung by the great Egyptian munshid, Sheikh Ahmad al-Tuni. The energy kept building, as light and rhythm cascaded through bodies and souls. Our group of dervishes became an intense unit of pulsating energy. At such moments of clarity, I felt that all was perfect. I could see why someone had done something that had caused suffering. Everything made sense, even my mistakes and foolishness. In its boundless ocean of energy, life could be a perfect dance. Physical reality is but a small reflection of a much vaster reality.

Walking down the hill in the early morning after the mulid, the dawn light illuminating the skyline of Cairo with soft gold, I did not feel any fatigue. I warmly greeted a small girl sitting on the bench of a wooden cart, holding the reins of the donkey that would pull the load of garbage and trash collected at that hour. She was one of the Zabbalin, mainly Christians from Coptic villages of Upper Egypt who dwell in shanties in dump sites of Cairo, surrounded by huge mounds of garbage that they sort through for items of any value. Most of what they collected would be recycled, including the food fed to their pigs. Although smudge-faced and dirty, as well as living in an unhealthy environment these children often seem quite cheerful. Though obviously sleepy, the girl smiled back.

Only after I went to bed in my small dark cave-room at the Oxford did I feel fatigue overtake me. I could not move for two and a half days. Astral travels revealed glimpses of an infinite universe during that long sleep. I understood what a Sufi sheikh had told me: "I can travel without moving my body. So why do I need to go anywhere?" It took six hours of effortless perseverance to launch myself into such an orbit. No airplane could take me on such a trip. The ticket was purchased with joy and devotion, by just repeating the movements and chanting during the zikr.

Whether in a small room or in front of a large audience on a stage, or even when acting in films, I learned to humble myself to this source of creativity. While singing for a folkloric concert in Cairo, I was surprised by a chorus of forty Egyptian men chanting in a semi-circle behind me during a Sufi song I had composed. These men had performed during other segments of the show, but we had never rehearsed together, or even spoken to each other. Dressed in long white djellabias, they chanted "Allah Hay" in deep voices, in perfect rhythm to my song. This vocal accompaniment spurred my singing to greater heights. It was as if we were all directed by a divine conductor. When the song ended, the audience arose in a standing ovation.

My reputation as a healer began during a mystical morning following leila kebir at a large mulid in the Delta town of Tania, at the great mosque of Sayyid Ahmad al-Badawi, a favorite Sufi saint from Fez, Morocco. Ahmad al-Badawi settled in Tanta in 1234, founding his own Sufi brotherhood, the Badawiyyah or Ahmadiyyah. I was initiated in Tanta into this Sufi sect.

It had been a long exciting night. The energy was still buzzing as people gathered inside the mosque for the dawn prayer. I was walking around the Saint's tomb—called a macam (station)—dazed and exhausted from lack of sleep during the weeklong festival. Three glowing elderly men, appearing like the three wise men in a nativity painting, approached me, smiling.

The first man kissed my right hand and placed it on his head, atop his white cotton crocheted skullcap. Understanding enough Arabic to realize that he was asking for blessings, I could not imagine why anyone, especially these three luminescent beings, would want my energy when I was so tired. What could I do? Remembering that surrender is a prerequisite in Islam, I closed my eyes.

Within seconds, I felt a sensation of light streaming through me and into the man. When I opened my eyes the man smiled and kissed my hand, then the next man stepped up. Again, I felt the energy flowing through my hands into the recipient. I was surprised at how refreshed I felt. After laying my hands on the third man, I went back to the home I was staying in. relaxed and recharged. There was no separation between the healer and the healed.

From then on, more and more people asked me to lay my hands upon them. I used a few healing and channeling techniques that I had learned through yoga and healing studies, including those learned from a Moroccan Sufi master, Jabrane, who I had studied with in Denmark and Germany.

This healing practice became a grounding rod in the midst of multitudes. It was also an acceptable means for touch, as Muslim men are often taught that it is forbidden to touch women, other than immediate family relations. Some of the strict fundamentalist men would not even shake my bare hand in greeting. If I offered my hand, they would wrap their right hand in the skirt of their djellabia and shake my hand reluctantly through the cloth.

However, as time progressed some Sufi men began to see me as a sister, embracing me in the manner in which they embraced other men—pressing first the right sides of our heads together, and then the left sides. This felt natural to me. Many Sufis are spontaneous and openhearted, not full of orthodox restrictions. However, to some strict Muslim observers this act of affection was considered taboo, and to dirty minds it was "bad".

My reputation as a healer grew; people in the streets besieged me. They would call from their mats as I passed by, sometimes clutching the hem of my skirt. There were times when I did not want to go into the streets, even when I needed to buy some food. Most people were sincere; their faith encouraged me to use the gifts of channeling. Others just liked the attention or were curious. Discerning the difference was often a challenge.

Such healing energy appears to be a natural presence in the universe, available to whoever is sensitive enough to gather and distribute it. Love is the greatest healer. Faith in the power of Allah;

in the healer faith creates a field of receptivity for healing. Faith is the cohesive bond which permeates the Islamic world Most of the people in Egypt are very poor, yet they have faith that Allah will provide. They share what they have with one another, even with strangers. Worship is shared, as is food, home, work and family life. There is power in unity. Life takes on another dimension when all is seen as Allah.

It was sometimes difficult for me to get from one place to another due to persistent demands for my attention. One night during a mulid at Sayyidna al-Hussein, I walked across the square to get to Sheikh Mohammed's hidema that lay behind al-Azhar mosque on the other side of the heavily trafficked wide road. As I crossed the midan (arena, open area, plaza) people called to me, urging me to join them, sometimes walking over to me with big smiles, and beseeching me to come over to their tent or mat Between handshakes and embraces, I struggled to get through the sea of shining faces. Carrying my guitar on my back was tiring. I was scheduled to sing for Sheikh Mohammed's hidema, so I tried to be quick with each person. Nevertheless, the journey from the midan through the road underpass to al-Azhar—perhaps about 500 meters—took me two hours. By the time I reached Sheikh Mohammed, I was exhausted. After reviving with tea and hot food, I was able to sing.

These were times when I wished I were invisible. During my last six months in Egypt, I could rarely go out onto the streets of Cairo without being stopped by Egyptians asking me for healing. Nor was there a fisherman on a lake—or the Nile River—to spirit me away in a boat.

EIGHT
POVERTY AS A JEWEL

"New organs of perception come into being as a result
of necessity. Therefore, O man, increase your necessity,
so that you may increase your perception."

(Rumi)*

Sufi tale, which I found in the library of the American
University in Cairo, illustrates a prevailing attitude of the
Egyptian dervishes toward poverty and wealth:

A merchant went to visit a Sufi master bemoaning his rate, of
which a series of misfortunes had reduced him from a state of great
wealth to a condition of poverty. After listening to the merchant's
complaints, the Sufi master replied: "I have paid a high price for
poverty by my own choice. Poverty is a rare jewel, which only few can
understand. Instead of complaining, be grateful, for now you have the
opportunity to discover, that which is of true value. The things that
you have lost were not necessary for your spiritual development. They
have only clouded your mind and you have lost touch with your true
sett; as a jewel is lost in a pile of rubbish. Now that the garbage has
been cleared away, perhaps you can find your true nature, which was
buried beneath your material wealth, greed and selfishness."

Throughout Sufi writing, one finds stories of holy men who. by losing position, wealth and social acceptance, thereby find truth. For example, Mohammed Jalal-al-Din-Rumi, the beloved Persian Sufi poet and mystic who founded the Mevlevi Order of "whirling dervishes" in Konya, Turkey during the thirteenth century, turned his back on a highly respected position as an Islamic leader in order to decipher his true nature. Spurred on by his mentor, Shams el-Din, he took up the practice of ecstatic dance and solitude. However, he never really lost his status even when people wondered if he was losing his mind. In "Fihi Ma Fihi," Rumi writes: "Man experiences pain, urges and demands. Even if he possessed a hundred thousand worlds. he would find no rest. Meticulously man ceaselessly engages in every kind of trade and craft. All these pleasures and pursuits are like a ladder, because the rungs of the ladder are not a place to dwell, but are transitory. Happy is he who awakens soon enough to become aware of this fact. For him the long road becomes short and he does not waste his life on the rungs of the ladder."

Even before Rumi's time, poverty as a form of emptiness was considered a necessary experience for spiritual unfoldment. When I found myself in Egypt upon the Sufi path, I had not intended to embrace poverty. Yet, in this environment of one-pointed love for Allah, it was natural to shed material comforts. The music, dancing, the ever-present love found within this framework were food for my soul. Rumi said that we could find no ease in any other thing but "heart's ease", which is the "beloved". This is the jewel. which shines as a steady flame, illuminating even the darkest recesses of the mind, bringing inner peace and a pervading atmosphere of love.

The price for poverty as I experienced it was: loss of prestige and respect in the eyes of people who value material success, suspicion and fear from those who have plenty—afraid I might want something from them, being labeled an impractical, foolish and eccentric vagabond, discomfort, fatigue, hardship, insecurity, and the inability to obtain what I needed sometimes.

On the positive side I learned faith, which included trust in the eternal abundance of the universe, the value of love put into practice, compassion, generosity, receptivity, loss of anxiety and stress, freedom from being possessed by possessions, and an ability to live simply with little in the way of lodging, food or clothing. By learning to surrender, I learned faith.

To say that I chose a path of poverty purposely to eliminate selfishness and desire would not be true. There were long periods of time when I did feel free, but then a little, or big, hook would reach out and dangle me in a pool of desire, or at least wishful thinking. These hooks tended to snare me most often when I was with other people who were caught up in desires, or when I was in a marketplace of tempting treasures. It was most difficult to be among Americans and Europeans whose reality was centered on comfort and prosperity. All rich people were reminders of such values.

When I saw guests at the hotel counting out hundreds, or thousands of dollars, or other valuable currency, I would feel poor in comparison. I would question my life style and even my sanity. Perhaps I should be working in Europe or the U.S., at least at a steady job in Egypt—singing or dancing in a nightclub or hotel where money flowed more abundantly than at mulids, or maybe teaching English. I spoke four languages—to some extent at least—and had two degrees from a university in California. However, it was life among the dervishes that rapturously held my attention. Without the crystal colors of mysticism, life has always seemed rather gray and flat to me. There were westerners who admired my freedom from materialism, also my devotion to a mystic quest. Residents at the Oxford Hotel were intrigued, watching me come and go, dressed in Egyptian dresses and scarves, checking to see if! had a pound for the taxi fare as I left the hotel, confident that Allah would provide the way back. There were those who saw me return late at night or early in the morning, exhilarated and joyous. Sometimes I did not return for a week, or a month or more, bringing back tales of wild adventures where one event led to another, until I was desperate for sleep and a respite from the struggle to communicate in Arabic and being in such a close-knit society.

It took me a long time—maybe more than a year—to become aware of poverty in Egypt. My first few months were spent in Luxor, singing and dancing for hotels and cruise ships, which brought me in contact with businessmen, lawyers, tour operators, felucca owners and tourists, who all had money.

Many of the homes that I visited were old and rough, but clean and livable. Even when I visited tiny mud huts along the Nile, where families sat on dirt floors, I did not think of those conditions as poverty, but rather a preference for simplicity; such as I had experienced while living in a tipi, and later a tiny cabin, on my mountain in northern California. That life-style had been my choice. The mud huts were more natural and aesthetic than the cement block apartment buildings in the cities and towns. The Egyptians always seemed to have something to eat; they spent a lot of time preparing food, eating and drinking tea. Since they invited me to share their space, food, and spiritual practices with smiles of joy, the thought of poverty did not enter my mind. It was in large cities—in crowded, dirty rooms,

illuminated by ugly florescent lights and radiation from TV sets—
that the concept of poverty registered in my mind. I did not consider
myself poor, even though I had very little money, sometimes none.
However, I was in a position to leave these circumstances or change
them, whereas these Egyptians lived from one generation to the next
in such conditions, with little education, and no means of escape.

Village dwellers were much more relaxed and content than the
occupants of city ghettos. The closeness to nature and the ability to
procure fresh farm food provided a nurturing environment.

At the mulids, I was not aware of poverty for a long time
either. Though people slept on straw or cardboard mats, the festive
atmosphere did not invoke images of poverty. Later I realized that
those with money had a tent or a temporary space in a building
for their clans. Human warmth would so envelope me that I would
accept invitations to share food or visit homes without thinking about
my hosts' social or economic position. Because sacrifice and sharing
are more common among poor people, their understanding of love,
as the greatest jewel of all, is fostered through interconnectedness
with other human beings.

One Saturday afternoon, after praying in the mosque of Sidi
Ibrahim al-Dasuqi, as I walked outside I realized how hungry I
was. As if in answer to this need, a man with a wife and two small
children sitting on a cardboard mat with a ragged umbrella for a roof,
hailed me to join them. It had been pouring rain for a few days. The
streets were rivers of mud. This family's cardboard floor was partly
submerged in mud and water. The tired children weakly raised their
heads from sleep as their parents made room for me to sit upon
some folded clothes. The woman was preparing a delicious meal of

eggplant, felafel, ful (beans), and dark farm bread. They were also grilling a large fish, a rare treat that a kind man had brought them.

While the food cooked over hot coals, the man showed me his stump of a leg, cut off at the knee. He said that I had laid healing hands on it once, that it was less painful since then. He hoped to someday have a small hand-rolling cart so that he could get around easier and take better care of his family. He showed me his small three-wheeled skate board that was soaking wet, unable to skirt over water when it rained, slow and awkward even during dry weather. The man told me that his legs ached from the cold wetness.

The cripple's wife was kind and sympathetic, pleased to have a visitor. They told me that they go from one mulid to another, sleeping on streets or the ground on cardboard. The energy of the festivals, sharing with others of faith and eating healthy meals when possible, sustained and illuminated their lives. They radiated an inner joy, even while telling me their problems. This man just wanted to be able to roll himself around above water and mud.

One can eat well in Egypt for little money. Gagir (water cress), potatoes, lentils, rice, mulihiya and rough brown bread can all be bought for a few ersh (pennies). Questioning why I spent so much time with poor people, when I could have been wining and dining with the rich, I realized that their spirit of generosity and compassion won my heart. Those who valued money and success often seemed misguided, even poor. Without the one-pointedness of opening and reaching toward Allah, people tend to become attached to material things to the exclusion of spiritual values. They search for recognition from others who are also obsessed with comfort. There were exceptions; Sufis who were materially wealthy but also spiritually awakened.

Had I not encountered poverty, I might not have experienced the fountain of universal abundance. Where there is emptiness, something usually fills the void. As a troubadour, I was usually recompensed, but there were times when I was down to my last ersh or gave it to a beggar.

One day I had only five ersh left (worth two and a half cents), having felt too exhausted to leave the Oxford Hotel to go out to eat during the past two days. Realizing that I was weak from hunger, I summoned up enough energy to gather my guitar and a few cassettes of my music, to go to Khan al-Khalili bazaar to sing. As soon as I exited the hotel, a beggar approached me. My heartstrings tweaked, I gave him my last five ersh. Within one minute, as I continued down the street, an Egyptian sidewalk vendor, one I'd seen before but never met, invited me to share his dinner of meat, potatoes, green beans and salad; a veritable feast for this hungry woman. Sitting next to his kiosk on a mat, it took little time to empty the aluminum bowl that we shared, with time for joking while we ate. With renewed energy, I went to the bazaar to sing. I rarely sang in the bazaar, except in some of the nicer cafes and restaurants in the evening. That day singing on the street, I sold a cassette of my music to an American tourist and earned fourteen pounds in tips; quite a decent sum for a penniless dervish in Egypt.

Howaria is the Sufi way of traveling from one place to another. This term probably comes from the Arabic word howa, which means wind or air. Following invitations and suggestions of destinations, I enjoyed drifting like the wind. Spontaneity is developed in such a life-style. A wandering mendicant changes environments often. The opportunity to see how different people live, without getting caught into daily mundane routines keeps life fresh. At the same time, fresh energy is contributed to a rooted household. Experiences are varied and a large circle of friends is gathered by moving about.

The best way to follow the howaria path is to move on every two or three days. Egyptians are very hospitable, especially during the first few days of a visit. Although my hosts never wanted me to leave, I knew I would be energized by a new, excited welcome at the next place. Charmed easily, my curiosity lured me upon many a winding path. Frequent travel could also be tiring, especially when carrying my guitar, clothes, and gifts for my hosts, tambourine and presents from others along the way.

A well-seasoned traveling dervish, my lover-brother, El Arabi, who often accompanied me, would usually leave his clothes, if he had any with him, at the first house that we went to, and walk off wearing two djellabias and carrying his sacred staff. Often he was given fresh clothes at the next house, to either use or keep, while the host's wife, daughter, or mother washed the dirty clothes. If he needed something later on from a stash he had left behind, he would return to pick them up, sometimes not for months or years. This reminded me of my own belongings that l had left in various countries during my travels—stashes remaining in Germany, Switzerland, Denmark, England, Israel and Egypt.

A dervish will use whatever is available, wherever one is. The more that you let go of things, the more that comes your way. Whatever was needed materialized, especially if I was not looking for it. It is a form of living indigenously, facilitating non-attachment, and curtailing expectations.

After leaving Egypt, while living in Wells, Somerset, England for three months, I was introduced to an American man of knowledge and

New Age vocabulary. He told me about the New Age University that he was starting. When I asked about the possibility of scholarships or grants, he flared up: "There is no room in our university for 'poverty consciousness'. We do not want needy people."

His monologue, expressed in trendy new age phrases, such as: "self-nurturing," "independence," "self-love," "prosperity", continued. Since I had been exposed to approximately fifty million poor Egyptians, I got up and left, not wishing to contaminate this rich man with poverty vibrations.

I wonder if Mother Teresa, St. Francis, Jesus, and other humanitarians were concerned about being contaminated by the poor, or accused them of poverty consciousness. When a person is giving or expressing his/herself in some creative way, his/her cup is overflowing, so input of unwanted energy is not likely.

The ancient Persian Sufi poet. Rumi, writes, "that merely to become aware of the power of love and to relate oneself to others is not enough; man must translate his state of being, kindness, benevolence and love into human conduct and creativity."

Perhaps qualities of sharing, caring and self-confidence can be taught to some extent in a seminar, but I wonder just how deep the grain goes on a human level. The transcendental ability within each of us is fostered through experience rather than theory.

Just before leaving for Egypt, I had signed up, and paid for, an EST training seminar in Israel, thinking that I would be back in three weeks. This seminar was going to focus on prosperity. which I felt would be beneficial. It is ironical that instead of returning to Israel and perhaps increasing prosperity in my life, I joined the poor in

Egypt. Yet, I feel that this association has been the richest experience of my life. thus far. The 'jewel' of such an experience was a feeling shared with other dervishes, as we embraced the magic and mystery of creation. It is easier to see God in someone who is seeing God in you.

How can our soul be nourished in a society that cares more about money than sentient beings, including the planet itself? Even a street cleaner can be happy in a caring society. In united struggles, a humanitarian spirit is ignited, even though suffering may be involved. People are hungry for the 'great heart'. If we lived in an awareness of the inter-relatedness of all of life, there would be no threat of extinction of any living species on our planet. Only greed could have brought us to the brink of possible annihilation. If we do not quickly learn to live in a state of awareness of the whole. we shall leave this cycle of existence with our wealth in ashes and our jewels buried with us.

Modem society praises poverty in dead saints and prophets, but when it is nearby this condition is labeled 'poverty consciousness', 'loser', 'bad karma', or 'victimization'. In Egypt, I observed that saints and prophets gain status through martyrdom. This is also found in Christianity in western countries. Yet, anyone poor or suffering nearby or underfoot—especially if it is under the foot of one's ambitions—is considered a misfit to be shunned.

If the poor person encounters misfortune in the presence of friends, it is embarrassing. The better-off friend is apt to put some distance between him/herself and the misalliance. From a distance, friends might send a package of underwear, or letters urging their friend to get out of a poor country and come to a land where money flows more abundantly.

I allowed myself to be charmed from poverty among the masses of Egypt to a more solitary space on the "Penniless Porch" of Wells, Somerset in England, where I lived for a few months during the first year after I left Egypt. Ah, how rich I sometimes felt in that drafty stone arched gateway to the majestic Cathedral; rich in the joy of singing for humanity, for the celebration of life through music and a few warm hearted contacts. A cup of hot tea brought to me when I was cold—though rare indeed, providing a vast contrast to the numerous offerings of tea in Egypt—would rekindle the flame of universal love. It is sometimes my choice to go through discomfort, even hardship, in order to experience the joy of sharing. Perhaps this is what the Sufi masters meant by the 'high price of poverty' and the 'choosing' of such. Sanai, a great Sufi master, wrote in his Hadiqa about the signs of the path: "If you ask me, oh my brother, which are the signs of the path, I would answer you very clearly and without ambiguity. The path is to look at the truth and break with lies, to tum your face to the living universe, to despise worldly rewards, to spring your mind free from any ambition of glory and fame, to stoop to His service, to purify your soul from evil and fortify it with discrimination, to leave the house of those who talk too much and go to the one where people are silent, and to travel from God's manifestations to God's attributes and from there to His knowledge. Then, at that moment, you will have crossed the world of mysteries and arrived at the door of poverty. When you are poverty's friend, your deep soul will have become a penitent heart. Then, God will extract poverty from your heart and when poverty is gone from there, God will stay in your heart."*

NINE

"Come, come, for the rose bower has blossomed;
come, come, for the beloved has arrived."

(Rumi)*

uring the first three months with the Sufis, I was unaware that a mysterious kohl-eyed dervish was watching me. Our meeting took place during the first days of a mulid for Sayiddah Zaynab, at the mosque of this female saint, the granddaughter of the prophet Mohammed, also known as Tahra.

At that time I had an Egyptian boyfriend, Kamal, who was studying English at the British Consul School, working fur customs at the airport, while striving to leave the old ways behind to become a modern westerner. He was intelligent, industrious, handsome and magnetic. However, once I had entered the dervish fold, I was not very interested in spending time with someone who was pursuing the goals of a capitalistic society with all its trappings. He called the simple life-style and ritualistic mysticism that entranced me "old ways." Perhaps they were "ancient ways." We were going in opposite directions and met as our paths crossed.

One evening Kamal came to the Oxford Hotel just as I was leaving for Sayyidah Zaynab, so I invited him to come along. I took him straight to the hidema of Sheikh Mohammed. This hidema was created inside the courtyard of an old house in the district of the mosque of Sayyidah Zaynab. With a tree in the middle of the courtyard and the brightly colored arabesque cloths covering the surrounding walls, the top open to the sky, I found this setting enchanting.

Less than a dozen people were gathered there that evening. We ate quietly as food was served. While the men sat near the tree smoking their water pipes after dinner, I was asked to sing. By this time, my friend, Kamal, had excused himself and left, having looked ill at ease during the entire hour.

Among the listeners smoking with the men at the tree. was a man watching me intently through kohl-rimmed, fiery, yet soft, brown eyes. When I finished singing, he approached me. Looking intently into my eyes with a soulful expression, he asked me for a bell from my ankle bells, which I use for rhythm while singing. He invited me to join the group near the tree and share the water pipe. Relaxing, I found myself laughing at semi-understood remarks and jokes. I left in a happy frame of mind.

A few days later at Sidi Ali Zayn al-Abidin, the receiver of the bell again made contact with me. He asked me to pose for a photo with him. Peering over my shoulder in the photo is a boy who appears to be cupid. "Mumkin enti min ana sawa sawa tul illail." "Maybe you and I can stay together all evening," El Arabi asked rue. Smiling, I agreed.

Taking staff in hand, this tall handsome turbaned man escorted me around the mu lid, where we visited various hidemas of friends of his. He introduced himself as "El-Arabi", (the Arab). Perhaps the name was taken from the famous Spanish-born Arabic Sufi poet and mystic, Ibn el-Arabi. More probably, he identified with Sayyid Ahmad al-Badawi, also called Sheikh al-Arabi.

El Arabi guided me around the mulid every evening for a week Everyone seemed to know El Arabi; they were delighted to see him bring the agnebia to their circles. A sensitive sensual flower was growing in my heart, it seemed in his also. From that day on, we spent much time together, wandering amidst the tombs that form the environment for many mulids. A graveyard romance flourished.

Graveyards have always attracted me. When I lived in New York City in my early twenties, I would sometimes dance on tombs in a small graveyard on 14th Street, across the street from the apartment building where I lived at that time. There, on large flat tombstones, I practiced flamenco footwork., zapateados. Occasionally I slept in the graveyard to refresh myself with silence and peace, caressed by mystical sensations.

At the age of sixteen, El Arabi had begun his dervish wanderings from one mulid and home to another, preferring the freedom to roam rather than living in a tiny room with his mother and sister in Alexandria. Poverty, plus lack of education, did not foster work opportunities. A spiritual person by nature, El Arabi found his place among the Sufis. He introduced me to numerous sheikhs and their followers. Singing for the hidemas of each sheikh endeared me to their folds, resulting in numerous invitations to homes, hadras, intimate ceremonies and mulids, in various provinces of Egypt.

Soon I found myself deeply in love. Primping before the mirror in my tiny hotel room, my heart danced with the anticipation of joining

El Arabi, and the mystical magnetism of our attraction. We became a popular couple. Our personalities complimented one another; people enjoyed basking in our love. After a large mulid in Cairo, El Arabi invited me to a hadra in the outskirts of the city, hosted by Sheikh Mohammed. As we entered the outdoor arena, I could hear my favorite Sufi singer, Sheikh Ahmad al-Tuni, emoting mystical poetry. After sitting with several circles of dervishes—drinking tea, eating, laughing and joking, I was asked to sing. The fresh audience was delighted. In the wee hours of the morning, many Sufis went upstairs in the hosting house to find a floor space or couch to sleep on, while others slept outside on colorful floral-patterned mattresses. El Arabi took me to a balcony upstairs. Laying down a couple of blankets., we curled into each other's arms. Relaxing, feeling our energies merging, El Arabi gently placed his hand on my Mound of Venus and whispered, "Mumkin?" (Maybe?) "Aiwa," (Yes), I replied. He quietly entered me, entangled in the coarse wool blankets; within a few moments, he was finished. I had fantasized that our lovemaking would be like an entire zikr session—a long, spiritual, sensual. ecstatic love dance. El Arabi went to sleep, awakening twice to enter me for a few moments and drift off again.

A few other people were sleeping nearby on the balcony. Since sex is taboo out of wedlock among Muslims, although furtively practiced at times, El Arabi needed to be secretive and quick in case someone woke up. Later I came to the realization that he had not had much sexual experience, at least not with a woman in love.

The morning sun woke us. Those inside were up and about, preparing and eating a breakfast of salty cheese, brown farm bread, tomatoes, ful (beans) and salty olives. This was followed by endless cups of overly sweet tea. After breakfast, Sheikh Mohammed and I

TARA SUFIANA

walked out onto the balcony to survey the rooftop vista overlooking Cairo. Not noticing the cross on top of a large domed building, I pointed and said, "mosque hunak"' ("mosque there"), in my broken Arabic. Sheikh Mohammed quietly corrected me, telling me that it was a Christian church and commenting, "The Christians also worship Allah. All worship is good. I am a Sunni Muslim." (Most Sufis in Egypt seem to be Sunnis. However I never heard them talk much about differences between Sunnis and Shiites; only a couple of mentions about the differences in beliefs regarding the lineage of Islam from the Prophet Mohammed. I never heard Sunnis criticize Shiites, nor visa versa.)

El Arabi and I parted at Opera Square, from where we could catch buses to our different destinations. He was going to Tanta for a ragabiya—a smaller mulid held six months after the large mulid. He asked me to meet him there as soon as I could get my things together at the Oxford and join him. El Arabi looked into my eyes beseechingly as we parted, as if to say, "Don't disappoint me. Do come."

After retaining my hotel room, five days later I took a train to Tania. At the mosque of Sayyid al-Badawi I sent word through the dervish grapevine to let El Arabi know that I had arrived. Within an hour, he found me eating with a group of Sufis. Delighted, even surprised that I had actually come. he guided me, arm-in-arm, to the house where one of his favorite sheikhs presided.

This was my first meeting with Sheikh Shamubi. Sitting against bolsters on a bed in a small room, the large sheikh impressed me with his warm kindly welcome. His twinkling eyes and relaxed manner put me at ease. By the compassionate love that emanated from him, it was easy to see why he had a large following of Sufis. The people

90

at the house were surprised to find a foreigner in their midst, but followed Sheikh Shamubi's acceptance, serving me tea and dates. Sheikh Shamubi was going to take a nap in preparation for the long night's festivities. When I told El Arabi that I was also tired, he took me to a bedroom where I could nap on a double bed. Thinking that the bed was for me alone, I was surprised when one woman, and then another, lay down next to me to sleep.

Once I awoke and saw El Arabi laying on the large rug, sleeping on his back, his crimson turbaned head resting on a bright red and green flowered bolster, his carved staff lying beside him as if to designate his space. My heart lit up with love at the sight of his beautiful pharaonic face, with sculptured high cheekbones. Within this being was a spirit that my spirit felt at one with, the source of our shared love. The women had disappeared during my nap. Whenever we were alone in the room together, El Arabi came to my bed and entered me. The couplings, though still brief, were becoming deeper and more loving as spirit, heart and bodies merged.

For a week, El Arabi escorted me around the ragabiya of Sayyid al Badawi, visiting his friends. His fame as a wise, humorous, charming and powerful sheikh grew. He kept me working hard. At every gathering, he would unzip my guitar case and hand the guitar to me. While I tuned up, he would tie my ankle bells around my ankles in preparation for me to sing. Sometimes he kept me going all night with these presentations, including his and my dancing. We were becoming stars on the dervish stage.

One of my favorite hidemas was at the house of the well-respected Sheikha Karima, in Tania. Why she was the head sheikha rather than her husband or sons, I do not know. Her position had probably been bestowed upon her when her father died. Her persona was both queenly and authoritative. During mulids, her house was always filled with people. Zikr sessions, which were often led by her or one of her grown sons, were numerous and powerful.

One evening after a long zikr session with Sheikha Karima, everyone began to lie down on cushions and mats on the floor, lining up in a row lengthwise to sleep. Instead of returning to the house where El Arabi and I were staying, El Arabi motioned to a mattress for me to sleep on. He lay down in the opposite direction on another narrow mattress, with his head touching mine, his feet extended toward the rest of the row of bodies. I was aware of the current of love flowing through our heads. With a last loving look into each other's eyes, we sighed blissfully and relaxed into dream world.

As the mulid gathered momentum, the house filled with more and more people. It was difficult for me to sleep in a roomful of women, especially since some of them snored. The roof was the only place uninhabited by humans. Only a couple of goats, a handful of chickens and one sheep lived up there. I built a small room out of a pile of bricks I found on the roof. El Arabi helped me place a couple of boards over the three small walls of brick. Over these boards, we draped blankets for a roof. A large cloth became the door. We placed our small personal belongings—combs, incense, prayer beads, bells, creams, kohl and soap and a few other small items—into niches that the irregular lines of bricks formed. This was our first homemaking experience together, joyful in its simplicity.

El Arabi did not usually sleep with me there; other household members might have frowned upon such intimacy without marriage. He went to the mosque or to men's groups at night before the mulid fully commenced. However, he often visited me. It was our special place. We rarely saw another person on the roof. One woman came to feed the animals. I rarely saw her because I slept late and was out during evenings.

One afternoon I found one of the eldest daughters of the household messing around in my little room. I let her know that this displeased me. She was offended and said that all should be shared. even my space. She also confessed that she loved El Arabi. She was jealous of me. Her husband was working in Saudi Arabia and she did not see him very often. Several months later, I heard that she had died in a fire in that house when a small kerosene stove toppled over. Even though our relationship had been strained, I was sad to hear that such a disaster had befallen her.

On the morning of the last day of the ragabiya, a torturous bleating and the voices of men awakened me. Opening my door-curtain, my eyes dazzled by brilliant sunshine, I stepped into a pool of blood swirling in front of my doorway. To the right of my little hut I saw men slicing the throat of the one large sheep. This sheep was the sacrifice for the leila kebir feast.

Although I did not enjoy this grizzly scene—especially since I felt affection for this roof-mate—it does seem more natural to kill one's own animals than buy plastic-wrapped meat in a supermarket. The owners often become fond of animals that they keep for months or years in their homes. At least they have a connection with the life and death cycle of what they eat.

When the mulid was over, El Arabi seemed as reluctant as I was to dismantle our tiny home. From the roof, he began to toss boards over the roofless top of an unfinished room below. When he threw an attractive floral print carpet on top of the boards, I protested in my poor Arabic: "La, mish kwaiyis. Sijjadi helwa." ("No, that's not good. The carpet is beautiful"). "Mumkin siijadi al ard." ("Maybe carpet on floor").

I was trying to communicate that I thought the rug was too beautiful to be used on the roof where it would not be seen; it could be laid on the floor. I guess he could not find enough straw mats to use for the roof. El Arabi did not seem to understand what I was trying to say. Perhaps he thought I was protesting the idea of staying there. He threw up his hands in despair, apparently giving up the idea to create a more permanent home for us, and said we would go to Dasuq for another ragabiya. I wished I had never opened my mouth.

We piled all our things onto a horse-drawn carriage: clothes, guitar, water pipe, a small kerosene stove, a colored straw mat, and an earthen jug with a metal cup attached with string that I had bought with the idea that I could serve water to the people in the mosques as a form of service. We headed to the train station, from where we took a train north to the town of Dasuq, where the ragabiya at the tomb of Ibrahim al-Dasuqi, an eminent Sufi sheikh, was forming.

El Arabi took me to a noisy section of town where men were smelting iron and hammering metal. Perhaps they were making or repairing automobile and machinery parts. The noise was loud and harsh. We deposited our things in a small mosque, and then went to a room behind the mosque where a circle of Sufi men sat. After introducing me to the group, El Arabi brought out my guitar and asked me to sing. After singing a few songs, I was offered a room at the home of one of the sheikhs.

The sheikh led us to his large house near the mosque of Ibrahim al Dasuqi; there, one of his daughters took me to a lovely room with a double bed and large wooden wardrobes—such luxury after the tiny roof-hut in Tanta. Best of all was the peace and quiet. During the week that I stayed there, I only saw a few people. My room was on a small side street.

El Arabi, like me, had a longing to create a home space. He would arrange objects here and there whenever I was given a room. The rooms were usually offered to me alone, although I think the men expected that El Arabi would visit me. Even when we stopped at a house or hidema for just a day or two, he would hang our bags on nails on the wall. This showed a respect for our belongings, rather than just stash them on the floor, plus it kept our clothes cleaner and out of the way of other people.

The ragabiya at Ibrahim al-Dasuqi was exciting and fun. Sleeping quietly and alone in the large room refreshed me. El Arabi, like a Prince Charming, would come to pick me up, escort me throughout the festival, and then bring me back late in the night.

One morning near the end of the ragabiya, a gruesome scene shocked me. When I had first seen the little white booth facing the mosque, soon after we arrived in Dasuq, I had been appalled by gaudy colored paintings on the outside walls of the booth, depicting a man—probably a barber—slicing into a little boy's penis with a knife; even the blood was painted red. Presuming that it was an advertisement for circumcision, I was still unprepared for the scene I would witness.

The morning after leila kebir, I wandered up the street from the house I was staying in to the mosque. Directly across from the portals of the mosque, from which hundreds of men and women were flowing out, a large wild-eyed group of people was gathered in front of the little booth. They were shouting and yelling with savage glee. A large burly black-bearded man, the 'barber', was holding up a small baby boy; blood was dripping from the end of his penis. The poor baby was screaming his head off.

In Tanta, El Arabi and I had been handed a card by a barber. From the barber's expression and El Arabi's explanation, I fathomed that the barber was advertising his services for circumcision in case we had a baby together. Barbers perform many of the circumcisions for boys in Egypt, especially in the rural towns and villages. Acknowledging my distaste for such practices, El Arabi agreed that he did not think that circumcision was a good thing, at least not for girls.

When I first heard that girls were circumcised in Egypt, I had difficulty believing that this barbaric custom was still performed anywhere in the world. I later spoke with several Egyptian women who had been circumcised. A modem, well-educated, beautiful young woman from a rich family in Cairo confided that she had been circumcised. "I have only had a little outer skin of the clitoris snipped off. I still enjoy sex," she told me. "'There are varying degrees of circumcision for women. Some have their entire clitoris removed, but that is rare today. The degree of cutting depends on the doctor or barber. For the upper classes there is a choice due to education and the means to engage the services of more modem doctors and medical facilities."

Some Egyptian men and women expressed the attitude that this is a "clean" practice. A few men believed that the practice was for the purpose of subduing the sexual desire of women so that they would remain faithful to their husbands and be content to stay in the home.

They said that women's sexuality was for childbearing and satisfying the sexual appetites of their husbands. Male critiques of Egyptian women's sexuality ranged from statements such as, "they are frigid" to "they are too hot."

In small villages the practice of female circumcision may still be practiced in Egypt, perhaps even in cities somewhat. Even polygamy was practiced more in the rural areas. Although four wives are permitted in Islam, I rarely met a man who had more than two wives. According to the Koran, the husband must be able to provide fairly for each wife. Most men find this difficult to do even if they can afford more than one wife. A lawyer in Tanta told me that most crimes in Egypt are crimes of passion. Sometimes one wife is jealous and tries to murder the other wife, however this does not happen very often. Crime in Egypt is rare.

I stayed a couple of nights in a home in a small Delta town where an attractive young man lived with two wives. One wife stayed with the children, cooked and cleaned. The newer younger wife was more modern, working in a shop each day while her mother took care of her newborn baby. The older wife was unhappy. She told me that her husband preferred the younger wife and only slept with her.

Uneducated, this elder wife was nevertheless aware of her position as house cleaner and cook. Her two small children also looked miserable. She said that she had nowhere to go and no other man would want to marry her. She also told me that she loved her husband. I felt sorry for her. The husband did try to give her some attention, but it was obvious that it was out of a sense of duty and because she was the mother of two of his children. He would talk about practical matters with her, such as house and food.

Westerners often claim that women under the domination of Islam have no rights and are subservient to men. This is not entirely true. The situation depends a lot upon the strength of the women in the household, on their support system from members of their family, and also upon education and intelligence. Mothers are respected, especially as they get older. Many men seem to be attached to their mothers, even after they are married. In a household where several women dwell harmoniously together, there tends to be a matriarchal dominance. A Lebanese businessman living in Cairo said to me: "Westerners criticize the Islamic code which allows a man to have more than one wife, but in America a man will often have his secretary or another woman as his mistress. Which is more hypocritical?"

Although western women have more freedom than their Muslim sisters do, in general their freedom sometimes fosters confusion due to so many choices and a complex life-style. Time for self-searching and inner peace might be easier to obtain through a life of simplicity, with fewer distractions.

For a month, El Arabi and I roamed the Delta. Following him, I surrendered to the magic, the timelessness that permeated the atmosphere among the Sufis. We usually began the day eating breakfast with our respective host and family or a small circle of friends. The zikr music played continuously on a cassette recorder. While eating, mending clothes, helping with chores, or listening to conversations, I would move to the music. My energy flowed as tensions were released.

I was ecstatic with love. Like the radiation of the sun, it spread in waves between El Arabi and me and the people surrounding us. Our love seemed to expand throughout a town or city, across lands and throughout the universe. Mingled with the magical feeling of sharing, we sensed that our love was meant to serve others. Little time was spent facing each other; we strode side by side in service of spiritual and earthly work. Love was a blessing directed from a higher source.

When the ragabiya in Dasuq was finished, Sheikh Sharnubi invited El Arabi and me to visit him at his country villa, not far from Dasuq. We boarded a public minibus to the tiny village. Upon arrival, we walked slowly along a small canal, enjoying the peace and quiet in a rural landscape after the intensity of the festival. Within an hour, we came to a charming small mosque, decorated with colorful, hand painted flowers, designs, and rural scenes. Three small mosques stood near each other, one each for Sheikh Sharnubi's's departed father, grandfather and great-grandfather. At least three mulids a year would be held at this site.

We entered the most beautiful mosque. The inside of the dome and the walls were decorated with brightly-painted folkloric scenes depicting fanners caring for their fields, crops, animals. and peasant families in their homes.

El Arabi and I were both tired. After circumambulating the macam (the tomb of the deceased Sheikh) and saying some prayers, we lay down on the floor to rest. Unable to sleep, I placed El Arabi's head in my lap and gave him a massage, channeling healing. Afterwards, El Arabi began organizing our things on a window ledge, with the idea of making the little mosque our temporary home. Then we followed a path gently curving uphill to Sheikh Shamubi's villa.

As we entered his large house, we found it overflowing with happy Sufis. After hugs and some verbal exchanges, they insisted that we stay at the villa in comfort. They may have also thought that the mosque—where we told them we would sleep—was not a proper place for lovers to dwell.

I told El Arahi that I did not want to sleep in a roomful of women, no matter how comfortable the bed was. He went off to try to find another space, while I socialized at the Sheikh's house. Within fifteen minutes, he returned and led me outside and across an open area to a row of sheds. Opening a door at the far right, we entered an unfurnished earthen-floored room. Next to the animals' shed, this room was simple, but private. With blankets and quilts that El Arabi borrowed from the Sheikh, we prepared a bed on the floor, brought in our few belongings and placed a candle in a glass bottle. Then we joined the group for dinner, music and talk, retiring early.

The following morning I bid adieu to El Arabi and the other Sufis, as I was scheduled to give a concert at the American University in Cairo. I promised to return in two days to join them for a small mulid in a neighboring village.

Many students-Americans and Europeans as well as Egyptians— gathered in the lovely courtyard of the American University that afternoon to hear me sing my self-composed songs. The fragrance and beauty of blossoming trees was inspiring. The concert was a success.

For two nights, I slept in my hotel room, taking care of a few matters in Cairo before returning to my lover and Sufi tribe via sherut (collective taxi). Six or eight people can ride together at a cost not much more than a second-class train ticket. The very poor ride on buses and third class trains for a pittance.

With joyful anticipation of reunion with El Arabi, I walked from the taxi depot toward Sheikh Shamubi's villa. As I passed a neighboring house along the footpath, the family came out and insisted that I come in for food and tea. Within ten minutes, El Arabi entered the house, came straight to me and kissed me, demonstrating how glad he was to see me. Someone must have sent word to him that I was there. While walking together through a lush orange grove to Sheikh Sharnubi's house, El Arabi told me that he awoke in the night searching for me. "Fen Tahra?" (Where's Tahra?), he gesticulated his longing.

At the villa, a large group was preparing to go to the neighboring mulid. Sheikh Shamubi was admirable in his role as tribal chief. He listened attentively to those who came to ask for advice and tell him about their lives. He appeared to be genuinely concerned about each one, responding with compassion and fatherly advice, even though he was quite young, perhaps forty. Members of his clan sparkled with light and enthusiasm.

At nine p.m., we piled into minibuses provided for the half-hour excursion. The small mulid was at a farmer's house on the banks of a tributary of the Nile. Colored lights illuminated the house, macam and the river. Inside the house people gaily talked as food and tea were served. The music and zikr-dance took place on straw mats beside the river. Near the end of the evening, I went to the roof of the house to look at the moon and stars. El Arabi found me on the roof. As the music crescendoed into a final peak, we joined into an ecstatic tantric union in time to the music.

It was early morning when we piled back into the rnicrobuses to return to the villa. El Arabi nodded, then slumped into sleep against my shoulder. We staggered into our rustic room and crashed into bed exhausted. Having drunk too much tea, I got up to go outside to the toilet cabinet. My prowling caught the attention of the caretaker who had shown displeasure with the sleeping arrangement of El Arabi and me. Now he barged into our room, yelling at El Arabi to go to the mosque for a chanting session with the men. Poor El Arabi was so tired He was angry with me for having created this situation by going outside to pee. Off he went to the mosque.

So tired that I could not sleep or think straight, I went outside to lie in the sun close to our room. While a few goats munched on some tufts of nearby grass, I composed a song linking Mohammed, the Prophet, with the sliver of the new moon. Muslims see the moon as a symbol of the prophet:

Here comes Mohammed, the first silver gleam of his eye.
Brighter than a star, we can see him in the moon.
His face reflects Allah in the sky.
Though his face is ever changing as the life that we know,
we can feel his presence deep inside.
It's the light in your heart, which can shine anywhere,
brighter than we see with the eye.
Mohammed, Mohammed, Prophet of Allah,
Your face we see at night, a reflection of the light,
the one and only one, the one and only sun,
Allah! Allah! Allah! Allah!
Allah Mohammed Rasoulillah! Allah Mohammed Rasoulillah!
Nur, nur, nur, nur, nur! Nur, nur, nur, nur nur! (Light)

It was just a few days before Ramadan, the month of fasting for Muslims. Men are not supposed to have sex or even think about woman sexually during this period—except for their wives, perhaps. El Arabi had been brought up in this tradition, had mentioned it to me, perhaps thinking that he should not see me during Ramadan.

While I was lying in the sun composing the song, El Arabi appeared with an armful of onions he had just harvested, indicating that he was capable of physical labor, in case I ever took him to my "villa"—as he called it—in California. He asked me to join the other Sufis for the final gathering before departing. Feeling so tired and in the midst of the composition, I remained where I was. Later I realized that by not joining the group, I alienated myself from the others as well as El Arabi. He told me that we would not go to Alexandria to meet his family as planned, but he would escort me back to my hotel in Cairo.

Feeling miserable as we stood in the empty room with our sacks packed on the floor, I took his zikr beads from a nail on the wall where he had forgotten them and placed them around his neck. Off we went, rattling along the dusty road in the back of a small canvas covered taxi truck, dust and wind searing our eyes and irritating our nostrils. El Arabi sat across from me on a small wooden bench, glaring at me with a look of anger, desire, confusion and disappointment.

Perhaps if I had said, "Let's go to Alexandria," he would have taken me. We were both too tired to think clearly, each longing for a bed and silence. Trying to act cheerful, I hoped our relationship would continue after we had some sleep. At the Cairo bus station we parted. agreeing to meet at Sidi Ali for a last hadra before Ramadan.

After sleeping in my hotel room for a few hours, I went to Sidi Ali. El Arabi was not there. There was no message from him. He was probably sleeping somewhere. Many dervishes who roamed a lot were going home to their families for Ramadan after this last hadra.

During Ramadan, many evenings found me roaming lonely through rough streets and graveyards that El Arabi and I had frequented together. No matter how many days passed, I still believed that nothing could sever the bond of love that we shared.

During previous Sufi studies, I thought that I understood the lover's longing to be reunited with the 'beloved' as comparable to the longing of an individual soul to be reunited with God. Now I understood with my flesh and blood, heart and soul, a physical manifestation of what I thought could only be spiritually experienced.

"The water has been cut off from this world's river;
O Springtide, return and bring back the water."

(Rumi)*

TEN

*D*uring this period of separation from El Arabi, I experienced a strange dream. Wandering through crowded brightly lit rooms at a mulid, I saw El Arabi's reflection in a mirror that I was facing. He was standing in a large room, dressed in red balloon pants and a red jacket. His head was wrapped in a red satin turban, one he often wore and later gave to me. His eyes were glowing like red-hot coals. Silently watching me, he conveyed a message; I was to continue to attend mulids and mingle with dervishes. He disappeared, and then reappeared into the next room I entered. This happened repeatedly. Each time I saw him, as my heart lit up with joy, he disappeared. No matter how many people surrounded me with love, I felt lonely when he departed.

During Ramadan I shuffled between two worlds, one devoutly Islamic, the other secular. It was not easy to fast in the pension amidst so many foreigners eating all day long. Farouk, the Egyptian travel agent, who lived in a room across the hallway from me, was also fasting. We encouraged one another by sharing this discipline. Sometimes we chatted late into the night in his room, sharing tales of our lives and philosophies, over bowls of delicious creamy rice pudding. This helped to soften the long hot days without food or water.

Cockroaches were taking over my room, eating clothes, even synthetic fabrics, and a long wide veil draped above my bed as a canopy. They ate through plastic bags into food and managed to get into lidded jars. The cockroaches were growing large while I wasted away from fasting and lovesickness.

During Ramadan, many Muslims congregated around Sayyidna al Hussein mosque, where countless rows of believers were fed the fast-breaking magreb meal of the day, immediately after sundown. Sitting with a group of Sufis on a large straw mat, we drank delicious coconut milk with chopped dates—a traditional fast-breaking drink. Next, we were served rice and vegetables, a small salad, beans, bread, and tea. After I had abstained from eating all day, I felt a special clarity. The month of Ramadan is also a time of socializing, especially near the Sayyidna al-Hussein mosque, filtering down to the bazaar. All classes of people would mill around the square at night, eating at outdoor tables set up by the restaurants for Ramadan, gathering in cafes for tea or coffee and conversation. There were often music programs and wandering minstrels. Vendors and musicians put forth their best efforts during this time of generosity. Sometimes I sang in the cafes. Many people stayed up all night until the mussein 's voice could be heard at dawn, calling the faithful to prayer, signaling the beginning of the day's fast.

The atmosphere is celebratory all over Egypt during Ramadan, from dusk until dawn. Special television programs and lots of other entertainment give thirsty, hungry devotees something to look forward to each evening. A quarter of a mile east of Sayyidna al-Hussein a complex of buildings hosts a large variety of performers: singers, musicians, and comedians—many of them famous stars. These shows go on all night.

Tired of my dark hotel room and longing for the more participatory music and zikr-dancing, I decided to go to a mulid in Alexandria where I could also swim and sunbathe on the beach. The mulid at Sidi Abul Abbas al-Murcie was different from others that I had attended. It was characterized by official ceremonies and more pomp. Dignitaries walked or rode horses in processions to the mosque. Commoners bowed somewhat, acknowledging respect for these patriarchs of Alexandria. Dervish dancing near the mosque seemed to be viewed more as a show for the officials than for the joy and love of Allah. The dignitaries watched the dervishes as they well might watch clowns in a circus or a musical spectacular. Still, they enjoyed this entertaining form of traditional Sufi practices. I think the dervishes sensed this class division, as they did not seem to lose themselves in a state of ecstasy in the zikr, as is the purpose. Awareness of the audience prevented total immersion. Women were rarely invited to join in. I was invited to dance, although I felt somewhat restrained when I did participate.

The tall-spired mosque of Sidi Abul Abbas al-Murcie is beautiful. Three or four smaller mosques, wherein other beloved saints are buried, surround it. Each of these mosques hosts smaller mulids at other times of the year. In a few tents behind the mosque, the dervishes held their own hadras, more enthusiastic and genuine, but still less spontaneous than at other festivals. Many dervishes were leaving after this mulid to go to an even larger one in Upper Egypt, near Asyut. Their excitement was so contagious that I decided to go to this grand festival. During the final morning of the Sidi Abul Abbas al-Murcie mulid I slept on the floor of the mosque for a few hours. At ten a.m., I boarded a train for Cairo. Ramadan was just ending. The train was so crowded that I climbed into the luggage rack above the seats, as soldiers sometimes did; spreading out my sleeping bag, I fell asleep. Some Egyptians tried to get me to come down, probably considering this unladylike, but I realized that once I was inside my sleeping bag neither my face nor my sex showed I was just a long sleeping bundle.

At the Cairo train station I ran into a Sufi sheikh I knew. He insisted upon paying for my bus ticket to Asyut. where he was also going. The next bus did not leave until six p.m. and it was only 3 p.m. We ate falafels and salad, and I browsed around looking at vendors' wares.

It was a long bus ride, packed with saiidi (people from Upper Egypt) fellahin. They slept so easily on the bus. I could only doze a little. We finally reached Asyut at one in the morning. This mulid coincided with the one in Alexandria, so it was already leila kebir, the big night.

Many fellahin, along with Sheikh Wahid and I, piled into the small rural truck jitneys, which met us at the bus stop in Asyut. For twenty minutes, we drove east from the Nile River, across dry barren flat land dotted with a few clusters of sparse tree foliage, until we came to the tent-filled encampment of the mulid. Sheikh Wahid took me directly to the hidema of Sheikh Mohammed; he was proud to be the one to bring me safely to the nest of my tribe. As soon as my Sufi family recovered from their surprise to see me at this remote outpost, they warmly welcomed me to join them. Sitting on their large rug, eating a bowl of soup by the lovely tall trees along the bank of a creek, I felt grateful for the camaraderie we shared.

As soon as I finished drinking my tea, I was asked to sing. After twenty minutes of singing, I was quickly led to the main stage in the center of the festival and asked to sing over the microphone for more than a million Egyptians. The arena was vibrating with excitement. In that roaring vortex of energy I could not hear my guitar very well, but I could tell it was out of tune. After a brief attempt, I gave up trying to tune it in such noise and chaos. Never mind. The crowd was waiting to hear the agnebia sing, an unprecedented event there. When I began singing words that were an expression of their religion, they were overjoyed, clapping and singing along; the guitar was barely heard without amplification. Only my voice was loud through the sound system. A foreigner learning their Arabic language and music, expressing it with reverence, was a confirmation of their faith in Allah. This mass scene under the stars was deeply moving for me also, an experience of spiritual unity. At that moment, I was as Egyptian as anyone was. We were all one in the spirit, one with Allah.

The great munshid, Sheikh Yasin al-Tuhamy, sang next with his group of musicians, and we zikr-danced until after dawn. A room was offered to me in an upstairs room of the house of peasants near Sheikh Mohammed's hidema, I climbed up some rickety stairs beneath large trees that embraced the little room with their majestic peacefulness. Feeling protected, I fell into an exhausted happy sleep. The mulid continued for leila latima (the night after the big night), quieter than the previous night, but still exciting.

When I awoke the next morning, I remembered that my American friend Rick, from the Oxford Hole was teaching English at a school in Nag Hammadi, approximately one hundred and fifty kilometers south of Asyut. Rick bad asked me to visit him whenever I could. I decided to pay him a visit on my way back to Cairo.

Upon arriving in Nag Hammadi by train and bus, I hailed a taxi. The taxi driver could not find the apartment building. It was already dark and he could not understand what I was doing there. Women in that village did not go out at night, at least not unescorted. I was relieved when he finally found the building, Rick came running out and we embraced joyfully. The taxi driver was staring in disbelief as I paid him. Rick and I walked arm in arm to his apartment.

It was a modem ground-floor apartment. Rick had created a pleasant environment, as he always does with his habitations. He opened a small bottle of imported brandy. We talked and laughed until late that night Then Rick took me to a small bedroom where I could sleep.

Awakened early in the morning by loud noise coming from the kitchen, I heard Rick protesting to angry male voices. As my door opened, a shaken Rick peered in. "Tara, I'm sorry, but you have to leave. The police are here, saying that people are talking about a woman visiting me in the night. It is shocking the whole town. They want to escort you out of Nag Hammadi."

Exhausted from the festival and our late night chat, I gathered my few belongings together. Unable to hug Rick goodbye, I passed through the kitchen where two angry-faced police officers stood They ushered me out the door and into a police car. My stomach and head churned as we drove to the police station. After waiting for more than two hours in a dark drafty hall, a brusque man called me into the police chiefs office, where I was harangued with questions as if! were a criminal. I was admonished for going to a man's house when I was not married to the man, scolded for wandering around alone like a gypsy. The chief also shouted that I set a bad example for their native women. My passport was taken into another room, where men's voices continued on and on behind closed doors. Perhaps they were trying to decide what to do with this wanton woman. This small town was close to Asyut, the hotbed of Islamic fundamentalism. It was especially ironic because Rick was gay. We were just friends. I could not tell the police this.

Extreme fatigue had turned into agony. Rick had promised me a relaxing vacation in a quiet village; instead, I was harassed for hours. It was getting dark when I was finally released. I was too exhausted to travel; too late for trains or buses. The police finally agreed to let me stay in a nearby pension for the night. They escorted me there, telling the manager to make sure that I did not go out. The pension was situated right across from a noisy cinema; the volume was turned up so loud that the dialogue of the films blared into my room until very late. The vociferous all-male audience prevented me from sleeping that night. After this experience, the Oxford Hotel would be a healing sanctuary.

The following morning I took a train back to Cairo, having covered almost two thousand kilometers in three and a half days, plus several kilometers of dancing. I stayed for over a week in my hotel room to rest and unwind.

Returning to Alexandria to escape the summer heat of Cairo, I found the beaches packed with millions of Egyptians vacationing in the cooler weather and sea breezes. On the beach, most of the women remained fully dressed, in observance of the Islamic code that prohibits women from showing their bodies in public. Ironically, many younger women were wearing tight-fitting dresses of synthetic jersey fabric that clung to their wet bodies, outlining every curve and each nipple. Watching them sitting in a few inches of surf, I realized that the effect was much sexier than a bikini. Yet, an Egyptian woman on the beach chastised me for wearing a two-piece bathing suit.

Such dress codes, including the veil, do not come from the instructions of Sayyidna Mohammed, the Prophet, as most people think. The Messenger advised women to be modest. He did not mention covering everything but the eyes. Someone recently told me that the wearing of the veil originated in Syria among Christians. Egyptians and other Middle Easterners picked up the custom while living there.

In the book, "Searching for Hassan", by Terrence Ward, his guide Akkbar tells him, that in Persia, before Islam, the chador—perhaps called something else at that time—"was a custom of high-class women, the aristocrats." Apparently, when the Arabs arrived during their northern migration, they adopted the local Persian traditions. Over the centuries, the wearing of the chador and veil became part of Islamic custom.

Walking along the east harbor one day, I found myself on top of a cluster of large boulders. Although no one was swimming in the area, I decided to jump into the sea for a refreshing swim. I peeled off the dress that covered my bathing suit. As soon as I undressed, voices shouted, arms gesticulated "la"(no). I thought perhaps these people thought I was not a good swimmer, or should not be in a bathing suit in a downtown harbor. Ignoring the warning, I plunged off the rocks.

As soon as I hit the water, I was overcome by the stench. I was swimming in a sea of feces. Who knows what else? Rather than water, I was immersed in a thick brown soup. I swam farther out from shore to get to cleaner water. The water was less murky, but I still had to return through the thicker sewage to get to shore. By now, many people were on the rocks, staring in disbelief at the stupidity and wretchedness of this agnebia. When I finally climbed out onto the rocks, dripping brown gook, some of the observers—keeping their distance—explained that this was where the city's sewage emptied into the Mediterranean. It could have included sewage and garbage from farther up the Nile tributaries as well.

There was nothing to do but put my clothes back on over the bathing suit and try to get to my room to shower as quickly as possible. Along the way, I dashed into a small shop to buy strong yellow soap. I felt wretched as I walked through throngs of people, feeling the pollution seeping through me, embarrassed about the odor that steamed through my wet clothes. Even a long shower did not remove the feeling of being permeated with shit. The manager of the pension where I was staying suggested that I try the clean beach at Agami, a resort for middle class to wealthy Egyptians and foreigners, about twenty kilometers west of Alexandria.

The next morning I took a bus to Agami. Disembarking from the bus, I was greeted by a soft ocean breeze. A dirt lane to the beach led me to clean sand stretching east and west along the blue sea. With few people around at that time, I stretched out on my towel. soaking in the peace; it was quiet except for the sound of waves.

Toward sundown, feeling rested after long swims in clean water, I walked south along the beach toward some hotels and restaurants. Choosing the nicest looking hotel on the beach, I walked into the foyer, thinking that I might be able to get a job singing. After inquiring at the desk for the manager, I waited in a pleasant lounge while watching the light of the setting sun dance on ripples of sea.

It was not long before a large Egyptian man with a warm beaming face descended the stairs and extended his right hand to me. He introduced himself as the owner of the hotel. As we sat chatting amicably, he ordered coffee for us. When he found out that I was a belly dancer, who also sang with guitar, he offered me a job. I could perform that very evening. If he liked what I did, he would hire me through the summer season until he closed the hotel in the autumn. He explained that since I was not Egyptian, my job would have to be unofficial. I would be a 'guest artist', paid in cash at the end of each week.

The charming Mr. Fawzy guided me around the hotel complex; first to see the bar upstairs where I would sing some of the time, then to the spacious nightclub where I would dance and sing. We climbed up one flight of carpeted curved stairs where he showed me a hotel suite with three rooms and a bath. This was mine for the duration of my stay, he told me. Since it was Ramadan, when most Muslims are strict about abstaining from alcohol, the hotel was not as busy as usual. I appreciated Mr. Fawzy's outgoing warmth and generosity. After showing me my rooms, Mr. Fawzy took me to the large restaurant on the oceanfront, telling me to order whatever I wished to eat. I sat at a table next to the large glass-wall facing the sea, enjoying a fabulous seafood dinner while watching the sea change into pastel hues of gold and rose as the sun set in the western sky.

After dinner, I returned to my suite to prepare myself for the evening. My guitar was with me. I had brought a long flowing dress that I could wear for dancing with a glittery scarf tied around the hips. Mr. Fawzi told me that during Ramadan belly dancers wear long dresses—usually a djellabia rather than a belly dance costume—tied and decorated with folkloric sashes, jewelry and spangled scarves.

"Your clothes and things from your hotel room in Alexandria will be brought here tomorrow, so you needn't have to fetch them yourself," Mr. Fawzi told me.

Although the nightclub was not packed that evening, the audience was appreciative. In my flowing dress, I felt more like Isadora Duncan than a belly dancer, which suited me just fine. An orchestra played Oriental music. Mr. Fawzi was surprised when I sang religious music in Arabic. "Why this is wonderful," he exclaimed. "How appropriate for Ramadan!" He was even more amazed to discover that I was a Sufi, spending most of my time at mulids. I was his Ramadan nightclub-act. After the show, which included many acts, Mr. Fawzi invited me to share Ramadan pre-dawn food with him and some of his personnel in his hotel suite. We were a merry group, eating and talking, partly in English for my benefit. Mr. Fawzi was delighted to learn that I was also observing summe (fasting) for Ramadan. This sharing of the ritual included me into the hotel family.

Mr. Fawzi had a large house on the beach next to the restaurant and nightclub, where he lived with his wife and two teenage daughters. "I keep a suite in the hotel for entertaining business associates, and to sleep alone in during Ramadan. I lake Ramadan seriously. I do not want to be tempted by sex, even with my wife. I love alcohol, but do not drink during Ramadan. This is one month when I give my life to Allah. That is the least! can do; just one month out of a year."

It was a month of regeneration for me. Swimming a lot in the Mediterranean Sea, plus eating good food during the night, I became relaxed and healthy. I was experiencing Egyptian society among the middle and upper classes.

One day Mr. Fawzi's wife invited me into their house for lunch. She was preparing a salad of greens, avocado, tomatoes and other vegetables, as well as fresh vegetable juice in her modern juicer. Besides all that, she also served a delicious whole grain bread, yogurt and fruit. This was my kind of food, health food that I had had little access to in Egypt, especially since I did not have my own kitchen. Mrs. Fawzi and I quickly developed a friendly relationship. She spoke excellent English. It was a pleasure to be able to share our dialogue easily in English. Mrs. Fawzi suggested that I sleep in their spare bedroom, rather than in the hotel, except when they had overnight guests. Their house was much nicer than the relatively sterile hotel suite.

The Fawzis had two teenage daughters who enjoyed my presence in their home. Their friendly smiles and greetings cheered me. This well-educated wealthy Egyptian family was similar to American and European families in many ways—quite a change for me after spending most of my time with Egyptians who did not speak any language except Arabic.

A few days after I arrived in Agami, I discovered unfinished rooms under construction above the ground floor of the Fawzi house. Another floor was being added; at the top was a roof with a fabulous view of the sea. At this time, construction was not in progress. I asked the Fawzis if I could move upstairs into an open-aired room, where the windows had not yet been installed. They wondered why I would want to be alone up there, when I could be part of the family fold downstairs. Of course, I could still share meals and help myself in the kitchen. I spent most of my time in that airy space, listening to the ocean surf, reading, watching the sea glinting gold in the sun, swimming and sunning by the water.

After a month, wanderlust overlook me again. Sometimes I went to Sufi gatherings in Alexandria on my evenings off. The Sufis told me about some small summer mulids in the Delta that I had never attended.

Mr. Fawzi encouraged my spiritual practices. He agreed it was a good idea for me to go to a mulid after Ramadan. I did not make a commitment to return to the hotel, which would close in a month anyway. I left Agami to egyptsy throughout the land once more.

During Ramadan, Egyptians often think about food even when they are not eating, many indulge with gusto when magreb arrives. Nevertheless, spiritual practitioners of Ramadan fast with reverence: praying, meditating, reading the Koran, conversing about the teachings of slam, such as the Hadith (sayings of the Prophet) and eating lightly. With the help of abstinence and devotional practices, their inner light becomes brighter and lighter as the days of Ramadan progress. Their thoughts, as well as actions, are not on food, sex or other physical survival matters, but on Allah. Many of these people are Sufis. While the men devote themselves to religious matters, the women prepare the food and take care of the family. The men spend much of their time during Ramadan in mosques. If they return home to eat, they need not be concerned with cooking.

Egyptian variety shows were aired on TV during Ramadan to entertain and amuse the fasting devotees, especially the women who stay home a lot The contrast between religion and sexuality was mind boggling. Sexuality can certainly be spiritual, but some of the spectacles that I saw presented sex in a coarse manner.

One afternoon when I was in Luxor, during my first five months in Egypt, a family on the west bank of Thebes invited me into their little mud hut to share a meal. Their eyes were glued to the TV that sat on a low stool upon the dirt floor. The young mother was nursing her baby. Although it was a hot day, the woman was covered from head to toe in a traditional black dress. On the TV s=n a young voluptuous Egyptian woman in a very short dress with a plunging neckline was singing and flirting with a handsome Egyptian male singer. With her bosom heaving in his face, she fawned over him lasciviously. There was no reaction expressed on the mother's face. Her husband was outside tending his fields. An Egyptian once told me that these dramas have nothing to do with reality for Egyptians. Such programs are almost like science fiction to them.

In Cairo, the Egyptian television station is a mere five minute taxi ride, or twenty minute walk, from al-Azhar Mosque, the Islamic religious educational center of the world. Situated across the street is Sayyidna al-Hussein mosque, where Muslims gather during Ramadan to drink their first drop of water and eat the first meal of the day.

Contradictions between traditional Islam and modem westernized values do not deter me from practicing religious prayers and customs. The essence of all religions springs from the same source. To observe discrepancies between beliefs and human behavior is part of life's schooling.

Having seen so many foreign women half-naked and 'sexually liberated' on TV, such as the American "Dynasty" show, it is no wonder that Egyptian men consider foreign women available and enticing. This is not to say that foreign women are not also respected. Sometimes Egyptian men put them on a pedestal, especially if the men have spoken with educated women, sharing ideas rather than only sex. The men are not only attracted to European and American women, but in many cases, they also hope for a chance to work in a western country, where they can earn a decent wage. However, the average Egyptian family is close-knit and frowns upon such a loss of their men, fearing that when a man leaves Egypt for a western country the old traditions and family ties could be lost.

Through her letters, my mother was encouraging me to leave Egypt. "If you don't want to return to California, why don't you go to Spain? You loved it there during your Flamenco period. Sounds like you're wasting a lot of time hanging around with those dervishes."

Mother was usually right; I rarely followed her advice. Mother was not much more conventional than I was, but she was practical.

*   *   *

Adventures and risks challenged me, beckoning me as a mountain beckons a mountain climber. Sometimes such challenges became my teachers; at other times, my actions were more like a form of self-flagellation. I seemed to think I needed to test my courage, to overcome fears by forcing myself to do things that were difficult for me, physically or psychologically, as if I would sink into a mire of comfort and mediocrity if I did not take risks. Adare took me to the top of Cheops Pyramid to dance for the Sound and Light show.

At a party in Ein Hod, Israel, a few weeks before I left for Egypt, I had met two Israelis who had just returned from Cairo. While sharing some of their adventures, one of them exclaimed. "I can visualize you dancing on top of the Cheops pyramid during the Sound and Light show. Can you imagine the expression on the tourists' faces during the climax of the historic film, when the lights hit the top of the pyramid, and there you are, dancing like an ancient pharaonic priestess? That show could use some live drama." His suggestion stuck in my mind. While partying with a group of Europeans at a bar near the Oxford Hotel one night, at three in the morning we decided to take a taxi to the pyramids to watch the sunrise from the top of Cheops. Intoxicated on Coptic Egyptian brandy, four of us—one Italian man, a German, and an American young woman and I—piled into a taxi on Talaat Harb Street. We were soon sailing down Shara al-Ahrnm, the road to Giza, with little traffic to obstruct us at this late hour—just a few cars and taxis carrying passengers to and from the numerous nightclubs that line the road. I mused upon the idea that I could be belly dancing in one of these nightclubs as I watched a few Saudi Arabian men wearing long white shirt-dresses and white kaffiyahs (head cloths tied on with black or gold cords) file out of one of the clubs. In the summertime, many men from oil-rich Arab countries come to Cairo for cooler weather, the freedom to drink alcohol and to watch belly dancers; both are prohibited in Saudi Arabia and other countries on the Arabian Peninsula. Filtered between the gaudily decorated nightclubs, perhaps trying to copy Las Vegas—such as a concrete model of the Eiffel tower adorning the top of one of the nightclubs—stood ugly cement storied apartment buildings or businesses. It certainly was an unattractive route to the ancient pyramids of Egypt.

Arriving at Giza, nine miles from central Cairo, we paid the driver, walked the short distance to the first and largest pyramid, and began to search for a feasible route to the top. Intuitively, I went to a different side than the others, guided to some large stone blocks upon which I could, crawling, slowly raise myself up from one block to another. The Italian man, who was trying to follow me, called out that he was too drunk to climb and was going to go back to the Oxford.

At this early morning hour, the large boulders still retained some warmth left from the penetrating Egyptian sun during the heat of the day. A quarter moon shed enough light to reveal the general outline of the boulders as I climbed each one slowly, probing the crevices for hand and footholds. I glanced down toward the ground occasionally. What if I came to an impasse and had to go back down into those shadowy areas? As long as I was climbing toward the light, I could see where to reach a hand or place a foot.

I carried a plastic gallon bottle of water. The stillness and altitude began to work their magic, to pull me into the presence of the pyramid. Continuing to wend my way slowly in the darkness and silence, it took me less than an hour to reach the apex, the flat area where the pointed top has been removed by nearby villagers to build homes, so I was told. Having attained the summit, I began to vomit. The exertion of the climb, combined with too much brandy during the evening, had exacted a toll. Embarrassed to bring recycled brandy to the Great Pyramid as an offering, I promised to return with better gifts. This was a night of purification. After washing the stones with most of my drinking water, I sat facing southwest, away from the numerous lights along Shara al-Ahram and Cairo in the distance. From this angle, all I could see was the expanse of desert sand, reflecting light from the moon, and sky with stars and moon above. A feeling of timelessness overwhelmed me.

The others from our late night party had not reached the top. I was alone, space and solitude contrasting dramatically with the chaos and clamor of Cairo. As I meditated, the desert began to take on a golden glow from a sky turning pink and orange as the sun rose. While distant sounds of traffic began in an awakening city, I lay down on the flattest stones, staring at the vast expanse of sky filled with stars before I dozed off.

I awoke from sleep under a broiling hot sun in late morning, feeling like an egg frying on the hot stones. Thirst summoned the energy to descend. It was easy to see my way down in the bright light of day, even with sweat dripping down my face and body. I knew I would return.

At the bottom of the pyramid, I found myself in front of a small museum. Entering the cool stone building, I drank deeply from a water fountain, and then washed in a clean restroom. Feeling refreshed, I wandered through the museum as any tourist might. Yet, my experience of the previous night superseded the acknowledgment of artifacts and historical narratives.

The evening of the next full moon, I took a lightweight sequined costume with me in a small backpack. Accompanied by Harry, the photographer, I climbed to the top of the pyramid before the Sound and Light show began. Harry planned to record my dance on film.

Climbing in the early evening light of the setting sun was easier than climbing at night, except for the Egyptian guards below firing shots into the air, commanding us to come down. This tumult below made it difficult to concentrate. We continued to ascend. The voices dwindled, as we became mere specks in their eyes. After changing into my sequined costume in the shadows behind some boulders, I performed a short ritual and meditation during the glorious sunset across the desert.

At dusk, the Sound and Light show began. I waited patiently until the background music of the documentary aroused excitement, spotlights focused on the top of the pyramid. Rising from my hidden spot, I danced into the light. Dramatic music on the soundtrack, accompanied by a man's voice narrating the history of the pyramid, was not the best for dancing. However, invoking the Goddess, I manifested a touch of 'her story', an expression of ancient mysteries. It was difficult to tell whether many people in the audience saw me dancing. I did hear some calls of surprise and appreciation. Harry was filming with his video camera. He also brought a 35 mm camera for still photos. Unfortunately, the camera batteries were low. There was not enough light, so the films and photos resulting from this experiment were too dark.

The third time I climbed to the top of the Pyramid, I was alone. Again, I climbed before sunset with gunshots firing into the air, the police and other people yelling for me to come down. I continued my ascent. In a crevice between boulders on the top of the Pyramid, I placed a photo of El Arabi and me as a prayer for reunion with my beloved, whom I had not seen for several months. I sat and meditated until it became dark, and the film began. This time I danced in costume for the "Son et Lumiere" show, with narration in French. Flooded with the light of the full moon, I experienced a feeling of oneness with the galaxies and ancient Egypt.

When the show was over, the floodlights—which glared from the direction that I must descend—did not go out as they did after the other show. I waited an hour, then another hour, periodically trying to ease my way down without being able to sec the stones beneath my feet, my stairway from heaven. The light blinded me. It was getting cool, and I had not brought a wrap or sleeping bag. Toward midnight, cold and thirsty, I said a brief prayer and began descending gingerly, feeling my feet touch one boulder—until I felt I could stand on it— and then another. Such patience was necessary.

After my feet had found a few such boulders, with my weight still on the stone my one foot was on, I stepped down into emptiness. My foot kept searching for solid footing; I had the sensation that I would fall out into space. My foot finally found a tiny ledge. This was the first time I had felt fear on the pyramid. I needed to sit and rest for a few minutes. The ledge was too small to completely relax on, no larger than one buttock. I perched there, practicing long deep breathing—breathing out fear, breathing in invisible guides.

Opening my eyes a few minutes later, I glanced toward the right, away from the direct floodlight, where I could barely see a piece of rock below me. Edging toward the rock with the hope that it would be enough of an edge to hold me, I placed one foot on it, slowly letting my weight follow. When it held me, I breathed a sigh of relief. I saw that I could descend. though precariously. As I gingerly groped my way down beneath the glare of the floodlights, it became easier to see. By the time I reached firm ground at the bottom I felt giddy and light, thanking the guiding spirits that I felt had helped me. There was no one around to scold or congratulate me. The desert, the pyramid, and I were bonded in our shared experience.

Although this experience was unrecorded by cameras or accolades, I had done what I set out to do. This freed me from a fantasy that might have bothered me to this day if! had not at least attempted the ascent Both the initiate and priestess within were appeased. Though not my first experience of temple dancing -I had danced in and around the mosques, temples of the ancient Pharaohs, plus temples in other countries-the pyramid involved the most effort and risk.

*   *   *

Numerous Egyptian men asked me to marry them. The first pursuers I met were often seekers of success, money and sex. Some of them did care about me and might have made fine husbands; I was not interested. Later, when I was among Sufis, as well as Egyptian men who were not interested in going to another country or getting rich, marriage proposals still beseeched me. Some of these men already had one or two wives.

A believer in love, rather than making practical decisions concerning mating, I preferred to follow my heart. Upon reflection, I realized that such practical, affectionate unions could bring about a pleasant situation. I could have the protection of a man and his family. The other wife, or wives—if there were any—were already trained to do household chores. Since I was a foreigner, a respected singer and dancer, and also holding the title of Sheikha—bestowed upon me after three years with the Sufis, I might not be expected to do housework or other menial chores. As my Arabic improved, I might have also been an intellectual companion to my husband. People listened attentively to my discourses in broken Arabic. Of course, this situation would only succeed if the other wives were not jealous. Sometimes they were relieved to be free from the attention of their husbands, preferring the company of sisters, mothers and children.

However, I was in love with El Arabi. My belief in a soulmate governed my love life, no matter how much I would try to rationalize myself into a more practical and less emotional situation. If I had ever wanted to extricate myself from a marriage, it might have been difficult. Divorce is not always easy for women in Egypt.

A marriage between a Christian Egyptian friend and a Jewish English girl has survived the test of several years, although it has not been easy. During my first month in Luxor, I met Khaled through other acquaintances. One evening he invited me to his home, which doubled as a small pension that he and his wife, Naomi, operated. It had a cozy living room with elegant wool carpets on both floors and walls, depicting scenes of rural Egyptian life: donkeys and farmers, fields and palm trees. Arranged around the room were hassocks of tooled gold embossed leather, water pipes and a few papyruses behind glass frames on walls. I moved into the pension the next day.

When I came home at night from my singing and dancing jobs, there were usually Egyptian friends and/or foreign tourists that Khaled lured from the train station, sitting on the rug or hassocks and reclining against cushions, eating and drinking tea, smoking water pipes and talking. When I arrived, Khaled would offer me food and tea. After I relaxed a bit, he would put on a Zoher Zecki cassette or some other belly dance music, knowing that I could not resist such enticement when he requested that I dance for the guests. Sometimes I also sang. I enjoyed these intimate evenings; meeting people from different countries, as well as gaining more understanding of Egyptian mentality and improving my Arabic. Having a live-in oriental dancer and singer also enhanced Khaled's self-esteem and stature in the local society. Naomi, his English wife, was an intelligent, attractive, quiet young woman. Naomi and Khaled had met when she came to Egypt as a tourist, after a visit to Israel. Khaled had charmed her into marrying him. They went to London for a while to earn some money, and then returned to Egypt, where they preferred to live. Although they experienced some turbulence in their relationship, they loved each other and remained together.

Our friendship would continue six years later when I was living in England. One day when I was in London, during January of

1990, I decided to sing by the entranceway to the British Museum, which was close to the hostel where I stayed. I was vaguely aware of someone selling Egyptian Papyrus at the other side of the gate, but had not paid much attention. As I began my first song, a young man approached me, 'Tahra, is that really you?" His sly smile spread across his face as our eyes met. "Khaled! Wow!" We embraced and laughed. We had always had a joking relationship. "Naomi and I are living in London now. She has a well-paying job. I also have a good job, plus I sell papyrus on the side. You must come to see us."

He took me home with him that evening, a fifteen-minute subway ride from the British Museum. Khaled and Naomi were buying the upper floor of an old brownstone house on a quiet street lined with large old houses. Entering the living room was like being back in their living room in Luxor; the same carpets, round brass table top on folding wooden-legged frame, brass trays, leather hassocks, water pipe, and large cushions furnished the room. "Look who I've brought home," Khaled called to Naomi, who came out of a back room, her round black eyeglasses framing her brown eyes like an owl. A warm hug followed her amazement. Over an Egyptian dinner, we reminisced and caught up on recent developments of our lives. Naomi was working as an executive in London. This nourished her self-esteem as well as her bank account. Khaled managed dormitories at a local university. Both of them were saving to build a tourist hotel in Luxor.

When in Egypt, Naomi retained her western persona. Luxor is a tourist town so Egyptians are accustomed to westerners. Though Egyptian women in Luxor wear long dresses, skirts and headscarves, I rarely saw a woman with her face covered.

The popular western notion concerning the wearing of veils, which few women in Egypt still wear, is that the purpose of the veil is to cover the woman's face so that other men cannot see her. Though this may be the conventional interpretation, even among Muslims, the wearing of the veil was not included in religious instructions from the prophet Mohammed. He simply advised women to be modest.

A practical reason for wearing a veil is to protect one's face from sand and wind. Even men in Arabic countries often wear a scarf around their head and face to keep out dust and sand. During the khamsin winds, which come in the spring from the Sahara Desert, even in Cairo, one is compelled to cover one's face to keep from choking. Another insight regarding the veil is that by focusing attention on the eyes. the soul is more clearly visible.

When I did not want to be recognized, I covered my face with part of a shawl or scarf. This concealment was also a centering device. It helped me to withdraw my mind from the external world and go within. Still able to observe the life around me, without others observing me as much, I felt more sensuous and mysterious. It kept me from talking much, which enhanced my awareness of subtle and psychic energies. Even tying a sash or rolled scarf around my head— usually around the edge of a cap or other loose flowing scarf—I feel more centered. Sometimes when I was tired during long nights at mulids, I would brush or comb my hair—cleansing my antennas— and rewind my scarves, or even tighten a scarf around my temples to renew my energy.

I can see how a woman who doesn't dash around or talk much would feel more sensual than a western woman who is busy with career and other enterprises. I can even understand why an Arabic man, raised in this tradition, might say: "A woman's place is in the home." A man stressed from dealing with the world at large can recharge his batteries by contact with a woman who is in touch with her center. 'Doing' needs 'being'.

In the bible, it is mentioned near the end of the New Testament, that Jesus said: "The Comforter will come." I interpret "the Comforter" as the feminine principle, the 'goddess' within. Patriarchal societies could certainly use some comforting.

Arabic men seem to be more in touch with feminine energy than their western brothers are, even though western women consider them macho. Egyptian men protect female energy by protecting their women, also providing their source of comfort.

The western woman, who tries to emulate men, does not help to feminize or balance the world, even if she calls herself a feminist. Why should a woman think that she has to be like a man in order to have power, when she is essentially powerful? According to Yogi Bhajan, "a woman is sixteen times more powerful than a man." Does a woman who tries to be like a man think that men are more powerful than women? Then there are women who think that money, position, fancy hairdos, and beautiful clothes create the new woman. True independence comes from the awareness of a much deeper many-layered woman within.

El Arabi once said to me: "Perhaps a man is the setting for a woman, who is the jewel" as he placed a silver ring with a turquoise stone on my finger. Could there be any greater recommendation for the value of a woman than these words from an Arabic man?

eleven

Love, love alone can kill what seemed dead,
The frozen snake of passion. Love alone,.
by tearful prayers and fiery longing fed,
reveals a knowledge schools have never known.

(Rumi)*

few days after I had placed the photo of El Arabi and me on top
of Cheops Pyramid, I saw El Arabi briefly at a mulid in Fayid, a
small town north of Suez, on the western shore of Great Bitter Lake.
As I sat with a sheikh from Helwan, smoking a long-stemmed water
pipe decorated with colored plastic flowers, El Arabi walked into the
tent smiling slightly and said, "Asalam alaikum," Then he walked
quietly away with his companion.

Two days later at a hadra at Sidi Ali, El Arabi approached me. Acting
aloof; I wandered to the cemetery area behind the stage to practice yoga
and deep breathing on a large flat tomb. When I returned to the arena
of music and zikr, El Arabi wooed me with shy awkward charm, trying
to pierce my pretended indifference. I succumbed to an appointment.

Again, we spent a period of time together, almost every day. This
time I slept in my room at the Oxford Hotel in Cairo, meeting him

during arranged times. It was romantic to anticipate our meetings, without being over-tired from sleeping here and there among celebrants. Sometimes we took short journeys to visit friends of El Arabi, sheikhs and their families. I could manage an occasional overnight stay, knowing that I had a room to which I could return. Our visits into homes and Sufi centers taught me about the culture, customs, and spiritual practices that varied somewhat from region to region. Sometimes I learned a new song. I could speak Arabic more fluently by now—an amusing broken Arabic that often brought smiles to the faces of Egyptians.

One morning in Cairo, El Arabi took me to visit a rich sheikh noted for giving money and gifts to poor Muslims when their need was apparent. El Arabi and I were both tired from a late night. We looked scruffy indeed when we arrived at the sumptuous flat of the famous sheikh. This sheikh was a television sheikh, known by millions for his recitations of the Koran. When we arrived, we were led inside, left to wait for an audience with the sheikh who was administering nuptial rites for a young couple. When we were finally seated on a gilt-framed velour divan in front of the sheikh, El Arabi was questioned in Arabic. An interpreter questioned me in English as the sheikh asked me probing questions about my conversion to Islam. I shared some of my beliefs and philosophy, explaining that I did not consider myself converting from anything to something else, that embracing spiritual traditions was a natural process. I told the sheikh and his entourage that my parents had never told me that I should be a Christian or anything else, that, in fact, they were agnostics. I had always been free to follow whatever spiritual inclinations I chose, that I'd been the only person in my nuclear family to attend churches or spiritual gatherings. Egyptians often assume that Americans and Europeans are Christian or Jewish.

Muslims rarely seemed to understand my unorthodox spirituality, except for Sufis who understood through their own direct experiences. My statements appeared to disturb orthodox Muslims rather than clarify my position. From the time they are born they are raised as Muslims, unquestioning Muslims assume that Christians and Jews likewise acquire their religious beliefs. Some Muslims claim that Buddhism is not a religion, because Buddhism does not use the name God.

With this famous sheikh, I extolled the virtues of love, compassion and devotion, which I found among the Sufis and Muslims in Egypt. Sick with influenza, feeling miserable, the sheikh did not seem pleased with what I said. El Arabi suggested that I give the sheikh a healing treatment. Before the sheikh had time to object, I walked behind him, raised my arms up in yogic eagle pose, began the breath of fire to energize, and chanting the fatah prayer (the opening sura of the Koran) in Arabic, I lay my hands upon the sheikh's fevered brow. Waves of energy flooded me. As I touched a few key acupressure points on the sheikh's head, shoulders, neck and chest, I chanted, "Ya Shafee, Ya Kafee!" ("Oh, Healer, O Remedy!"), and swept his aura in the manner I had learned from a Moroccan Sufi master, Jabrane, in Denmark. When I finished the healing treatment, the sheikh spoke a few words to a servant, who went out of the room and returned with a beautiful white djellabia for El Arabi; he handed me twenty Egyptian pounds. Giving alms is one of the five pillars of Islam. El Arabi knew how to receive such gifts with grace and dignity, leaving the givers smiling or laughing. We thanked the sheikh and left.

At the Khan al-Khalili Bazaar nearby, we bought cotton long johns and socks. Our legs and feet were starting to get cold during the winter evenings. We must have made a funny picture in the narrow bazaar street, in front of the stall full of underwear, two tall lanky figures trying on the white long johns under our djellabias.

The following summer, as hot as the winter had been chilly in Cairo, I decided to visit Alexandria to cool down. While visiting the tourist sites—Pompey's Pillar and the underground burial tombs of Korn al Shuqafah, I found myself in Karmuz, the poor district of Alexandria where El Arabi was born and raised. El Arabi had once suggested that I visit his mother and sister when I was in the area. I wandered for more than an hour through impoverished sections of Karmuz until I found the house. A beautiful teen-age girl answered the door. When I told her I was a friend of El Arabi, she introduced herself as his sister, warmly inviting me inside. His mother was cordial, but cool. She may have already heard about my affiliation with El Arabi, displeased with such a romantic alliance with her son.

This home, consisting of one small room—about ten by twelve feet, and an even tinier cubicle for a kitchenette, had sheltered ten children and parents. El Arabi's sister insisted that I sleep there that night, sharing the double bed with her. Her mother slept on a narrow, hard, couch-bench.

Before we fell asleep, three of her brothers arrived, probably curious to see El Arabi's agnebia paramour. The Egyptian message system works quickly, word usually spread by small boys sent as couriers. There was certainly no telephone in the house. The brothers slept on the floor in front of the double bed. When I got up to go to the toilet in the night, there was no floor space to walk on. I had to step over the sleeping bodies.

El Arabi was the first born in this tiny home in a dilapidated building in the slums of Karmuz. After his father died, when El Arabi was sixteen, he was expected to take care of the family of eleven. Instead, he began roaming as a dervish. By the time, El Arabi was twenty, he rarely returned home from his wanderings, preferring to eat and sleep on the ground or in tents, mosques, and homes of friends. There he immersed himself in spiritual camaraderie and celebration of mulids. To be responsible for the welfare of that large family would have been a burden for anyone. He loved his mother and his only sister. In any ways that he could, he tried to help, mainly by visiting occasionally. El Arabi's brothers lived normal lives, marrying and working. They pooled their money together to take care of the mother and sister. For part of Ramadan, El Arabi returned to his family. He once told me that he was afraid to go home because it was a "calabooshe" for him, meaning that his family, especially his mother, did not want him to leave. He felt imprisoned there.

We had a similar problem wherever we visited. Our Egyptian hosts never wanted us to leave. They would promise gifts for the next day to entice us to stay; perhaps a new dress or djellabia, or money or a ride to where we wanted to go. The 'next day' could become a week or more until we managed to tear ourselves away.

Sometimes El Arabi expressed demons when he was over-tired. Don't we all? Once, when I found him sleeping on the roof of a house we were staying in during a mulid, I accidentally woke him up. He jumped up, startled, roared like a wild beast, his face contorting into a monster, then curled up on his side and went back to sleep.

Downstairs, Sheikh Mohammed tried to calm me as I cried, telling me that I must wait patiently until El Arabi awoke. I was also over tired and should have been asleep. In less than an hour El Arabi came downstairs refreshed and calm.

Even with my limited Arabic, El Arabi and I sometimes shared deep communication. One evening during a mulid in Cairo, we were sitting in the upstairs of a small mosque with a small group of dervishes. When I expressed a need to go to the bathroom, a young man offered to escort me to the toilet. On the way back, I stopped to pray. El Arabi came rushing into the prayer room, speaking angrily to the young man, scolding him for not bringing me right back. I tried to calm El Arabi, leading him over to a glass compartment that enclosed a Madonna and child statue. In broken Arabic, I tried to help El Arabi understand that the young man did not keep me from returning immediately. I wanted to pray. "Ana ketir mabsut min salat," I told him. "I am very content when I pray." Sitting there in front of the saint's shrine, I felt so much love for El Arabi. In the depths of my soul, I felt that I was his wife. "Ana az walad min inte," I said in my broken Arabic. ("I'd like to have a child with you.") El Arabi looked at me tenderly. We felt so close during that moment

It was a delight to discover that El Arabi was a fine poet. One evening at a hidema at Sayyidna al-Hussein, El Arabi and I were reclining on some bolsters against the wall of an upper room in an unfinished building, eating and smoking a shishe (water pipe) with other Sufis. My right arm was draped gently over one of his shoulders, our love connection flowing strongly. El Arabi was speaking rhythmically. Everyone in the room was listening. After ten minutes of this musical discourse, little of which I understood. a man near me said that El Arabi was poeticizing his love for me. The words that he translated revealed poetic beauty and intelligence. I vowed to improve my Arabic in order to better understand my poet-magician-lover.

In spite of the limitations of verbal communication, I felt that I understood El Arabi, that my soul knew his soul. I could also feel his presence when he passed behind me, or when he was entering a room, even with my eyes closed and preoccupied with singing or conversations. Sometimes dreams would reveal when or where I would see him again. El Arabi found me one evening in a tent of dervishes in a distant graveyard in Cairo, because he saw where I was in a dream that he had when he fell asleep in El Fishawy Cafe, near Sayyidna al-Hussein. He arrived at the tent exclaiming how he had seen me there while he slept. Several times, he found me with such dreams. Then too, we often lost each other, due mainly to interference from others.

One night I arrived at eleven p.m. near Sayyida Nafisah, hopefully to meet El Arabi for a nearby mulid at Sayyida Zakina. On this cold rainy January night, El Arabi came staggering up the street, exhausted and sick with influenza, accompanied by a group of male disciples. Instead of realizing that he was ill and should be sleeping, I was eager to partake in the festivities. He took me to a hidema where we ate a little. Then we wandered through a few streets until we found ourselves alone, beside a roofless, dirt and grass space enclosed by four stonewalls. He opened the small gate, led me inside and pressed me against one of the stonewalls, smothering me with passionate kisses. An inner voice told me that this was not the right time for passion, even if he did need comforting. I was resisting his embraces when three men suddenly intruded. The men grabbed me lustfully, while shouting obscenities to El Arabi.

To my disbelief, El Arabi fled, leaving me in the clutches of the men. However, he returned within a minute with a few young men he knew. The attacker stopped harassing me. Theo the whole group of us walked down the dirt street. As we got to a fork in the road, someone directed us to go toward the right. I sensed that something was not right in that direction, maybe police. El Arabi suddenly went into a sprint, fleeing down the left fork, calling over his shoulder, "Yella, Tahra!" "Come on! Lets go!"

I was shocked that El Arabi would run for his own safety, even though I'd already been told of some of the harassment and danger which can befall Egyptian men in the hands of the police. I had been told that an Egyptian man can go to prison for just kissing a woman in public, or anywhere, if not married. I had heard that men were often beaten, even incarcerated for acts that could be construed as sexually oriented. El Arabi's kisses were not devoid of sexuality. I ran faster. Keeping pace as fast as I could, I followed El Arabi to the hidema where we had eaten supper earlier. El Arabi quickly rolled out a mat and lay down to sleep. He told me to take a taxi to my hotel. I went out into the courtyard and broke down in tears. My body and mind were trembling with fear and tension. Two young men came out and asked me what was wrong. "El Arabi," I whispered, with gasping sobs. I was in a state of shock and needed comforting. The young men went inside and returned with El Arabi. They all walked out onto the street with me to help find a taxi. There was no place or time for comforting. Looking back, I feel that I was selfish to have exposed El Arabi to more danger in case the police or others were looking for him.

Too exhausted to return to the mulid the following evening for leila kebir, I returned the night after for leila latima. I wandered up and down the streets and prayed inside the little mosque where the saint was buried, but I did not find El Arabi. A Sufi informed me that El Arabi had left with his friend Iman after Leila Kebir, to recover from influenza at Iman's house in Heliopolis. Six months passed before I would see El Arabi again.

By this time, my Arabic had greatly improved and my dervish song repertoire had grown. I was regularly invited to sing for festivals and hadras, which eased the loneliness of separation from my beloved. There were millions of Egyptians—mostly Sufis—to nourish me with love. Sometimes people would tell me that El Arabi had traveled to another country to work, or that he was married, or was killed in an automobile accident near Qena. "Forget him," I was often advised, including by my mother in California. I never did. I felt that our love transcended earthly barriers. We were eternal lovers bound in an inseparable cosmic love.

When I was tired of the company of so many people, I would travel to the Sinai or Bahariya—a hot springs oasis in the desert southeast of Cairo—for peace and quiet, sun and swimming. The hot mineral baths, desert serenity, and palm-fringed oasis of Bahariya were healing. During one visit to Bahariya, I hitchhiked a ride to Farafra, another oasis farther south on the same road. By the time I returned to Bahariya the next day in the back of a small truck through the hot desert for more than a few hours, I was well baked.

Sometimes I needed even more solitude, away from tourists and local Egyptians. This I could find in a cave or a secluded spot in the Sinai, near Sharm al-Sheikh at the Red Sea. I would swim for four or more hours a day and lie on huge boulders in the sea or on the shore, feeling the sun penetrate my body, while the energy of the rocks slowed me down; the gentle sound of the water lapping upon the shore and rocks soothed my mind. Swimming in salt water healed and relaxed my nervous system. Since I did not like to go to a tourist beach to buy food, I would sometimes fast for several days.

One morning I awoke thirsty. Some of the numerous crabs were already scurrying around the rocks that I crawled over on the way down to the shore to retrieve my bottle of water. Although I had dug the plastic bottle, filled with water, deep into the sand to keep it cool and stay put, it was gone; it must have floated away in the night. Nor had I eaten for five days. Spotting the arrival of a van with a couple of tourists, about 200 meters away, I walked over to them. "Do you happen to have a little water that you can spare? My water seems to have been carried away by the sea." "Seems like you should be better prepared," the young man answered with an American accent. The sight of ice coolers full of delicious fresh food and frosty cold drinks provoked my thirst and appetite, but I decided to ignore such physical needs and trust in Allah. I did not want anything from anyone unless it was offered willingly.

I returned to my citadel, formed by a towering rock formation on the beach. Finishing my yoga session, with the early morning sun's rays shining directly into my face, I leapt naked into the wild, blue, wind-ruffled sea. Swimming south, where I rarely met anyone, I felt invigorated by the white-capped waters, unusual for the calm Red Sea. I forgot my thirst and hunger, feeling free as a dolphin as I swam, dove, sang and danced in the water.

This was my usual all-day journey. I would swim into the shore every now and then, exploring natural tall rock formations lining the shore. Many of these carved-by-the-sea structures had openings into which I could enter to explore caves. On the shores. I discovered magical stones and plants and played with the swift-dashing crabs.

In the sea, I entered an underwater dream-state as I swam around the coral reefs, watching the beautiful colored fish and multi-colored corals through my snorkel mask, often diving deep into mysterious caverns of coral.

In the afternoon, I turned back toward my rock cathedral camping spot. Midway back, a half-full plastic liter bottle of water floated from the open sea toward the shore, into my arms. It seemed like a message. By trusting in Allah, I would be provided for. I swam to a lovely beach with my bottle of water. There, upon the edge of the sea, with the gentle waves caressing my feet and legs, I raised the bottle of water in gratitude to the Great Spirit—a prayer of thanks upon my lips—and slowly relished the trickles of fresh water gliding through my mouth and down my throat, relieving thirst with pleasure.

A solitary figure strode toward me with snorkeling gear in hand. Unabashed by my nudity, a friendly young man smiled and said: "Oh, I thought you were a mermaid when I first saw you sitting there on the shore." Off he went to snorkel.

The cove I was in possessed a magical aura, as if the high sheer rock walls protected it from intrusion on the western side, facing the direction of the road and humans. The cover's semi-isolation appeared to be reachable only from the sea, by either swimming or boat. No signs of trash or campfires were apparent.

Feeling sleepy from my long journey, I lay down on the sand in the shade of a cluster of mammoth boulders, alone with the spirits of rock, sand, sea, sky. Protected by these giant rock cliffs, I dozed off, caressed by the soft Red Sea air—a perfect temperature for my naked body.

Upon awakening, my eyes glanced upward. Above my head, poised on a small rock ledge—a protuberance of the rock formation—lay a small round onion, an offering upon an altar. When I reached up and took it in my hand, I could feel its vibrant life force. The onion seemed to appreciate my recognition of its essence; we felt bonded in that moment. Delicately. I peeled off the thin *dry* skin, relishing the aroma unfolding; the perfect onion glistened with moisture in the late afternoon light. Biting into the crisp juicy onion, I savored the powerful energy that seeped into me as the juice trickled through my mouth, carrying its essence throughout my body sweetness. Delicious! Never before had I been so aware of the power of an onion. My mind became clear. Flooded with gratitude for the gift of this humble bulb, I swam back toward my campsite with renewed energy.

I glided into a small cove past my camping spot, noticing a group of tourists watching me. After six days alone, I had become so comfortable with my nudity that I did not even think about it. Beach clothes and bathing suits looked cumbersome to me. As I stepped out of the water, a man wrapped me in a towel and handed me a fresh peach; never has a peach tasted so delicious.

I began to enjoy the boisterous merriment of a couple of stocky German men. They showed me a spot where they were diving into an underwater cave with oxygen tanks on their backs and fins on their feet. I expressed a desire to dive into the entrance, through the short passageway they told me about, and up to the surface from the other side, without an oxygen tank. "That's not a good idea, too dangerous," one of the men said, I finally convinced them that it would not be difficult. "Well, you better use my flippers," the other man insisted. I'll wait for you at the other end of the cave to make sure you come out." Diving into the small opening, through the channel of the cave—similar to a birth canal—I felt a touch of apprehension. It was not such a far swim, just the awareness that I could not rise for air until I reached the end of the cave. When I came out the other side into the arms of one of the German divers, I felt as if I were being born; he was the midwife. Laughing and joking, we walked to their land rover, where they offered me a large ripe mango and mineral water.

Before sundown, the Germans left. I walked back to my rock tower to don clothes and prepare for the dark. The fruit I ate had whetted my appetite for something more substantial. Less than two hundred yards from where l camped a group of tourists were unloading two vans. Wandering down the beach to the group, I learned that they were from Israel. We discussed familiar places and events there. Spotting a pile of numerous loaves of bread, I asked them if they could spare a piece of bread. The woman in charge of the food squinted her face with discomfort. "I have to be sure that I have enough food for the tourist group. I guess you could have this small crust of bread and an apple." Thanking the woman, I left her surrounded by heaps of food that might have fed an army for a week. There were eight people in her group.

Preparing to sleep early, I meditated as the gold reflections of the last rays of setting sun shone upon my citadel. "Hello there," a friendly male voice called out from nearby cliffs. I was not in the mood to talk, wanting to calm my hungry stomach to sleep. Two young men climbed down to my perch. friendly, happy to meet a female who could speak English.

Discovering that I was American made it an even more joyful occasion for the two young American servicemen. They could not understand why I would want to be there alone. When they saw that I had no food or water, they exclaimed, "You must come to eat with us at the Multi-International Forces Base, where we are stationed." "I've already had fruit and bread." I replied. "That's nothing, especially for six days."

The twenty-minute walk seemed a long way at the moment, with feet cut by coral and rocks; their friendly chatter lifted my spirits. Off we went along the shore and up a steep hill to the military base. What my eyes beheld upon entering the dining room appeared to be a mirage. On a huge table in the middle of the very large room were heaped all kinds of fruit; almost every variety that I had sampled anywhere in the world. There were the usual European and American fruits plus kiwis, pineapples, melons of every sort, coconut, all kinds of grapes and berries and, and... "That's for dessert," they said, as they veered me toward the cafeteria counter. "First we take a tray and go down the counter for the main courses."

It was difficult to choose from the vast variety of meat, casseroles and vegetable dishes. I selected a few slices of roast beef, a small tile! mignon smothered in mushrooms, spears of asparagus, broccoli, scalloped potatoes, and a few luscious salads. My plate was brimming over even though I took small portions of each item. By the time we got to the myriads of desserts—cakes, ice creams, gelatins, puddings, custards, rum sauces and whipped cream and pies—my eyes were popping.

During the five years that I had been in Israel and Egypt, I usually ate very simply. The vegetables in Egypt were usually overcooked and swimming in tomato sauce. Whenever I was offered meat, which I rarely ate, it was stringy and tough.

When I did not eat with Egyptians I subsisted on yogurt, ful (beans), tiny salads of tomato and onion, fruit from the market, felafel and kushary (a macaroni dish cooked with tomato sauce, lentils and rice, with fried onions sprinkled on top). For more than a year, I did not have much appetite. I could barely look at kushary since I had lost a tooth in a bowl of it, due to a small stone in the rice that cracked my tooth off.

As the soldiers and I sat in that spacious banquet hall eating our food, I could not help wondering if such a bountiful food source was not a prime enticement to lure young men with hearty appetites into military service.

The feast I was now offered was overwhelming. Salivating, my appetite increased amidst all the food. As I began to eat, I realized how much my stomach had shrunk, especially from the past six-day fast. I felt embarrassed to be able to eat so little of the food on my plate. The two soldiers jumped to my rescue. collecting plastic bags. wrapping up what they could, then gathering fruit, numerous small plastic containers of yogurt, chocolate and plain milk, fruit juices, crackers and cheeses, and dumping all into the large bags. "Let's go," they said. "This food should keep you nourished for at least a few days."

Passing the Israelis, still surrounded by mountains of food, the woman who had given me the apple and bread sheepishly told me that she had come over to invite me to join them for dinner. "I am well fed, thanks anyway," I smiled.

Back at my camp, the soldiers and I sat and talked for a while under the starry night. "I feel so good to have been able to help someone," one of the soldiers said. "We have no real work that makes us feel as if we are being of any use to anyone or any country. There is no war going on here. When we stand on lookout duty for eight hours, there is nothing to do or look for. There is no enemy or action out on the sea, and we know that no one is coming. We are not allowed to read or smoke. We have to keep looking out into space—only sky and sea, where there is nothing but an occasional swimmer or domestic boat. Feeding you has been the only service that I have performed in six months." Nearing curfew, they left, glowing.

I slipped into my sleeping bag, relaxed with food, some tender care and the security of knowing that I had enough food and water for several days. I would be able to stay alone, write, read, practice yoga, meditate and swim. I spent twelve days at my rock outpost, feeling less lonely than I usually do among people. My friends were the stars, the sea, the crabs scurrying over the rocks near the water, the beautiful colored fish of many varieties swimming through the coral reefs, which I never tired of watching as I snorkeled. Peace was my constant companion.

On subsequent visits to the Sinai, I became acquainted with Herb, the beach director and swimming instructor for the military beach that was unofficially named "Herb's Beach", after him. Herb was a legend in the area, known for his prowess as a swimmer and for his intelligent philosophical discourses. Most of all he was famous for his solo swim of sixteen miles to an island in the Red Sea at the age of sixty. His body was strong, firm and agile, better than many of his young proteges. He also taught soldiers techniques of survival in the sea. Sometimes he brought me fruit or yogurt and interesting books to read. Having studied massage in California, as well as occasionally working as a masseuse, I posted a sign at the military base beach shack, advertising massage on the beach. Clients came to a space that

I set up in a quiet cove around the bend of Herb's Beach. I was able to earn some money while vacationing.

During this time, I felt inspired to write about some of my experiences with the Sufis in Egypt. An English woman I had met at the Oxford Hotel encouraged me to write an article for a woman's magazine in London. Lying face down on a towel on the beach, words flowed forth like a stream. Later in the day, riding on the back seat of a crowded bus to Cairo, the flood of expression continued. In the midst of noise and chaos, with an Egyptian man trying to engage me in conversation, I kept writing. I finished the article by hand in Cairo. While visiting an Italian friend at his apartment one day, I saw a typewriter in his office. "Could I come over and write my article on your typewriter," I asked. "Sure."

It took several typing sessions to finish the article, creative and joyful work. Before sending it to SHE magazine in London, I showed it to Herb during my next visit to Sharm al-Sheikh. "I didn't know that you could write this kind of stuff, Tara," Herb exclaimed. "This is really good." I felt encouraged.

Within a few weeks of the mailing, I received a letter from SHE Magazine. The editor was thrilled, saying she wished to publish it in the November issue. They would pay one hundred English pounds. This could stretch a bit in Egypt. I was becoming a writer.

Tara Sufiana singing for a festival in Egypt

Dancing on a tomb among the dervishes

Channeling healing energy for a circle of dervishes

Alhamdulilah!

Zickring with the dervishes

A crumbling Cairo wall

Procession to a festival in a Delta village

Asalamalaikum!

Zikr-dancing with the dervishes

Procession to a mulid in the Delta, Egypt

Dancing with the Sufis

Tara at a macam tomb inside a mosque in Egypt

Tara dancing on a tomb stage for a festival in Cairo

τwelve

If to be a lover is to be a poet, I am a poet;
If to be a poet is to be a magician,
I am a magician;
If to be a magician is to be thought evil;
I can be thought evil;
If to be thought evil is to be disliked by
worldlings, I am content to be such;
Disliked by worldlings is to be a lover of
the true reality, more often than not;
I affirm that I am a lover.

(Anwari)*

One evening at a small mulid in Cairo, I chanced to meet Iman, El Arabi's friend from Matariyyah, a slum area that sits on the ancient site of Heliopolis, where Greeks built a temple to worship the sun. I had always liked this respected, though poor, sheikh. El Arabi and I had visited him several times. Iman, which means faith, belief; lived with his wife and two small children in a dismal two-room lower floor of a dilapidated house. He earned a little money selling felafel and ful from a cart that he wheeled around the streets. He tried truck driving for a while, which did not bring in much money, nor did he enjoy this work. It saddened me to see his hope for a better life diminish during the four years that I knew him. His spirit dimmed with the fatigue and dreariness of trying to survive at unsuitable jobs. He was a wise, elegant man, who needed better surroundings and a decent place to gather with his disciples, not to mention a better home. His handsome face was becoming strained with the worries and problems of survival.

In the midst of the hullabaloo of the festival, Iman came up to me smiling, telling me that he had seen El Arabi in Alexandria; El Arabi had sent greetings to me. I had learned by then that when El Arabi relayed greetings through someone it meant that he wanted to see me again soon. "Humph, he sends greetings of affection, followed by a period of time together, then he leaves again," I responded. "Sayyidah Zakina," Iman replied, with a knowing expression of the seriousness of when El Arabi and I had run from the mob. El Arabi was only trying to survive and keep out of jail— for a kiss.

In Alexandria, I had witnessed a police officer hitting a young dervish in front of Sidi Abu! Abbas al-Murcie during a mulid. I had left my guitar in care of the young man while I went off to zikr-dance. When I returned, the poor fellow was in tears, as a policeman was cuffing him and accusing him of stealing my guitar, which was slung over the back of the dervish in its hand-made cloth case. The police officer just shrugged when I told him that I had asked the dervish to hold my guitar while I went to zikr. Furthermore, he had no right to assume that the young man was a thief I took the dervish to a food canteen next to the mosque and bought him some food and tea, trying to reassure him. He remained frightened for a long time. He could barely eat.

How could I, a westerner, understand what it was like to be a poor disrespected Egyptian man? I had Consulate protection, tourist privileges. while he was at the mercy of the whims of those in positions of authority.

During the middle of the next mulid in Cairo, in honor of Sayyidna al-Hussein, while I was joyfully embracing a Sufi couple in the al Hussein square, El Arabi appeared. He came up to me and shook my hand, saying that he had been to Mecca for umra—a small pilgrimage to Mecca that can be taken at anytime of the year. He had just returned. We did not seem to know what to say to each other and stood there awkwardly for a few moments before parting.

Feeling sad and alienated by this stiff encounter, I went on my way to sing for various hidemas. While I was dancing for a large hidema, El Arabi came to me. When I finished dancing, he took my arm as if we belonged together. It was as though there had never been a separation. He ushered me off to another hidema, where he prepared the water pipes and fire; cleaning and stoking the pipes with a tobacco-molasses mixture, then lighting them with hot coals for each participant in the circle of men. He was excellent at this task, a master of fire performing a ritual. I became very high in the loving vibrations of this warm-hearted group of people, even snuggling into the arms of an elderly gentleman like a small girl in the arms of her father. El Arabi was watching me from his position as fire tender. Later he came over to me, looked deeply in my eyes, and said: "You are the spirit of Isa (Jesus), Mohammed and all of the saints. You are a great light here at the mulid of Sayyidna al-Hussein. I honor you." This was an overwhelming statement, encouraging me to expand into an even stronger state of universal love. Our personal love bloomed again as we shared many hours together each day.

One day we stood on the terrace of a majestic Mamluk tomb. This large stone structure also housed a Sufi khanqah, a place where Sufis gathered. The largest room served as a hostel where Sufis could sleep. El Arabi picked a rose from a blooming bush, handed it to me and formally proposed marriage. I shyly accepted.

The next morning, as we had agreed, El Arabi came to the Oxford Hotel, tall and elegant in his djellabia and turban. We went to the nearby Swiss Consulate to arrange for marriage papers. A secretary told me that the translator was away on vacation. I felt that it was necessary for El Arabi to understand our contract. El Arabi seemed to take this setback as a sign that we were not supposed to be officially married, at least not then. He whisked me into a taxi to take us to a noonday dervish gathering at the small mosque of Sitta Fatimah Nebawiya. We walked to the saint's macam to pray. Aware of my own hesitation to marry El Arabi, feeling that he may have noticed this—therefore this hesitation on my part had canceled our marriage—I broke into uncontrollable sobs. El Arabi assured those around us that I was simply in a state of rapture with Allah. They nodded their heads with understanding and respect for such devotion. As we sat in the sun outside with other dervishes, I calmed down.

We wandered through the narrow streets together, occasionally meeting people that we knew. One English-speaking male acquaintance of mine said that I looked radiantly beautiful, as though it was my wedding day.

Whenever El Arabi made a suggestion or asked me a question, he listened attentively to my answer. He took my reply as a guideline for making a decision, but I often hoped he would try to change my mind about an idea that I had negated. El Arabi, like me, preferred to follow the will of Allah. Decisions were not necessarily made logically. We could see many viewpoints concerning an issue; if we were not guided by intuition, we became confused. One evening, when I asked him a question, he cried out, "I don't know what I want."

When one is poor, or chooses a difficult path, it is not always possible to have what one wants. Sometimes I felt that I had lost touch with 'what I want'. This condition is also influenced by the wish to be free of desires or attachments. When friends ask me what I want to eat or drink when we are in a restaurant, I often do not know what I prefer. Westerners are surprised at this lack of connection to my desires. When one has had to do with whatever is available, or has had many disappointments, one learns surrender, detachment, and acceptance. The perfume of love is smelled best when one has been separated from the fragrance for a while. The longing for reunion with the beloved is the cosmic game of 'hide and seek'. When something precious comes our way and we keep it for a while, we sometimes take the treasure for granted. It looses its luster in the eye of the beholder. The polarization and magnetism of romance can seem preferable to a more stable relationship. In my relationship with El Arabi. longing fed my passion. When I gave up my room at the Oxford Hotel to travel with El Arabi and other dervishes, or journey alone to visit homes where I had been invited, I felt a sense of freedom, spontaneously following a path that revealed itself from moment to moment. I felt comfortable with my Egyptian clans and tribes. My improved Arabic was good enough to communicate. During this ·wandering dervish' period, I did not speak English for more than a year. While attending hadras and mulids, little bits of paper would be thrust into my hand with directions—often unintelligible—to a village or home. The person handing me the paper would ask me to come to an address at such and such a time, or whenever I could. I scribbled in the phonetic spellings so I could pronounce the words.

The easiest way to find a place was to take a sherut to the town, either showing the driver the scribbled paper or trying my best to pronounce the words from my phonetic spelling. When I arrived at the village, town or city, I would head to the most central mosque and inquire about the hidema or person I wished to visit. It never took long to find someone who knew who or where I was inquiring about. A young boy was usually sent to relay a verbal message to my would-be hosts or else to guide me there.

El Arabi and I were sometimes offered a bedroom together in the homes of Egyptian families. At more than one home, we were given what looked like a bridal suite, with a red satin comforter on the double bed and drapes of lush red fabric cascading over our heads as a canopy. At a stonewalled windowless room in a small village in the Delta, strings of tiny colored twinkling lights—like small Christmas tree lights—were draped above the bed. The tiny red, blue, green and yellow light bulbs twinkled alternately on and off, while El Arabi and I made love and slept. At least he slept. We could not find a way to turn off the lights; I found it difficult to sleep under all that celestial activity. Our skin felt so silky in that comfortable bed. El Arabi and I rarely had a chance to be naked together; when we did, our bodies responded with bliss to a touch or caress; satin sliding across satin. Often we bedded on a floor under rough woolen blankets. The contrast between rough wool and the softness of our skin was especially heightened at such times. Our life together was a jewel of love in a setting of poverty, dirt, loud noises and harsh voices. It was not always like that, just most of the time.

On one occasion, we slept in a lawyer's house in a village near Tanta. We made a bed on a thick red carpet on the dining room floor. No one bothered us during that peaceful night. We felt bonded by passionate love even though I was bleeding profusely during my menses. I had heard that Egyptian men do not like to contact a woman during her menses. Passion overpowered El Arabi's initial distaste. It was probably a new experience for him—part of his schooling of life with a foreign woman. Even though we were lying on some bedding, in the morning we discovered that the blood had stained the beautiful carpet. Fortunately, the rug was patterned with scarlet roses. While we were scrubbing the carpet on our hands and knees, El Arabi had a concerned expression on his face. Then his mouth tilted humorously as he said: "Ahmar kwaiyis. Ward ahmar kaman." ("Red is fine. The roses are also red."). Our smiling eyes met with mutual understanding of the humor of life and the joy of our love.

Hospitality was never absent when visiting a home in Egypt. Even the poorest people served us food and tea, always welcoming. There was a feeling of spaciousness surrounding most of the homes we visited in the Delta countryside, with trees, birds and animals nearby. On one such visit, as El Arabi and I approached the villa of a Sufi friend we were greeted by two beautiful horses in front of the wooden gate. The villa itself had a few separate buildings. One building was for the household, where the women cooked and the family slept. One low separate room was used as a salon where men gathered to smoke water pipes, drink tea, converse and practice zikr. Family members served them food there when they were hungry. Another building—originally built as a barn—enclosed a large high-ceilinged room used for group gatherings, including zikr sessions. A large floral rug covered the earthen floor, except in the back where bales of hay were stored. That is where I chose to sleep. El Arabi and the other men fell asleep on the floor of the smoking room when they felt tired.

We attended a tiny mulid close to the villa; a charming fairy tale scene with lanterns in trees, colorful fabrics suspended on poles to form spaces for eating, music and zikr. Simple countrywomen in colorful dresses attended our needs with smiling faces.

Having noticed some mounds silhouetted against the night sky in the barren sandy plain edging the eastern side of the villa, I inquired about them. My hosts told me that they were ancient burial grounds. The following morning I took a walk to the mounds and peered inside the dark chambers. Constructed like honeycombs, layered shelves had been dug into the earth; each shelf was large enough for a body. I did not see any bodies or even bones. As the mound extended for perhaps a hundred yards, there was room for many bodies, a tidy way to set the deceased to rest. l was told that this beehive tomb was no longer used as a graveyard.

While leaving a mulid in the Delta, a wealthy sheikh invited El Arabi and me to visit his home in the eastern Delta with a small group of Sufis. The sheikh provided a minibus to take us to his village, Dondet, a two-hour ride. Upon arrival, the sheikh took us up a flight of stairs to the upper story of his house. There we found a clean, modern, empty flat. To my surprise, the sheikh said that El Arabi and I could live in this flat.

A fire was made, pipes cleaned, long grass mats unrolled, and rugs and cushions placed around the long entrance-room. While the men were preparing their social ritual, l went into the largest bedroom to practice yoga, meditate and arrange my things. As I was finishing my session, two men carried in a beautiful oriental carpet, red again. It covered the entire floor of our bedroom, creating an atmosphere of elegance.

In the evening, large trays of food were brought up from the sheikh's home below. A festive air permeated the gathering, with talk, laughter and music. After dinner, El Arabi rose from the circle of men, picked me up in his arms and carried me into the large bedroom like a bride. The sheikh entered the room with a ledger in which El Arabi and I signed our names. The whole evening seemed to be a marriage ritual. We spent a romantic undisturbed night in the double bed. Only the sound of the animals in the barnyard below broke the silence.

The second evening, a group of familiar Sufi men arrived. We zikred, sang and talked until the wee hours of the morning. To my chagrin, the men came into our bedroom to sleep on the floor, wrapped in blankets. Once again, I had to remember that in Egypt— especially among the dervishes—there is no such thing as 'mine', at least not when it comes to space. Snoring again disturbed my sleep; as much as I loved these Sufis, I was happy to see them leave the next day.

Perhaps we could settle down to homemaking. Alas, a group of local men arrived for the evening. El Arabi asked me to sing and dance for them, showing me off like some exotic bird until they finally left at three or four a.m. This scene went on night after night, as word spread that an agnebia was visiting the home of Sheikh Mahmoud. The stream of relatives and friends was endless. When it appeared that all of the villagers had met me, relatives and acquaintances from distant villages came to visit.

I still occasionally wore a man's djellabia that had been presented to me in Luxor. One evening El Arabi left the roomful of visitors for a few minutes. He returned wearing a red and white stripped long nylon jersey dress that a woman had given me during our travels. It was tight enough to sensuously outline my curves; on El Arabi, it clung in a long straight line, accentuated by the vertical stripes. "If you're going to wear men's djellabias, then I'll dress like a woman," El Arabi exclaimed with a straight face. We all burst into laughter at this funny prankster.

El Arabi and I would sit tall and proud on large bolsters on the bed in the smallest bedroom, which had become the social salon. The visitors would gather around us, sitting on chairs or the floor. Every night I was asked to sing. Often I was prodded to continue all night long. One day a blind singer came with an Egyptian woman who guided him around. For an Egyptian man and a woman to travel around together unmarried, was highly unconventional. I learned that she was married but did not enjoy the life of a housewife. She told me that she preferred to go to Sufi gatherings with the blind sheikh. Obviously, she ruled her own life.

The blind singer was delighted to sing his songs for me and to teach me one—a love poem, so beautiful that I sometimes cry when I sing it. Although it does not sound as poetic in English as it does in Arabic, here is a rough translation:

O Medicine, treat me,
I am speaking with my love when I am alone,
Do not split me or I will break.
Drinking love from the crescent moon,
I offer my spirit to you.

I offer my life for someone who remembers me.

The night is clear.

He is in my zikr.

My soul does not sleep even when I do.

When I depart from my love, I hide,

because I cannot say goodbye.

There is no morning for me,

My morning is night.

With God's power, we will stay together forever.

Even when we disagree it is okay.

Our love will not die.

(Song in Arabic, by Fazana Kabanu)

During the days, the men sat and smoked their water pipes and drank tea in a small structure made of poles and palm branches, outside, next to the house. Tired of sitting, I would wander off to explore the village. The narrow road-paths were dirt, often dusty. Most houses—of varying rectangular sizes—were made of adobe, brick or cement. There was a small marketplace where people gathered to trade fruits, vegetables, goat and water buffalo cheeses, utensils, dishes, brooms, etc. Trees scattered here and there throughout the village provided some shade in a dusty earth setting.

Besides television, weddings provided the main amusement for the villagers. There is never a lack of weddings in Egypt. Sheikh Mahmoud took El Arabi and me to a wedding celebration near his home. Beautiful large trees surrounded a large courtyard near a roomy pleasant house; probably that of the bride's or groom's parents. Most of the villagers attended. Music and dancing continued throughout the night, punctuated by the high trills of women, shrill to my sensitive eardrums. Sumptuous food for the guests abundantly covered long tables. For such a small village this was an elaborate party; the bride, groom and families dressed in fancy, frilly attire.

El Arabi suggested that we use the flat as our home base and travel around to Sufi gatherings from there. He could work in a local cafe making tea and coffee, preparing the water pipes and fire. Foolishly, I told El Arabi that I needed to live in Cairo to earn money singing, dancing and acting in movies. This lack of commitment to our partnership seemed to make El Arabi restless.

One morning El Arabi came into my room with a breakfast tray filled with various cheeses, ful, pita and tea. After eating, he showed me a tattoo on his left breast. The design was a heart, with a sword piercing its center and a rose emerging out of the top of one side of the heart. El Arabi told me that he loved all beauty; perhaps this tattoo symbolized his Sufi heart. The tattoo stared into my subconscious. The first meaning I gleaned from the tattoo was that the sword of suffering pierces the heart before the rose of love can bloom.

Trying to rationalize the tattoo as a positive symbol, I concentrated on the rose. Were there thorns? I noticed a few that might prick. The rose was in full bloom, with a short stem coming out of the heart. Ah, well, perhaps it is the sword of truth piercing delusion, so that love can bloom

El Arabi left the room for ten minutes. Returning, he gently lifted his djellabia to show me that he had shaved off his pubic hair. "Mumkin enti?" he asked ("Perhaps you?") He had brought razor, soap and a howl of warm water. My pubic hair had sometimes shocked Egyptian women who had bathed me at various homes. Perhaps one, or more, of them had told El Arabi that it was not proper. All Egyptian women-as far as I knew-removed their pubic hair and sometimes all body hair, except on the head, which they usually covered, except when at home with intimate family. They used a mixture of flour, honey, lemon and water, which forms a paste. After applying the paste and allowing it to dry. they ripped it off, with the hair attached to the paste.

With trust, I lay down on the beautiful flowered carpet while El Arabi began to shave off my pubic hair. A few minutes after he began I became paranoiac. I fantasized that he might also cut off my clitoris in his attempt to egyptianize me. I expressed this fear for a moment. El Arabi reassured me with a soothing voice that there was nothing to fear. While shaving me, El Arabi pointed to my clitoris and asked, "What is that?" I told him that it is a natural part of a woman's anatomy. I wondered how he could have managed to live for thirty eight years without knowing about the clitoris. Then he told me that he had never seen a woman's genitals. "Ente min ragil," I asked, meaning that I wondered if his sexual experience had been with men. He nodded his head "no", then expressed that he was unable to explain due to my limited Arabic. I began to wonder if he had been a virgin before I came along. Perhaps his experiences had been furtive—under clothes, or maybe he had seen or felt a woman who did not have a clitoris. I remained baffled.

El Arabi preferred not to confront problems that disturbed him. One sheikh told me that El Arabi did not like responsibility. He said that El Arabi was intelligent, kind, a great dancer, poet and storyteller, but also restless and inexperienced, one who avoided responsibility. El Arabi was not the only Egyptian who enjoyed the company of others to keep him from thinking about their own problems.

In both Europe and America, I have friends who prefer to move on rather than confront sticky situations. An English friend of mine says that she does not like to stay in one place more than two months at a time. If she stays more than two months somewhere, she says that friends and acquaintances begin to draw her into the trivia of their lives. She prefers to have time and distance away from household trappings. For me also, fresh situations and contacts have often felt preferable to the hassles of domesticity and proprietorship. I see how one could spend a lifetime just protecting and caring for one's possessions. Dervishes try to avoid such snares.

One evening, impulsively, El Arabi asked me if! wanted to go to a mulid in the northeastern Delta with him. We took a sherut taxi from our home base at Sheikh Mahmoud's house to a small town, and then walked across fields to a small dome-roofed mosque surrounded by small houses. Inside the mosque, we ate with some friends of his in a side-room used for cooking and eating. The festival was just beginning. There was a feeling of intimacy among the few early participants. An occasional tree dotted the dusty open field surrounding the mosque. El Arabi decided that he wanted to stay the full week. I needed to go to Cairo to sing for a concert; I promised to return for the big night. Returning on the night of leila kebir, I had difficulty getting through the throngs of people to the mosque where El Arabi and I had planned to meet. I finally squeezed my way into the mosque. When I could not find El Arabi, I had just as much trouble leaving. I literally fell out of the crowded mosque into El Arabi's arms as the mob pushed and shoved.

Everyone there called El Arabi my husband. Perhaps Sheikh Mahmoud really had married us, though not officially recorded. During the day after leila kebir a painful infection in El Arabi's right thumb was causing him great discomfort. As night approached, I urged him to come with me to a doctor's house, where I had been invited to sleep. He wanted to stay in the familiarity of friends for leila latima. The doctor's family kept me up most of the night with questions. I would have rather been dancing.

Exhausted, I returned to our flat at Sheikh Mahmoud's the next morning. Mosquitoes were invading the bedroom from the barnyard through the slits in the wooden shutters. Out of necessity, I built a frame of poles around the bed, draping mosquito netting over it. I crawled inside this canopy to sink into much-needed sleep. El Arabi showed up soon after, asking if he could climb into the bed with me. Although I was still desperate for sleep, we made love. Before I dozed off, El Arabi asked me if I wanted to go to Cairo with him for the birthday celebration of the Prophet Mohammed. I told him that I needed to sleep for a few more hours. When I awoke later, El Arabi was gone. The prayer mat upon which he had prayed was still on the floor of the small bedroom.

Sheikh Mahmoud insisted that El Arabi would return any day. I became ill with flu and spent most of the time in bed, feeling lonely and miserable, even though Sheikh Mahmoud brought me food from downstairs and was kindly. The buzzing of mosquitoes, braying of donkeys, snorting of pigs, and crowing of roosters was getting on my nerves. I did not get off to Cairo for more than a week. I wrote this poem while sick in bed:

Where were you my love,
when I lay sick and lonely
in a village in the Delta?

Where were you,
who I thought was my beloved,
my divine husband,
when the moon was full and
my breasts ached with longing?
Where are the eyes and lips
that spoke of love,
or the hand to hold
when I needed a friend?
Where were you,
who I revered as my Sidi, my Master,
When I walked cold and lonely through graveyards?

In the name of love,
you tease me with gifts of tin rings and plastic fish.
You carry me across the threshold,
toss me into the air and
give me puberty rites,
then leave me alone and ill,
while you go to the city,
to celebrate Prophet Mohammed's birthday.
You, who said that you were afraid
to go to America;
that I might leave you alone and lost.

Where is your presence to protect me
from other men's desires?

Where is the love of husband and wife,
for better or worse?
Is this love only an ego booster for you,
to show others what a lovely flower you picked?
And when it wilts in your hand,
you throw it away,
or leave it to lie
at the mercy of human dust.
You, who could breathe new life into the flower,
and water it with love.

El Arabi appeared while I was dancing at a mulid in Cairo a few weeks later. I felt angry that he had disappeared from Dondet without saying goodbye. El Arabi smiled sheepishly and handed me a beautiful long bead and stone necklace that he had brought back from Beni Suef during a visit to friends of ours. He explained to some Sufis standing nearby that I was a little angry that he had left Dondet without me. A woman's place is in the home. but what is so surprising about a man's wanderings, especially a dervish?

Strangely enough, I liked the feeling of my smooth-skinned, hairless Mound of Venus. I felt like a virginal young girl. However, later when my hair grew back randomly—not only across the mound, but further down my inner thighs, accompanied by some itchiness, I felt that nature knows best.

Egyptian women practice several beautifying rituals and cosmetic artifices. For weddings, the bride and her women attendees henna their hands, and the bottoms of their feet. I partook in this treatment a few times. The henna felt grounding to me, especially when applied to the soles of the feet. Using the same henna paste, women sometimes created designs on their hands. The Nubian women tattoo their lips with a bluish black color.

Although marriages are festive celebrations, the plastic faces of a bride and groom were often alarming. Sitting stiff and frightened—particularly the bride—in high-backed throne-like gilded chairs, posing for pictures, hardly created a portrait of nuptial enthusiasm. One man told me that the girl was often frightened, having had no previous sexual experience. Marriages in Egypt are often arranged for the financial and social benefits of family ties. Cousins often marry one another, which can lead to congenital defects. However, the married couples often learn to love each other, aided by the blessings of relatives and the responsibility of raising a family. The love between El Arabi and me shone like a beacon of love between a man and a woman from opposite sides of the planet. Some people shared in this glow, while others were jealous, furtively trying to separate or discourage us. With all the twists and turns of this relationship, I still enjoyed the delicious nectar of love.

ThIRTEEN

$\mathcal{O}$ ne evening at a Sufi gathering a young man suggested taking me to the home of a renowned sheikh who he thought I should meet. Although it was already ten o'clock in the evening, my escort assured me that the sheikh received visitors late into the night, Thursdays through Sundays.

The apartment was upstairs in a well-built old building at the end of a quiet street near the Nile River in al-Rawdah—a small island in the middle of central Cairo connected by bridges. Upon ringing a musical bell, the door was opened by a pleasant young man in a white djellabia. We were ushered into an elegant salon with a fountain issuing from a gilded metal palm tree on a table, between two gilded lamps in the shapes of palm trees. The kindly sheikh welcomed us while a servant served food and tea on a brass tray. The other visitors had left earlier so we were able to enjoy a pleasant conversation with the sheikh. He was delighted to meet a western Sufi woman. Surprisingly, he spoke fluent English. Wearing an elegant cream colored djellabia, Sheikh Halim was seated on a high plushy divan, smoking a large water pipe. Middle-aged, with a smiling face, he spoke quietly and intelligently. At the end of our visit—after midnight by then—he invited me to stay in his house for as long as I wished.

Having left the security of my small room at the Oxford Hotel, I had been wandering with the dervishes for a year. This vagabond life-style was beginning to take its toll on me physically. When I accepted his offer, at least for one night, Sheikh Halim led me to the middle room on the other side of the hall. Two young men were preparing mattresses to sleep on. The sheikh told these men—who worked there as servants in exchange for room, board and teachings from the sheikh—to vacate the room so I could sleep there. They did not look happy as they moved their mattresses into the larger room next door, which served as a dining area, TV room, ironing room, and place where visitors waited to see the sheikh.

Rooms can be reconverted at a moments notice in Egypt. Since meals are often served on movable low tables—or from a large, round, metal tray set on the floor—they can be set up anywhere. Any room with carpets, or straw mats, can be turned into a sleeping room. Shoes are usually removed upon entering a room, except for a kitchen or bathroom. If the room is needed for entertaining, the cushions and mattresses are arranged for seating, "Allah Karim!" ("God is most generous!"), I sighed, with gratitude for a room to myself in the lovely home of an intelligent sheikh who could understand English. This flat, on a quiet street inhabited by upper middle class Cairenes, was a peaceful place. Nile breezes wafted into the room through an open window, carrying floral scents of blossoming trees. No one disturbed me in the morning. By the time I awoke, Sheikh Halim had left for a three-day weekly visit to his countryside retreat near Tanta. His wife, who remained at home, suggested that I bring my clothes and things to their flat and live with them, as Sheikh Halim had instructed.

After an Egyptian breakfast of ful, salty cheese, olives and tea, I went off joyfully to collect my things from the Oxford Hotel and various homes where I had left them. I was still somewhat reluctant to commit myself to living there, so I did not bring everything.

Because I am a person who likes to have my own space, it was not so easy for me to wander from place to place in Egypt, with rarely a room to myself. When traveling, I make myself at home, wherever I am, even if it is only for a day or so. However, I never completely succeeded in training myself to sleep among people, so I was often tired.

I resided with Sheikh Hakim and his wife for a few months. For the first few days, I had the room to myself; then some visitors came. The young student male servants slept in the small room with me. I was feeling quite at home as the extended family and I learned to enjoy each other's company. Two of the students could speak some English. I would practice my Arabic with them in the quieter hours, without noise and distractions. Sometimes when the sheikh was out of town, Umi, the sheikh's wife, would put a mattress down for me in the saha salon so that I could sleep alone. Because there was an air conditioner in the saha room, Umi also slept there during hot summer nights.

Longing for solitude, I discovered the roof of the apartment building. Lying on a thin straw roll-up mat in my sleeping bag, I enjoyed gazing at the moon and stars in this quiet dimly lit neighborhood. My seclusion was short-lived; the household became suspicious that I was having sex with a handsome lawyer who lived in the same building. In the early evenings, he came to feed his pigeons, which were in cages on the roof, near to where I slept. I rarely saw him because he was usually through feeding before I retired. We only had a few brief discussions. Suspicion frequently plagued my life as a single foreign woman in Egypt, especially when I wanted to sleep alone, separately from the rest of the household members. It was customary for women to accept protection. Sheikh Halim and I shared some wonderful philosophical-spiritual conversations. His wife retired earlier than we did, not looking pleased about our tete-a-tetes. However, the sheikh never made any physical overtures toward me. In fact, he told me that sex was not good for spiritual growth. Umi seemed frustrated. Sometimes she talked baby talk and acted like a small child in the presence of her husband. She explained that this resulted from a trance state. The sheikh would smile as if charmed by her baby antics. and flatter her. I felt that she used this as a ploy for attention; the sheikh spent so much of his time talking to other people. Umi, meaning ·mother', in reference to her being a mother to all guests—although she had no children of her own—was an intelligent, educated woman, tall of stature, with an Afro-Bedouin appearance. On her bedroom walls, portraits of her Bedouin ancestors were displayed. Umi seemed rather fond of me, sometimes treating me like a daughter.

Becoming involved in the situation of a given moment, I would be distracted from my own projects. I would often lose touch with my inner needs; practicality and single-mindedness could fly away in the process. But when my heart center was open, I learned to embrace the people I was with and learned not only their customs, but also the similarities that humans share anywhere in the world, regardless of race, language, religion or life style.

One day while I was preparing to meet El Arabi at a mulid in Cairo—after a deep, loving, sharing the day before—I was so full of love that I was dancing, singing and sharing joy with members of the household. As I was getting ready to leave, Sheikh Halim asked me to come into the saha to speak with and dance for a visiting

American Muslim and her Arabic husband. Enthusiastically, I danced and conversed with the couple; however, I was late for my appointment with El Arabi. We found each other hours later, at the mulid. Regrettably, this tardiness on my part subdued the ecstasy that El Arabi and I had shared the day before and may have contributed to non-commitment. If I could not keep an appointment, then why should he?

Sheikh Halim often asked me to sing or dance for his guests during his Thursday evening Sufi gatherings. I felt like a court troubadour. It was a refreshing change from the huge crowds at mulids. Most of the visitors were well educated and wealthy. Although these intimate gatherings were pleasurable, when a festival beckoned I was eager to leave the confines of a room for the open air, wandering through streets, graveyards or the countryside. Preferring live music, dancing and the unrestrained energy of dervishes, I felt like a wild cat let out of a comfortable cage to roam freely. Sheikh Halim was kindly and understanding, yet disappointed that I was not a more lady-like stay at-home cat. To entice me into staying home more often, Sheikh Halim offered me the use of a chauffeured car to take me to mulids. He felt it would look more dignified if I just made occasional appearances. However, I would get restless. I wanted the freedom to come and go as I pleased.

It seemed that I had made a mistake to tell Sheikh Halim about El Arabi. "I have heard that El Arabi is a poor, eccentric. irresponsible dervish. Don't ever bring him here," the Sheikh exclaimed, frowning. "You should not be spending time with that dervish, but if you do spend any time with him, see him as a servant, not as a lover or husband." It reminded me of a fairy tale, where the princess falls in love with a poor fool and the father forbids such an alliance.

The sheikh's remedy for this situation was that he would arrange a suitable marriage for me. That situation never transpired, perhaps because he could not find anyone who would want to try to tame me.

During this period, El Arabi was in Alexandria. Our encounters were few. In the spring, El Arabi came to Cairo; our love blossomed with renewed fervor. In this state of joy, I also blossomed. Although I did not explain the reason for my joyful behavior, the household loved my exuberance. One day El Arabi asked me if he could visit Sheikh Halim. I just shook my head "no", not wanting to tell him that the sheikh forbade me to bring him to the house. A few weeks later, El Arabi told me that he had been informed that I was Sheikh Halim's lover. This false gossip poisoned El Arabi's trust in me. I realized that there were people who were jealous of our love, using lies and deceit to try to separate us. Slanderous gossip and lies about El Arabi had also caused me to falter in my trust and faith in him.

Although it was reassuring to have a welcoming home when I returned from the mulids, other difficulties arose at Sheikh Halim 's. The diet consisted of white rice, stringy meat and overcooked vegetables. Rarely was I offered a piece of fruit, so I began to buy my own fruit and vegetables. When I steamed vegetables in the kitchen, Umi would say that I should eat with the rest of the family, not use the kitchen. The food I was offered was getting worse and worse as I watched glasses of carrot juice, yogurt, lush fruits, nuts, delicious custards. and tapioca pudding pass before my nose on the way to Sheikh Halim and his wife.

One morning when I felt hungry, I walked into the kitchen. A part time cook was preparing stringy meat for lunch. I explained to the cook that I just wanted to get some fruit and cheese, which

I had bought, from the icebox. The cook said that Umi had given her and the other servants instructions to keep me away from the kitchen. The diet of white rice and meat was making me weaker and weaker—even too weak to go to mulids or hadras, where I could eat healthy food with the peasants. Alarmed by how thin and wan I was becoming, I went to several hospital clinics for checkups. The doctors told me that I had some amoebas or other parasites. They gave me flagyl pills, an antibiotic that made me feel terrible.

Nor had I forgotten my bout with bilharzia during my first October in Cairo. I must have contracted this disease in Luxor when I swam daily in the Nile River. I even drank the river water a few times, as the native felucca sailors did. Sometimes I sunbathed on a muddy, slimy, flat spot next to the river, where scorpions and reptiles crawled and nested. I had chosen such a hidden place, uninhabited by humans, in order to escape the attention of Egyptian men, who would not leave me in peace once they saw me in a bathing suit, alone. A month or two after arriving in Cairo, I was so sick from bilharzia that I could hardly crawl from my room at the Oxford Hotel to the Swiss Consulate around the comer. Seeing how ill I was, the Consulate employees took me to the Anglo-American Hospital. I recovered in three days due to peace and quiet, a few chicken dinners and good medicine.

Bilharzia is a disease caused by the eggs that snails lay. After they hatch, the tiny snail larvae eat the intestines of the host humans. I was told that sixty percent of Egyptians have bilharzia, many completely unaware that they have contracted this deadly disease. Some people are born with bilharzia, having never experienced good health to know the difference. This disease was often a cause of death.

Since my bout with bilharzia, I used the services of doctors in clinics when I did not feel well. I discovered that these over-worked, underpaid doctors, catering to the needs of millions of poor people, did not have time to give thorough medical care. Many of them were still in training. The average doctor in a hospital or clinic in Egypt earned about eighty Egyptian pounds per month—less than forty dollars at that time. Quite possibly, salaries have not improved greatly by now.

One day Umi discovered some gray slimy stool in the toilet after I was there, apparently not flushing well. Umi called her doctor. A charming well-educated man, who spoke English well, arrived at my bedside. Catering to a rich clientele, this doctor possessed the medical knowledge and time to give good medical care. He was convinced that I had hepatitis. He told me to prepare for a stay of at least two weeks in the hospital. I was shocked to discover that I weighed 105 pounds, at least twenty pounds less than my usual weight—not much for my 5'8" height. The doctor was distressed that I had waited so long to discover that I had hepatitis, indicating that my condition was very serious. The following morning a friend of Sheikh Halim drove me to the Fever Hospital in Abbasia. The sun warmed me as we drove. Receiving care relieved some of the stress from being ill. I was ushered into a large room containing several empty beds. To my delight, I would have this room to myself. A tall tree stood outside of a corner window, the green-leafed branches soothing my sick body and tired mind. Lawns and other trees could be seen through windows. I had not realized how much I needed solitude and nature, the best medicine.

Intelligent doctors and nurses cared for me without disturbing me very often. The chief doctor confirmed that I had indeed contracted hepatitis. He said I would be ill for at least two weeks, that I would need a minimum of one month for recovery. The doctor gave me some baby formula powder, pills and vitamins, especially Vitamin C. Since I had lost my appetite, it was easy for me to skip hospital meals of white rice, meat and mushy vegetables. I accepted my orange per day and gave some money to one of the workers to buy me tangerines at a nearby fruit and vegetable market.

An English friend of mine from the Oxford Hotel had contracted hepatitis while he was in Sudan. On the telephone, he told me that tangerines were very helpful for his healing process. I also asked a female custodian to buy me cauliflower and a few other seasonal vegetables, which I steamed in the kitchen each evening. The doctor said I needed to eat jam. Perhaps pectin is beneficial. A friend of Sheikh Halim brought me fruit yogurt, jam and honey on my first day in the hospital. Another friend of the sheikh brought me some other treats one day on a surprise visit. These strangers, who came out of a sense of duty, were my only visitors. Relishing the much needed solitude, I did not feel like talking or relating to people. Still, I longed for a visit from El Arabi. By telephone, I sent word through another sheikh to tell El Arabi that I was in the Fever Hospital.

Other patients invited me into their rooms for tea and fruit, chats and TV; I visited a few, but preferred to read or write in my journal, to meditate alone. Most of the patients enjoyed television in their rooms, with visiting friends and relatives talking while the TV chattered. Sometimes relatives slept overnight on empty beds in the patients' rooms. Each day I went to a quiet spot near a tree to practice yoga in the sun. Traffic from the busy road was barely audible because the hospital was set back on some acres of land, with wide lawns between roads and buildings.

Three days after my arrival at the hospital, tests of my condition were taken again. The results astounded the doctor. 'The tests show that you don't have hepatitis anymore," he said. "This is amazing. But you should still stay in bed for two more weeks to rest and recuperate." The fresh fruits and vegetables, plus peace and quiet, were healing me. Strength returned, although I gained little weight on the cleansing diet. I decided that I would never return to the Egyptian cuisine, a decision that I did not honor for long. As soon as I returned to the festivals, I ate whatever was set before me. However, I chose to munch on watercress, turnips, radishes and lettuce, rather than eat the heavier foods.

Parasites never completely left me during the five years in Egypt. These parasites feed off the body's nourishment, depleting one's energy. I was later told in a Swiss hospital that the parasites were friendly. "They will eventually go away by themselves if you eat a healthy Swiss diet," the doctor told me. I guess they did.

The mulid of Sayyidah Nafisah was taking place during my stay at the Fever Hospital. This was a festival that I did not want to miss. During the last five days of my hospital stay, I took the risk of losing my wonderful room. The call of bright lights and music urged me to dress, walk to the street and take a taxi to Sayyidah Nafisah. As soon as I arrived, a dervish guided me to a hidema located in a tent far from where the taxi let me off. When I asked my host sheikh where I could find a bathroom, the sheikh sent me to a building across from his tent. Opening the wrong door, I was surprised to find El Arabi sleeping in the room. I was feeling energetic and in a good mood. "What's wrong? Are you sick?" I asked him as he opened his eyes sleepily. Instead of coming to visit me in the hospital, I was arriving at his bedside. He smiled sheepishly, happy to see me. "Tabra! Sayirfik?

Enti kwaiyis?" (Tahra! How are you? Are you okay?) He went on to say that he had received word of my illness, but due to poverty and fatigue he had not made the trek by bus yet. Both of us were in high spirits as we wandered around the mulid, greeted by our favorite sheikhs, who were happy to see us together. "Enti menowar," (You are starlight.) one of them called.

At Sheikh Mohammed's beautiful large tent, we ate quietly, sharing food and conversation with a group of our favorite Sufi friends. The evening was just warming up when I became concerned that the hospital gates might close at eleven p.m. Reluctantly, I took a taxi back. The front door of my building was locked. Fortunately, I had left a window open at the comer of my room next to the tall tree. By climbing onto a large branch, I was able to crawl through the window.

Each evening I returned to the festival. Having learned that the hospital gates did not close until I a.m., I was able to stay later at the mulid, to zikr-dance and sing. By this time, the nurses had been informed by other patients—who had seen me leave all dressed up— that I was going out at night. They knew that I was a dervish and longing to attend the mulid. On the last evening of the festival the head nurse gave me the key to the front door so that I would not have to crawl through the window.

El Arabi came to visit me the following day. I was doing yoga behind a group of trees outside. The cleaning woman did not tell El Arabi where I was, so I missed his visit. That evening the doctor came to see me, saying he had been informed that I had been leaving the hospital premises at night. "You're in the hospital because you are sick, not well enough to go out. Leaving the premises until dismissed is against the rules." I promised the doctor that I would not go out again before I was released. Having seen El Arab warmed by his love, I enjoyed my remaining days in solitude. Three days later, Sheikh Halim's friend drove me back to the sheikh's house where I was warmly welcomed. They fed me well. Perhaps Umi felt guilty about the previous unhealthy diet.

The best food I ate in Egypt was with the peasants, especially in the tent of dear Sufi friends from Beni Suef. Sheikh Mahomet was a tall, black-bearded, handsome Sunni Sufi. His wife, Fatima, had the presence of the Virgin Mary. Sitting upon their beds of hay with their darling small daughter, they looked like the holy family one might find in biblical pictures. Fatima cooked the healthiest food that I ate in Egypt. She prepared fresh vegetables—lightly cooked—and delicious hot nourishing soups, such as lentils with vegetables. This little family exuded warm-hearted love. Although they were poor, they would not accept monetary donations from me for the food I ate.

During the second year that I knew them, Sheikh Mohamet acquired a new large stereo tape player. So happy with this new toy, he loudly played the zikr music cassettes. Too loud for my eardrums, I sometimes left before I really wanted to. Although Sheikh Mahomet's family was poor, they received gifts of food, money and other things for their hidema. With the new boom box, they acquired greater status and self-confidence. El Arabi told me that although they lived in a tiny one-room house, they always had good food, blankets, and cassettes. Helping to set up hadras near Beni Suef, Sheikh Mohamet began consorting with famous munshidin. He enjoyed his work as a sheikh, guiding others with zikr, words, and by his loving example.

Sheikh Mohamet zikred much of the time in his seated position upon a cushion. Most of the visitors who came to his hidema followed suit. While he zikred and spoke with visitors, Fatima sat on a rug, cooking on a small one-burner kerosene stove. During the mulids, Fatima usually went to sleep earlier than her husband did. The talking, loud music and zikring did not keep her awake. She was used to this life-style. I sensed that they shared a deep love, a happy marriage. People felt comfortable in their presence. One morning after a week-long mulid, I was surprised to find Fatima, a small woman, dismantling the large tent while Sheikh Mahomet slept. It was heavy work for a woman. Then she packed up all the blankets, pots and pans, dishes, and kitchen utensils. When he awoke in the afternoon, she fed her husband; together they packed up a small truck, borrowed from a friend, for their return to Beni Suef.

The men in Sufi society, especially the handsome ones, are quite fastidious. They spend a long time trimming and combing their beards and mustaches, and arranging their turbans. The result created a charming picture; actors in a divine drama, playing their roles with style. This ritual of preparation was a meditative practice in my life also—taking time to arrange my dresses, scarves and jewelry. Preparing myself in dressing rooms during my belly dance career had trained me. Others related to me with more respect and admiration when my appearance was pleasing; this is true in any country.

Another one of my favorite dervishes was a poor, yet luminous, sheikh from a village south of Mansoura. I first met Sheikh Fatah when El Arabi took me to his hidema at the Sayyidna al-Hussein mulid. He was sitting on his straw mat—which grew bigger as the years passed—peering over his little water pipe with his large lucid black eyes. His long hair hung in loose black curls beneath a woolen cap. He did not play music cassettes very often; I think he preferred silence. Sheikh Fatah exuded an aura of tranquility and wisdom. His quiet, plump, young wife served healthy food while nursing a baby. Whenever Sheikh Fatah offered me a cup of tea or handed me his pipe with his long, elegant, sensitive hands, I felt as though he was handing me a great gift. His eyes radiated compassion. When our eyes connected so did our souls.

When not stressed by time or distractions, every little joy, gift, gesture of kindness or heart-to-heart sharing takes on a quality of deep significance. A sincere smile or a small trinket warms the heart. Whereas among the westernized Egyptians, weeds of stress were growing, the spontaneity of the simple people of Egypt sprouted forth as plant shoots upon a fertile field.

FOURTEEN

The fires of the mulid were gradually dying down; a few embers glowed here and there throughout the graveyard. Strains of music wafted from a persevering group of musicians at a distant tomb. A hush descended as dawn broke, followed by the sweet songs of small birds. The January morning was gray and rainy; a light drizzle cleansed and softened the exhilaration of the fiery night. El Arabi and I walked hand in hand among the graves, across the barren hills of dirt and rubble. He seemed to be searching for something. I wondered where we were going. It was always a mystical journey when I followed him.

We passed a trash-filled area, a haphazard dump. Such piles of trash could be found almost anywhere in Cairo, especially in the poorer sections. People lived in many of these graveyards, including this one at Sidi Ali Zayn al-Abidin. Bones, flesh, rotting food, cans, bottles, plastic, paper and other refuse were all going through a metamorphosis together; a smelly soup in an earth cauldron. A light rain moistened the confetti-colored mounds.

El Arabi found what he wanted; a little plastic hut. Bending down to enter, he led me inside. An old man was sleeping in the corner. He did not awaken. El Arabi lifted his outer djellabia over his head and spread it on the ground, immediately pulling me hungrily down onto it, then passionately and hastily made love to me. His powerful desire was enough to ignite my inner fires. Even his scent, especially in the nape of his neck, caused me to melt into him as I buried my nose in his neck, inhaling deeply, merging essences.

The old man awoke and raised himself slightly on one elbow, looking over at us through half-closed eyes and mind. El Arabi and I were partially clothed; a bundle of damp, rumpled layers of entangled Egyptian cotton and wool djellabias. We rarely had a chance to feel our bodies skin-to-skin; but our souls were naked to each other. El Arabi acknowledged the man with a greeting, "Saba el heir." ("Good morning!") The old man nodded and went back to sleep, snoring, as if we were part of his dream. Rays of golden sunlight through chiffon wisp clouds suffused the plastic hut. Seeds of passion were left upon the ground, like the rain and decomposed bodies and garbage, a gift of fertilization for mother earth—all organic.

Upon my return from the hospital, life at Sheikh Halim 's was pleasant for a while. I came and went to mulids, and some engagements where I was hired to sing or dance; folkloric shows, weddings, hotels. Then some incidents occurred in the house, which estranged me from Sheikh Halim and Umi. One night after a Thursday evening saha in Sheikh Halim's sala, I discovered money missing from my purse in my room. Surprised that visitors or servants in a wealthy respectable home would steal money, I told Sheikh Halim. He did not believe that these young men would steal.

A few mornings later, upon awakening, I opened my eyes to observe a servant shoving something into his pocket near the dresser where my handbag lay. I got up and looked in my handbag. Money was missing again. As I accused the servant on the spot.

he denied taking anything. From then on, he was sullen towards me. Umi also began acting cooler. They needed servants. The sheikh was not in the best of health. Smoking the molasses-tobacco mixture in the water pipe so much must have put a strain on his liver. There were times when I felt tired after smoking a water pipe, yet I enjoyed the ceremonial sharing. Umi said that Sheikh Halim smoked in order to stay awake late at night with his visitors. Sometimes I gave the sheikh and his wife massages and healing treatments. which they appreciated. However there was some strain between us after I accused the servant of stealing, so I moved back to the Oxford Hotel.

Movie companies periodically came to the Oxford to recruit foreigners as extras in films. Whenever possible, I would go to these film sets to work as an extra. During filming, I was usually given a character role. Sometimes I suggested an idea, or a character would be invented for me on the spot.

When I was in my late teens, I studied acting at Hedgerow Theater in Moylan, Pennsylvania, not far from my family home. In my early twenties, I began acting professionally on stage and in films in New York City.

For my first film-acting job in Egypt, I sang a Greek song for a film supposedly set in Greece. In another film, I danced. In one film, I spoke English, playing an American. One time a film director came to the Oxford to engage me for an interesting part in which I spoke several lines of French with the film stars; I played the role of a Belgian Ambassador's wife. The last film scenario that I acted in before leaving Egypt took place on an airplane, in a seat next to Ahmed Zecky, the handsome star of the film, a favorite Egyptian comic actor. In this scene I spoke a few words of Arabic while he read my palm, much to his surprise.

As the handsome actor held my hand in his, palm up, both of us scrutinized my palm. "Nigmi," I said as I pointed to what appeared to be a star on my palm. Ahmed Zecky smiled warmly, looking into my eyes with his penetrating brown eyes, circumventing any need to remember the rest of the dialogue.

A typical day was spent waiting around on the set. Once we began a scene, my energy returned. In one film, twenty of us, dressed in renaissance costumes, sat around a long table laden with heaps of fruits and other dishes. Laughing and eating, we portrayed characters enjoying rollicking. bacchanalian fun.

No film or stage acting engagement was as fascinating to me as the dervish stage. At every mulid, there were numerous sets. actors, zikr dancers, musicians, lights and enthusiastic participants. No director—except perhaps the "divine director'—could produce such colorful and spontaneous scenarios.

One evening I entered Sheikh Shahid's hidema—built around a large tomb at the Sidi Ali mu lid—to find El Arabi dancing buoyantly in front of the musicians. Instead of wearing his usual djellabia, he looked like a gypsy boy with his pant legs and shirtsleeves rolled up, wearing a silver and black striped vest, and a wool-tasseled cap on top of his thick black curly hair. This jester, a fool dancing while the fiddler fiddled, enchanted the roomful of more than one hundred people.

El Arabi then asked me to dance for the sheikh and his group. In this large space, I could exuberantly express myself in free flowing motion and much whirling. Whirling takes me quickly into my center—the center of the universe—and after a short period, it feels as if the world is spinning around me while I am still, in a divine ecstasy of union with divine spirit.

Many years ago during ballet training, I learned to turn by 'spotting' (turning the head first, with the eyes quickly moving to the original front spot). Later I learned to turn without spotting, as the whirling dervishes do. The head, slightly tilted, stays with the body. The right arm is raised, with the hand pointing up and slightly out, and the left arm is lower, with the hand facing the earth. At first, this kind of whirling made me dizzy, but with a little practice, it became easy.

Since learning to whirl, I have experimented with additional movements, such as turning my head in little circles while whirling. I also enjoy moving my arms alternately up and down as I turn. I can take a piece of candy out of my pocket, unwrap it and put it in my mouth while whirling. I discovered that I can do many oriental dance movements—moving my hips, sliding my neck sideways or in rotations, or hand, arm or pelvic movements—without losing my center or the euphoric perception that I enjoy while turning. One foot is the grounding center—not moving from its position—while the other foot propels the body around. The whirling dervishes turn counterclockwise; the left foot stays in one spot while the right foot turns the body. I feel more balanced when I whirl in both directions, alternating. Rarely dizzy or tired, I find that whirling induces an experience of oneself as a center of stillness, while perceiving everything external in motion; as though the world is turning around me rather than I am the one turning. The individual becomes one with the Universe, one with the Divine!

Varying the dance movements can also be beneficial, stretching the body in many positions and directions. My head moves to loosen neck and shoulder muscles. Shoulders, arms and hands move to release tension and express themselves. Belly and hips roll. My pelvis thrusts sideways or in circles to the beat of music. My legs leap, prance, run, bend and stretch. My feet touch the earth in different ways to ground me, enabling me to move other parts of my body in balance. Listening to my body and letting it guide me as to what feels most harmonious, I stay in balance with nature, with my self. Dancing can prevent illness or promote healing. My mother told me that I was born dancing. She said that she knew I would be a dancer by the way I moved inside her womb, that I danced myself through the birth canal into the world—the easiest of her childbirths.

In Switzerland, after leaving Egypt, I healed myself of influenza by dancing. I was staying in an old stone farmhouse used as a vacation center in the Alps of the Engadine, when I became ill with the flu. I felt that! couldn't get out of bed—much less cross the hall to the bathroom—until a staff member told me that a party was beginning in the upstairs salle. I dressed and joined the festivities. After dancing for a while, mostly whirling, I began to feel better. The following day, I was almost fully recovered.

Dancing opens the flow of blocked energy, awakening chi When the mind stops worrying and we relax, when circulation increases through rhythmic movement, both fears and toxins are released. Then Mother Nature can do her work Most diseases are spawned in stress, fear, anxiety, fatigue, over-eating, and over-talking. Breathing is an important first step in healing, yet it is difficult to breathe when one has a cold. When a person does not breathe properly, he/she tends to think too much. Silence and rest are also good medicine. Without silence, rest is not as restorative, because our mind and spirit need quiet to be able to receive healing energy from the universe. With a lot of commotion and noise around, it is better to move with music, to dance the illness away, then rest afterwards.

Dancing professionally on stage for many years, I became accustomed to having my own space when I performed. Now I have learned to find my space in a roomful of dancing bodies. If there is not enough room for grand leaps, I find another suitable movement or else a space opens up for me. I merge into the interrelationship with my surroundings.

Yoga also balances and heals body and mind. Part of my yoga agenda includes standing on my head. For a few years, I stood on my head with my feet pointing to the sky. I found that I could stay in that position for as long as I wanted, until I got bored. Then I spread my legs apart in different directions, turning my body from the waist down—which is up when standing on my head—so that my legs cross; I can twist halfway around from the waist to the feet. Still on my head, I put one leg bent with the foot across the other leg, an inverted tree pose. I turn my feet in circles from my ankles and move my legs around. Bending my legs from my knees, with the feet towards the buttocks, puts pressure on the sciatic nerve, relieving tension. Such simple postures and movements restore vitality and mental equilibrium. After experimenting with various positions, my body tells me what it most needs. If I have been writing for a while, I get up every hour to stretch or zikr-dance. Even five minutes can relax tension, clearing my mind, opening my memory bank, allowing creativity and the subconscious to flow more freely.

The Egyptian Sufi way of clearing and healing is with zikr. Chanting moves energy from deep within the solar plexus. The 'hara'—called the 'seat of consciousness' by Buddhists—is located three inches below the navel. Chanting purifies the chakras—energy centers located within the body—as the energy moves up the torso, carrying negative energy out through the mouth with sound. Powerful rhythmic sounds made in unison with a group of people can quickly eliminate ego separation; we can share our common source.

How we move affects how we think and feel. Energetic motions foster an ability to be more assertive and strengthen will power (yang). Soft flowing motions caress and soften consciousness, enhancing receptivity (yin). By balancing our motions, we can find harmony in body, mind and spirit.

Even though I spent most of my time with the Sufis, occasionally I accepted a belly dance engagement, especially when I took a break from the continuous Sufi celebrations.

During a trip to the Sinai for a short vacation, I was dozing when the bus passed the spot on the road that was closest to Herb's Beach, where I usually went to camp. The bus stopped at a restaurant across the road from the Sharm al-Sheikh beach area; there I enjoyed a leisurely lunch. Afterwards I crossed the road to the tourist area, where hotels and campgrounds cluster.

That first night I camped there, in order to take a hot shower and eat well before returning to my hermitage near Herb's Beach. Many young people from Europe and Israel—even an occasional American—camped in this area, socializing at the restaurant, cafe, bar, and on the beach. Swept up in the carefree ambiance, I accompanied a small group of European students to a nightclub discotheque. That night there was no floorshow or live music; we still had fun dancing to platters and drinking a few beers. We were told that there would be a live band during the weekend. That is when I got the idea that my belly dancing or singing talents might provide me with employment. After introducing myself to the disc jockey, he responded enthusiastically to the idea of having a Swiss-American belly dancer to entertain the foreigners. "Go to the hotel over there tomorrow," he suggested, pointing toward a building closer to the sea. "Ask to speak to the manager, Mr. Shafi. He's the one in charge of this club."

After a half-decent sleep on the beach among late-night parties, and a breakfast of fruit, yogurt and tea, I crossed the beach to the large building which served as the hotel. On the way I passed a cluster of new-looking yurt cabins. Peering inside one, I saw a pleasant room with a double bed, drapes at the windows, a closet, a chest of drawers and night stands. An open inside door led into a bathroom. Such comforts would provide a refreshing change from the smelly cave or the rocky ledge where I usually slept near Herb's beach.

Delicious smells wafted from the kitchen as I approached the main hotel building. Inside the large restaurant, I asked to speak to Mr. Shafi. "Yes, Mr. Shafi is here," replied the headwaiter. "I'll see if he has time to talk to you." Within a few minutes, a portly Egyptian man entered the dining room, inviting me to sit down. We sipped lemonade as I told him about my skills and experience. His response was enthusiastic. "You could sing in the dining room, or on the outside veranda where guests sometimes dine during dinner hours. Then you could belly dance in the nightclub later with the Egyptian band that plays oriental music. It is against the law to hire foreigners; instead I can offer you a yurt to stay in, plus three meals per day here in the restaurant." This was luxury to me. I would not need money in this paradise.

I moved into the yurt with my few belongings: guitar, a small duffel bag of clothes and my sleeping bag—which I would not need there. The luxury of silky clean, finely woven cotton sheets, soft pillows, warm bedding, hot showers, and the sound of the sea outside my window made civilization look pretty good at the moment.

That night I began work, singing for guests dining on the large outdoor veranda. They enjoyed my multi-lingual repertoire, sometimes asking for a song in a particular language. Mr. Shafi was sitting with a group of Egyptian tourists, beaming with pride as they complimented the new talent.

Posters had already been spread around Sharm al-Sheikh about the new nightclub act. I had not brought a belly dance costume with me-assuming that I would be camping out in solitude, but I did bring a full, pastel blue and apricot colored skirt, plus a pastel blue satin hand-embroidered vest. A plum colored silk scarf adorned with numerous tiny gold coins served as a jingling hip belt. During the rehearsal, a staff member had taken a photo of me to put on the flyer. Everyone was pleased with my outfit. It suited the desert-beach landscape. That night the orchestra played well for my dance. They were so excited to accompany a professional dancer. Within two days, the nightclub was filled with tourists—Egyptians and foreigners—who had heard about the new belly dance act. I was the talk of Sharm al-Sheikh.

The structure that housed the nightclub consisted of one large round room covered with a palm-thatched conical roof. Its spacious smooth wooden floor was a delight to dance on. The area facing the sea was mostly open so I could look out onto the sand and sea—illuminated by a full moon that graced those first few days there. While I was dancing on the second night, a lone-silhouetted camel—with rider in djellabia and turban—strode across the sand outside; a fantasy scene that I thought I had seen before in a photo or dream.

Enjoying my popularity as a main attraction for tourists, I could still find serene moments lying on the beach, swimming, and snorkeling, with time out for an afternoon nap in my quiet room. I also discovered a charming little cave-like bar-restaurant, reached by descending a steep, winding stone staircase, with wooden railings, that zigzagged down a cliff to the sea. I sometimes sang there for tips between my dinner singing gig and belly dancing.

After a week or so of this perfect working vacation, I happened to pass a small makeshift tent on the backside of the hotel. As it was time for noon prayers, I decided to join the few men praying there. While slipping my sandals back on after prayers, a middle-aged man with a tightly pinched face came over to me and began scolding me. "Have you no shame, to dare enter this tent to pray? I saw you dancing last night, almost naked, in the nightclub." Almost naked? What would he have thought if I had been wearing a regular belly dance costume? "What were you doing in the night club," I asked. No one forced you to be there, watching me. My spirit was joyfully dancing, while your mind was seeing dirt where there was light." His face clouded with fury. I could see that he wanted to hit me. Instead, he threatened that I would no longer be able to dance in Sharm al Sheikh. "I'll be talking to the Police Chief," he shouted as he left.

Sure enough, the next morning Mr. Shafi told me that the Police Chief had visited him, saying it was not legal to hire foreigners—especially for entertainment coveted by Egyptian belly dancers—even if it was only for food and lodging. "I'm sorry Tara, but the Police Chief forbids me to let you stay here. These laws are not necessarily enforced if you keep a low profile. The incident in the tent angered a police official. You know Tara, that Egyptian men do not like an argument from a women."

After I gathered my belongings, I trekked off to Herb's Beach, feeling depressed by the incident. Herb was on the beach, tan and youthful as ever, especially for a man of 60. He commiserated with me when I told him what had happened. I also shared the news of my article being published by SHE Magazine in London; the article he had liked so much." "That's great, Tara. Now you will have time and seclusion to write more. I'll bring you some yogurt and fruit tomorrow," he added to my retreating form as I headed south toward my citadel near the cave.

FIFTEEN

During my five years with the Egyptian Sufis, I remembered many lucid dreams. One night I dreamt that I was welcomed onto a large sailing ship by a group of Sufis. The ship was tied up at a wharf, with the stem facing me on the dock; the bow pointed toward the open sea. Um Ahmed, a middle-aged woman, one of my favorite female Sufis, was sitting against the mast looking at me, smiling and waving gaily, inviting me to come aboard and sit next to her. Um Ahmed attended almost every Sufi gathering in Cairo, usually sitting with friends smoking a water pipe, watching the action. Umi means mother. When Um precedes the name of the child, such as Um Ahmed, it means mother of that son, or daughter, when there is no son.

Sheikha Dunya, who presided with Sheikh Mohammed over their hidema at mulids, was also aboard the ship. I had grown fond of this wise sheikha, even sleeping in her large double bed at her comfortable apartment in Cairo. We had also traveled on buses together. One day we went to visit Sheikh Mohammed in his Delta village, not far from Zagazig, north-east of Cairo. Sitting on a couch in the living room of Sheikh Mohammed's farmhouse, I could watch a water buffalo attached by a wooden harness to a water wheel in a well, walking in a circle around the well to bring the water up. Another time we visited Sheikha Dunya's son and his wife in a rural home east of

Zagazig. When she traveled, Sheikha Dunya always wore a chador, the typical Muslim black long dress, and head cover. Perhaps my colorful self-created dervish attire attracted too much attention when moving about in public. One day she asked, "Why don't you wear the traditional uniform? I can give you a chador if you will wear it." The chadors that the women wear these days are often made of sticky nylon or polyester. I grimaced just thinking about it.

Sheikha Dunya appreciated my singing and dancing. She would collect money from the guests who attended their hidema, then hand me money at the end of an evening. Rich people donated generously to their chosen sheikh's hidema. This was how the hidema supported itself. The donations paid for the tea, food, water pipes, music, and zikr. Sheikha Dunya organized the food and service. If someone handed a musician money, the money was for that musician, or divided with the other musicians in that ensemble. In a separate place from the room where guests sat or zikred, women cooked the food. Young boys served the tea and food.

Sometimes Sheikha Dunya and I danced together in the center of a room, receiving and feeding each other's energy. We danced occasionally between two lines of zikr-dancing, invigorated by the powerful chanting of men's voices. At other times, we danced—separately or together—in the center of a large tent, with the audience of guests sitting against the walls on large cushions. When Sheikh Mohammed wanted me to dance, he would bellow in his deep voice, "Tahra, Yella, raks," waving his large hands in a sweeping gesture as though to move my body from my cushion.

Sheikha Dunya was the mother of ten grown children. Considering her a wise woman, people consulted her for advice. After the dream about the Sufi ship, I went to visit Sheikha Dunya to ask her for an interpretation of the dream. In the dream, the ship stayed in port. I asked her why we did not sail. Through an interpreter, she said, "The ship is Prophet Mohammed's ship of Islam. The ship is not going anywhere because there is no need to travel. The Sufis are together on the ship so it doesn't matter where we are."

Later, I had another dream. The same ship, with Sufis on board, was sailing on a wild windy blue sea, not far from land. I felt that this sturdy seafaring ship, with a freshly painted white cockpit and deck, could sail anywhere. The sea was deep blue, with foaming, sparkling white caps. We were moving swiftly through the waves in the strong wind, gliding smoothly or heeling. The sky overhead was clear, bright blue. Although Dunya told me that I was a welcome member of her Sufi family, through an interpreter at another time, she said that my vibrations were different from other Muslims. I was not really trying to be a Muslim; I simply enjoyed the practices they taught me, and shared. Even when embracing the essence of a religion, I feel free to express disagreement with dogmas and theories. Undoubtedly, I act accordingly. However, I was never made to feel unwelcome among these people.

By this time, Sheikh Mohammed had initiated me as a sheikha; other sheikhs had also bestowed the title upon me, referring to me as Sheikha Tahra. Feeling a greater responsibility, I worked to channel healing and transformative energy wherever my path took me. In the heat of a hot July, in a village near Sohag, in Upper Egypt, I had the chance to experience being a sheikha in a different setting.

The sojourn began while sitting in a cafe near Sidi Mursi Abu! Abbas in Alexandria in the beginning of July. Two friends of the great munshid, Sheikh Yassin al-Tuhamy, invited me to join their hidema at the mulid of Sidi Fargali in a small village near Asyut, beginning the following week. Because the train ride from Alexandria took so long, I was tired when I arrived. When I found Sheikh Tuhany's hidema, a member of his entourage took me to a room in a schoolhouse where I could sleep. The music and activity were so continuously exhilarating during the festival that I barely slept the three days that I was there. The last morning I slept in a very hot room in a small hotel in Asyut, and then traveled south by minibus to a small mulid at the farmhouse of a sheikh who had recently died.

The mulid was organized by Sheikh Mohammed and friends to commemorate the passing of our friend, who had died at the Cairo train station after the Sayyidah Zaynab mulid. It appeared that he had a heart attack. This could be a warning against too much over excitement, lack of sleep, endless tea and coffee and shishe pipe smoking. I remember that this sheikh smoked the water pipe continually at mulids. I never saw him zikr actively, perhaps internally. Movement and music helped me to feel alive and healthy during such intense gatherings. Sometimes this powerful sheikh would invite me to smoke his water pipe with a circle of friends and then he would ask me to sing. He was the first one to hand me money for singing or dancing. Then he would urge others to give also.

There were about ten people preparing food and setting up the sound system when I arrived at the farmhouse. I ate a little, practiced yoga and rested in a mosque before being escorted to the house to meet the deceased sheikh's widow and children. The entire house had dirt floors, as most country homes do. Water can be poured on hands to wash over the floor. I have even seen children pee on such floors, water then poured onto the spot. A dirt floor helps to keep the house cooler. In the evenings, a fire is made to cook food or bum charcoal for water pipes. This house was large and dark. Cows, donkeys, goats, sheep, pigs, and chickens shared a large back barn like room.

At seven p.m. Sheikh Mohammed awoke from his nap and invited me to join him for salad, goat's cheese and farm bread. Many people had gathered by now. Sheikh Mohammed was the presiding sheikh for this ceremony. Because I had now been honored as a sheikha, he insisted that I sit next to him all evening, barely allowing me to get up to zikr a few times and sing. These country folk were not accustomed to foreigners or independent women.

In the morning, several people invited me to their homes to sleep and visit. One man spoke English. It was difficult to decide where to go. I was most charmed by a friend of Sheikh Mohammed, who lived in a village near Sohag. When his group's minibus showed up in the morning, I piled in with the rest of the Sufis, mostly farmers. High from the festival and our newly formed ambiance, we laughed and sang all the way to the village.

My host's name was Sheikh Mu'min. He had one eye that did not open all the way. He told me that he could only see a blur out of that eye; his other eye was fine. We arrived at his home shortly after dawn. He woke up his wife, asking her to make us some breakfast. His twelve-year-old daughter and two baby sons were still asleep. His wife kept looking at me quizzically, perhaps wondering if I would be a new wife. Sheikh Mu'min later told me that she was jealous at first, but after realizing that I was there in friendship and for sharing ideas and music, she was very sweet, accepting me into her lovely family.

I intended to stay there for no more than a few days. *As* it turned out, I stayed almost a month. Sheikh Mu' min had a saha for the local Sufis in a large room on the ground floor. This saha had been presided over for two years by the dear sheikh whose mulid we had just come from. In the same space where he had slept, I slept. In a small back room, my clothes hung next to his favorite brown wool djellabia. Along with Sheikh Mu'min, I became a presiding sheikha.

Mostly farmers, but also teachers, students and businessmen stopped by any time of the day or night—usually in the evening as the sun was setting, staying until midnight or later. We placed mats outside the door of the saha to view the stars, moon, and the tall date palms in the balmy night air, where a whisper of breeze might cool us. Inside, with a ceiling fan, I had the coolest spot in the house. However, tiny bugs that lived beneath my straw mat disturbed my sleep by biting me every night. Sheikh Mu'min and I shared a spiritual and mental rapport. With his sketchy understanding of English, he found what I said interesting; translating for others from my broken Arabic and English mix. Upper Egyptians, dwelling in the southern part of Egypt, speak Saiidi Arabic; a variation I found difficult to understand. However, these people were fascinated by my philosophy and ideas; they loved my songs in Arabic. Almost every evening I brought out my guitar to sing from my Sufi repertoire. Because of these early evening informal performances, I was well nourished and learned about village life in Upper Egypt.

One member of the saha owned a local store from which he brought me fresh fruits and vegetables, which he knew I liked. The smell of cooking meat on hot afternoons nauseated me, so I rarely ate with the family upstairs, preferring to eat mw foods or steam my own vegetables. All members of the family were handsome, except that their skin appeared porous, even oily from fatty meats.

The pretty—in spite of a greasy face—teenage daughter and I enjoyed each other's company. She liked to sing also. Sometimes I would listen to her or we would sing together, laughing at our own theatrical antics and jokes. Occasionally, a young nephew who studied at the University in Asyut came over to the house to practice English with me. He had an eager, bright sparkle.

Across the narrow dirt lane that passed by the house lived a few women who did sewing for the village on a sewing machine in a dark room. Baskets and bags of fabric and clothes were strewn in every room of the two houses. The women in that part of Egypt like to wear colorful, beautiful clothes; mostly full cotton pantaloons under calf length skirts or dresses.

Two of the seamstresses were widows. They were all Christians. One seamstress, who looked like a nun, invited me to her large upstairs bedroom. On the walls were prints of paintings from Coptic churches. A large cross hung over her bed. Coptic Christians had sometimes complained to me that they experienced prejudice in this predominantly Muslim country; however, the Christians were often prosperous. Although this woman was poor, she said that she had never experienced problems with local Muslims. "We are all one family," she said. love radiating from her gentle soul.

Each evening, our circle of Sufis shared ideas and spiritual experiences. We chanted, mostly with the zikr-songs I sang. I sometimes wondered if the late sheikh had guided me to his saha, thinking that a foreign female sheikha would be an interesting experience for these Sufis; also because he liked my music.

Sheikh Mu'min warned me not to go to wedding parties or hadras, although I was invited several times. One evening, when loud music over a sound system kept me awake, I wandered over to a nearby hadra. Many of the people looked shocked to see a foreign woman. After a Sufi acquaintance told the head sheikh that I was a true dervish, I was handed a cup of tea and pastries, surrounded by puzzled and shy expressions on the faces around me. After watching the men zikr for a while, I joined in. These simple villagers-many of them having never seen a foreigner, let alone a wandering female dervish—were surprised that I knew zikr.

A small group of Sufi friends was at the saha when I returned to the house. Sheikh Mu'min was furious with me. He scolded me for leaving, explaining that the people around there were naive; it was dangerous for me to roam about alone.

One day I walked into the upstairs living room to find a very handsome man sitting on the sofa. Soft spoken and gentle, yet with fire and light in his eyes, this man had a strong, well-built body and powerful face. A dark short mustache decorated his full-etched mouth. He spoke English well enough for us to have a pleasant conversation. A few nights later, he came to the saha bearing a gift of lovely ripe mangos for me. That night the other guests left early, leaving Rashid and me alone on the divan inside. After talking with me for a while, Rashid kissed me. As his passion rose, I became shy and embarrassed. I knew Rashid was married Sex without marriage, with a married man, would be considered taboo in such a small village. I went to take a shower, hoping he would leave. He followed me into the tiny back room near the shower. This time he became very passionate; his cotton djellabia hung on his rigid penis like a drape on a statue. When I urged him to leave, he regretfully did, promising me undying love.

The next day Sheikh Mu'min told me that he had witnessed the whole scene in the saha room from a peephole in the ceiling, which was the floor of his upstairs flat. He said that I should not tempt men or allow them any sexual license. "I saw Rashid follow you into the little room. What went on in there? You were in there for several minutes." I assured him that Rashid had only kissed me. Even though Sheikh Mu'min did not intend to be unfaithful to his wife, he acted possessive of me. It was clear that he did not want other men enjoying what he perhaps fantasized. The knowledge that he had been watching me through a peephole was discomforting. One time, Sheikh Mu'min had moaned about the fact that women want to make love all the time, insinuating that his wife was in a constant state of desire. Perhaps the women in that hot climate were somewhat preoccupied with sex, with nothing better to ease the monotony of daily household chores.

One day I traveled to a mulid in a nearby village, staying with an unmarried couple—a rarity in Egypt—from Aswan. The man was Nubian. He told me that he had left wealth and a high position in order to wander as a dervish. That evening I sang for the people who came to their hidema. The woman offered me her large bed in a big room; they all slept in the saha foyer. During the three days I was there, she even bathed me, combed my hair, and dressed me. Rashid—my eager suitor—showed up on the second day, asking me to come back to Sheikh Mu'min's saha. He said that he had spoken with Sheikh Mu'min, who agreed that Rashid and I could see each other at the sheikh's house, where Rashid could court me properly.

THE SWORD AND THE ROSE

Rashid also said that he was very serious about marrying me. He had already told his wife. "How did she feel about it? What did she say," I asked. "She was neither happy nor unhappy about it," Rashid replied. "I love her, and I also love you. One does not replace the other. I want to travel, learn English better and work in other countries. I would like to go to California with you. However I must earn at least one hundred and fifty Egyptian pounds per month to send to my wife." (That was about seventy-five dollars at the time.) Rashid appeared to be sincere. He stated that I must be faithful to him if I was to be his wife.

A few days later I visited Sheikh Mu 'min's sister and husband in Sohag, the closest town to the small village I was living in. Again, Rashid showed up and urged me to marry him. He said that he would come to Cairo to visit me. Because I still felt that El Arabi was the only man for me, I told Rashid about my love. A week later, when I returned to Cairo, I learned that Rashid had come to see me at the hotel where I thought I would stay.

While in Sohag, a young man offered to take me to a Christian mulid at a famous monastery located in nearby arid hills; we rode there on his motorcycle. On that hot summer day the half-hour trip to the monastery was refreshing. We walked around the mulid for a while, observing the Coptic monks chanting and swinging their incense braziers in the large church sanctuary. Then we wandered amidst numerous small tents where people sat selling their wares: vegetables, fruits, crafts, and religious icons. The tents were mostly white, instead of the predominately colored ones—at least on the inside—seen at Muslim festivals. During that day, selling and buying seemed to be the focus—rather than serving tea, food, and music. Refreshments and instruments would probably appear later in the evening. Herc the energy was tranquil; there was no wild tassawuf (dervish) music, either live or tape-recorded. One man played a simple bamboo flute.

Just as we were about to leave, we walked past a police tent. Perhaps the police officers were bored, having nothing better to do than check on a foreigner. They asked us to come inside the tent for questioning. When I produced my requested passport, the police noticed that my visa was a few days overdue. Two of the police officers drove my escort and me to the police station in Sohag, leaving the motorcycle at the mulid site. I felt so sorry for my frightened escort who they put in the back of their truck. In the cab, both the driver of the police van and the policeman on my right gestured in lascivious pantomime, accompanied by dirty insinuations that the young man and I had participated in sex together; such thoughts were undoubtedly introduced or influenced by U.S. television programs. I felt disgusted. Little did I know that I was in the hotbed of Islamic fundamentalism.

When we arrived at the police station, I was held waiting for more than two hours in a tiny cement-walled guardroom at the front gate. When I was finally ushered into the Police Chiefs office, he told me that I must go to Cairo or Luxor immediately to get my visa renewed. Before I left Sohag, I saw the motorcycle owner. He assured me that he had been released after a couple of hours of questioning, and had picked up his motorcycle. Alhamdulilah!

Two police officers escorted me to the train station the next morning to be sure that I boarded the train to Cairo. The train was crowded and slow; most of the time, it barely moved, stopping at every little village or whenever sheep, goats, donkeys or cows were crossing the railroad tracks. Because the seats were crammed with people, I sat on the floor on my rolled, cased sleeping bag for a few hours, my body aching. At the next railroad crossing, I got off the train, and walked to the road to hail a minibus heading north. "Sheikha Tahra," someone yelled from within a minibus pulling up. Pushing his way through the crammed bodies, he then helped me step onto the bus. Excitedly he told the people in the bus about me in Arabic. They kept staring at me. I was tired and hot.

It was noon when we arrived at the next village as the muezzin was beckoning the faithful to prayer. I entered the small mosque near the bus stop, cooling my body and mind with water and prayer. Mosques are oases of peace in the chaos of Egypt. My sanity and center have often been restored in quiet mosques. However, this tiny mosque was overcrowded for the dor (noon) prayer. After everyone left, I stayed to meditate for a few minutes. In such mosques where they have no area curtained off for women, the Imam (the mosque priest) would sometimes hide me behind a door or in a nook or cranny, such as on this day. Sometimes the Imams seemed embarrassed by my female presence, yet felt it might look bad if they discouraged prayer. If I visit a Muslim country again, I will stay out of mosques when only men are praying. Women are supposed to be praying in their homes. If one does not have a home nearby, then where should a woman pray?

I maneuvered myself north by taking one minibus after another, from village to village. All along the way, people were waving to me from the sides of the road, calling out, 'Tahra". In each village, there were people who knew me, or knew of me. It appeared that since I had sung for some big mulids in Upper Egypt, I had become a folk legend up and down the Nile. Although accustomed to familiarity with Egyptians in northern Egypt, I had not expected such welcomes in the southern areas—called Upper Egypt because the Nile River flows from south to north.

Arriving in Mallawi in the late afternoon, I decided to see if I could find the Egyptian doctor, Kamal, who had guided the two Australians and me to my first mulid, almost four years earlier. He had given me the address of his pharmacy, where I went to inquire. The pharmacist called Kamal on the telephone. Kamal instructed the pharmacist to take me next door to the hotel, owned by his brother. There I could wait for him to send someone to pick me up and drive me to Kamal's farm; in the meantime, I could take a shower and relax in my room.

My escort arrived in a buggy drawn by two horses. It was a wild and dusty ride across the Nile by bridge, and into the eastern desert near al-Amarnah—where Akhenaten, the heretic Pharaoh, had created his City of the Horizon, a center for sun worship. After a bouncy hour's ride, we arrived at a stone house surrounded by trees and plants. The driver took me up an outside flight of stone steps; he rang a bell. We waited for some moments before Kamal came to the door in a bathrobe, looking a bit drowsy. Dismissing the driver, Kamal then showed me into a little sitting room to wait until he got dressed.

Fifteen minutes later he invited me into the large center room; a combination living-dining-kitchen room, more like an American or European country home than an Egyptian house. A pretty, young woman came languorously out of the bedroom, eyeing me suspiciously. Kamal introduced us. "This is my new Danish wife, Marianne, who I married last month in Denmark."

As we sat around the wooden table in the center of the room, eating dark volkornen bread and Danish cheese, the new wife warmed up to me. We began to laugh and enjoy the visit. Both Kamal and his wife spoke English fluently; it was relaxing to speak in my mother tongue after a year of communicating mainly in Arabic.

It was near midnight, the stars shining over the dark desert, when the horse and buggy whisked me back to my hotel. The next morning I boarded a second-class train to Cairo. As we headed north, the landscapes of green trees and towns became more familiar. Near Sayyidna al-Hussein Square in Cairo, sits an old inexpensive hotel where only Egyptians stay; some of them are long-time residents. I visited a few hidemas there during the large Sayyidna al-Hussein mulid; that is when I met several Sufis who lived in the hotel, as well as the owner and workers. An exception was made for me, a foreigner, to rent a room there occasionally.

While I had been in Upper Egypt, after the Sohag experience, the police had visited the hotel, instructing the owner not to let me stay there. Big Brother was watching me. It seems that someone in the Egyptian government—or at least the police force—was not pleased by my integration into Egyptian Sufi society. Sufis were mavericks of society in the eyes of fundamentalist Muslims.

When I returned to Cairo, I went to the hotel to see about renting a room. I liked the location and it was generally quieter than the Oxford Hotel. As soon as I entered the hotel foyer, the desk clerk eyed me suspiciously. "You can't stay here. The police will not permit it. By the way, a man named Rashid was here yesterday looking for you."

At the Passport Control Office at Mugama—a collection of government agencies in a large building at Tahrir Square, I was given a run-around from one office to another, and then told to come back in three weeks for my visa. A woman worker stamped a temporary visitors permit in my Swiss passport. I was still unaware that there was any real problem, thinking that the delay was due to bureaucratic complications.

Happy to get out of Cairo, I took a bus in the direction of a small mulid in the Delta, near Benha. There was no public transportation from the main road to the tiny village. The bus dropped me off at the entrance of a dirt road. I waited in the dark under a grove of tall trees to see if someone going to the mulid might come along in a vehicle. Just when I was thinking about giving up and hitchhiking to Benha, where I could find a place to sleep, along came a truckload of Sufis I knew. They were delighted to take me to the mulid.

Upon arrival, one of the Sufis guided me to a brightly lit tent full of colorfully robed men and women. The microphones and loud speakers were better than average for a small mulid After a cup of tea, I was encouraged to sing. This woke up the relaxed farmers, who had never seen or heard me before. The evening warmed up quickly, with several groups of musicians keeping us zikring all night.

As dawn approached, people began leaving. A tall handsome man walked beside me, shyly speaking. He invited me into his house on the left of the dirt lane, awaking his wife to serve us some food. After eating goat's cheese, greens, farm bread and tea, he took me to a simple small room on the roof, where I could sleep. The call of the muezzin from the nearby mosque awoke me at dawn and again at noon. It was getting too hot to sleep anymore, so I went downstairs to wash. The man's wife placed a wholesome breakfast before me at a table.

My host, Barud, was a local sheikh, earning his income as a tailor, also cultivating a small plot of land. His darling old rather twinkled joyfully at me, perhaps his first contact with a foreigner. The sweet wife of Sheikh Barud did not seem to be jealous of my presence. Two well-behaved adorable children also graced the home. There was no television set.

Barud's workshop was in a small dark downstairs room, containing an old heavy-duty sewing machine, fabrics, threads and other sewing supplies. After Barud finished farming chores in the evening, he ate supper, and then worked late into the night under a stark light bulb, making djellabias. Barud's handsome race looked tired for a thirty-five year old man.

His life-style reminded me a little of my life in America, where I homesteaded on my forty acres in the Coastal Range Mountains of northern California: planting, cultivating and fencing fruit and nut trees; digging a well by hand; building sheds and cabins; gathering wild herbs; and growing vegetables, flowers, and herbs. Actually, Barud had more comforts to begin with. For several months, I slept on the ground in a sleeping bag, then upgraded to a teepee before building a cabin. Nor did Barud have to haul water half a mile as I once had done. In addition, he had electricity.

Labor wages are very low in Egypt. Barud earned only a few dollars, at most, for a djellabia. Moreover, he had his family to support. His heart was in his plot of land in the fields east of the village; a pretty spot near a grove of trees. Barud's white donkey knew her way to the land. I felt honored to be carried briskly across the fields on the back of this lovely creature, arriving ahead of Barud and his children, who came by foot. Barud took off his djellabia in order to cultivate his vegetables and fruit trees. With his shirtsleeves and trouser legs rolled up, he could have been any farmer anywhere—happy on the land, happy with his children helping and playing. Although gentle, Barud displayed strength of character; at other times, he could be patriarchal and bossy.

On the third evening that I stayed there, Barud asked me to marry him. He told me that his wife was sick—something wrong with her womb or stomach—and that she did not want either sex or more children. I refused to take his proposal seriously.

When, one afternoon, I visited a nearby house and drank tea with a few men sitting on an outdoor mat, Barud was greatly displeased. He said that he felt responsible for me, that I was part of his household and no one else's. He was beginning to treat me like a second wife. Surprisingly, his wife appeared to be relieved to have me there as a substitute for his attention. Having already experienced similar scenarios, I did not wish to get involved. It was time for me to move on. I recalled an invitation from a sheikh who lived on a tributary of the Nile in the eastern Delta. This seemed like a good time to visit him; I was not far from the address he had written down. Like the Delta fan, I spread myself throughout the land.

At mulids, Sheikh Rahman would sit regally on gilded chairs or piles of posh cushions, smoking a large glass-bottomed water pipe, while devotees and servants waited on him. I never saw him arise from his seat except to leave a room. Although he looked anemic and unhealthy. a quality of understanding emanated from him. One evening at a mu lid at Sidi Ibrahim al-Dasuqi, I found myself alone with him in the large room of his hidema. During a quiet conversation, sharing his offered pipe, I felt a spiritual connection.

Arriving unexpectedly, I was warmly welcomed into his home, which was built on a bank of a branch of the Nile River, just off the street where the taxi let me out. Although larger than many homes I had visited, it was a simple two-story rectangular concrete structure. After food and tea, I was shown to a room on the second floor where l could stay. The rest of the second floor was still under construction; no work went on while I was there so I had the upstairs to myself. I used a candle at night and borrowed a chamber pot. My favorite time was sundown, when I sat outside on the terrace next to the Nile River branch, watching the orange-gold sun set through palm trees on the opposite bank.

Whenever I am near a body of water—even if not much larger than my own body—I feel an urge to swim. Against the advice of the household, I swam a few times in the same waters where oxen, water buffalo, donkeys, horses and other animals were daily bathed, in the same waters that collected trash, garbage and toilet wastes from humans. The only human bathers were a few men, a handful of boys and me—the most foolish of all, not being immune to the diseases and parasites that such pollution produces.

During my sixth evening there, while sitting with Sheikh Rahman and a visitor in his saha room, in walked El Arabi with his dervish friend, Johann, with whom he was traveling. We were shy with each other, each trying to act self-possessed, not needy. l went to my room alone while he sat with the sheikh. The next morning El Arabi told me that he had received word that I was at Sheikh Rahman's. He had come to invite me to go to a mulid in Cairo with him. He said he would return for me in three days. I replied that I would return to Cairo before then, that I could meet him at the mulid. Somehow, I got caught into the household scene, also singing for guests, so I did not leave for six days, leaving me only three days to get into the flow of the festival in Cairo. I never even saw El Arabi there.

So many times when El Arabi suggested that we do something together, I would complicate matters. I was in an almost continual state of longing, yet when he came within reach I could not seem to accept the manifestation of our union. It was as though I was attached to longing, or had spent so much time fantasizing future happiness that I did not know how to experience the realization of such fervent dreams.

SIXTEEN
SHARKS OF SAFAGA

*B*etween the mosquitoes and the persistently attentive manager of the Youth Hostel in Suez, I had not slept during the night before I boarded the nine a.m. bus to Safaga. My breakfast—quickly grabbed at the bus station—was a sandwich with greasy mush of indeterminate origin, salty hot peppers, plus a bottle of mineral water. The ancient rusty bus was full of Egyptians. In order to stretch out, my only choice was the long seat in the back of the bus over the hot engine. As the bus groaned its way out of the Suez bus terminal, I lay across the sea the engine already heating up beneath me. During a cool winter night, this long space might have been a comfort, but this day promised to be the usual July Egyptian scorcher. I was headed south, five hundred kilometers to Safaga, plus another sixty kilometers into barren mountains, if I could find transport.

I reconsidered my impulsiveness in undertaking such an arduous journey. The morning after a mulid in Fayid, north of Suez, I was feeling high from excitement and lack of sleep. I announced to some sheikhs that I wanted to go to a large festival in a remote part of southeastern Egypt, up in some mountains, not far from the Red Sea. They blessed me heartily, apologizing for being unable to accompany me there. One of the sheikhs drove me ten kilometers south to a saint's tomb on a barren dusty knoll, where a few dervishes cared for the small tomb. After invoking the spirit of guidance at the tomb, I hitchhiked a ride to Suez.

Now, with my buttocks burning over the noisy engine and fumes sickening me, I realized how exhausted I was. I had not slept for forty-eight hours. The sandwich was terrible, my thirst unquenchable. I considered leaving the bus at its first stop, three hours south of Suez, but after inhaling a few draughts of sea breeze, I dragged myself back to my oven-seat. I was too tired to even enjoy the beautiful sparkling blue vistas of the Red Sea as our route followed the shoreline.

A stubborn streak—even self-destructive—sometimes prodded me to put myself through great ordeals, even danger, in order to follow a quest. In order to complete a weeklong pre-Easter fast, ten years earlier, I had slept on a mountain in northern California during torrential rains and violent winds, in a tiny torn useless tent. I could have descended to my home in twenty minutes, but then I would have missed awakening on Easter morning to the wonderment of brilliant sunshine and green soft hills covered with wild flowers. which sprang up overnight. In contrast, this noisy bus going to God knows where and what, in a foreign country, was not an experience alone with nature.

It was five p.m. when the bus reached Safaga. Hot and tired, I headed across the nearby beach to the Red Sea. Removing the dress covering my bathing suit underneath, I ran into the soothing, healing salt water. Swimming straight out from shore among small fishing boats. I proceeded toward open water.

Reveling in the luxury of being alone, I heard a voice calling in Arabic. Turning my head, I saw a small fishing boat nearby. A young fisherman leaned over the stern and invited me to come aboard for tea. A beaming smile and kind brown eyes accompanied strong rope roughened hands, which hauled me onto the deck. While he heated water on a small kerosene stove, I stretched out my bus-cramped legs, and sighing, reclined peacefully, my head under the shade of a furled sail. The young man, who introduced himself as Fati, did not talk much. Occasionally I responded politely to a question, while listening to the music of gentle waters caressing the hull of the boat.

Sensing that I was tired, Fati offered me the hold of his boat to sleep in that night. He said he would soon return to his home and family. Pulling up a small hatch covering a portion of the hold of his boat, he showed me a cupboard-like space, just big enough to squeeze into and lie down. It was a protective womb in the sea. However, when I saw the dirty scratchy blanket and inhaled a musty oily smell, I remembered why I had come so far. I told the fisherman that I was on my way to a festival and must look for a lift. "Be careful of the sharks," Fati called, as I splashed into the sea. "Sharks?" My head rose out of the water. "Yes, these waters are full of them. Safaga is famous for its sharks. Last summer a shark killed someone here. You look pretty tasty." His eyes gleamed mischievously. Visualizing the silent swift creatures gliding toward me beneath the sea, I swam swiftly to shore, where I dressed. It was not far to the road.

A group of men was sitting at an outdoor table of a roadside restaurant. Glancing up, they invited me to join them. As my eyes feasted upon fish, salad, and rice, I realized how hungry I was. Some nourishment might help me on my way, I thought, as I sat down upon the chair they pulled out for me. While eating, a large truck came roaring down the road, heading north, horns blaring, bodies leaning out of windows and from the roof; voices singing, tambourines and tablas beating rhythmically. "They're returning from the mulid in the mountains. We have seen five or six trucks and there will be more, returning to their homes for Aiid," explained one of my hosts. "What, the mulid is over?" That also meant that I had missed a ride back to Cairo, where I had left my money and passport in my room at the Oxford Hotel. I must have been exhausted to come this far so foolishly with no more than eight Egyptian pounds (four dollars), and the one dress I was wearing over my bathing suit. In the course of conversation, an elderly gentleman at the table invited me to stay at his nephew's mechanic shop, two kilometers away. "There is a room there where I sleep when I visit him, also an extra bed that you can use. You'll be safe with me." the man smiled, revealing a few remaining teeth. There did not seem to be another choice, with so little money and too tired to think straight. We took a taxi to the shop. As I was led inside, past the junkyard of disassembled motorcycle pieces, the stench of oil and grease permeated the air. Uncle Gaddi led me into a filthy messy room. I longed for the cramped hold of Fati's boat. Gaddi lit a match to the little gas burner to make some tea, and then turned on an old radio hidden behind greasy djellabias hanging from nails on peeling-paint cement walls. When I sat down on the small metal-framed bed, which was supposed to be mine for the night, the entire bed sank to the floor.

After tea and too much talking, my host lay down on his bed and fell asleep, snoring heavily. This racket, plus my filthy bed across the tiny room from him, was not sleep inducing. I wandered out into the roofless workshop. Among the pieces of motorcycles, I found a wide board to lie upon, hoping that the moonlight and sea air might be of help. Cockroaches and other bugs scurried everywhere. A huge rat raced across the room, leaping—almost flying—over my head. I could not find a drop of water to drink. Sleep did not come.

By morning, l was feeling crazy with exhaustion. I walked to the beach across the road for a dawn swim. Then I walked down the beach to where I had swum to Fati's boat. The fisherman was nowhere in sight. Feeling hungry and hopeless, I lay in the sand. The sun grew hotter and hotter, my brain sizzling like a piece of liver on a hot skillet. While sipping on a plastic bottle of warmish water that I had collected from a nearby mosque, two young men came along and stopped to chat. Realizing that I was homeless in Safaga, they apologized for not being able to invite me to their home. It was Aiid al-Adha, the four-day feast commemorating the prophet Abraham offering to sacrifice his son to God. (At the last moment—before Abraham chopped his son's head off—God substituted a sheep.) Relatives were visiting each other at this time of family gatherings. Everyone in the entire Islamic world was gorging on roasted mutton. The two men offered me a tin of corned beef and a piece of bread, then left to rejoin their families.

Feeling lonely for the first time since I had arrived in Egypt, I sat on a piece of driftwood, eating a little of the corned beef and bread. As soon as I ingested a morsel of corned beef, a strange feeling came over me—not just dizziness, but also a sensation of dying. All over Egypt, millions of sheep were being slaughtered. Perhaps I was psychically attuned to the mass trauma of fear and death. Was I also a victim of this bloodletting ritual, I wondered? Alone on the beach I sank to the sand, then crawled to the side of a rowboat for a small slice of shade. Even there, it was blazing hot, the sun glaring off the sand a few inches away from my head. I seemed to be going through a rapid metamorphosis, growing older and older, dying. Suddenly I was aware of the presence of someone. I struggled to lift my head from my lying-on-my-stomach position. My eyes met the gaze of Fati, as he bent to see who I was. He was obviously shocked and scared to see me there, now an old woman, a dramatic change in the sixteen hours since he last saw me. He asked if I needed a doctor. "Aiwa," I gasped. "I think I'm dying." Fati could see my struggle for life. He dashed off. Lying there alone, dying on some forsaken beach in Egypt, while not far away rapacious Egyptian celebrants feasted on the blood of Abraham's sheep, I thought about all the Sufi songs I had created and was going to record; four and a half years of field work, from the fertile Nile valleys to the deserts, mountains, and cities, throughout this ancient land. Now my efforts would be wasted. As I felt myself slipping away from life, from my body, I softly spoke an Arabic prayer as my left hand dug into the sand—the only earth I could hold onto. I began to relax, letting go of fear, which felt like the clutch of death. Surrendering to the will of Allah, I felt a presence as life returned into my body.

A young man appeared with a lemon—the Egyptian cure-all for everything, especially anything to do with the head. He squeezed and rubbed it onto my face and neck, telling me that Fati had sent him. So, the doctor turned out to be a lemon—how refreshing! "I know a nice peasant family that live up the hill west of the road," the young man said. "I think you could sleep there." Along the way, we stopped for a 7-up. I even danced a little to some oriental music on the radio in the cafe, celebrating life. The day had passed; evening was approaching.

At the house, the peasant family was seated in a small circle on the dirt floor of a dark room. They invited me to eat their simple fare of rice and mulihiya. With some food in my stomach, I began to feel sleepy. The wife's mother took me to a roofless earthen floor, stonewalled room and gave me a blanket for sleeping on the ground.

A small pile of hay sufficed for a pillow. The donkey whose room I shared was most hospitable. After a long deep sleep, I awoke to early morning sunshine. "Since I'm here I might as well enjoy the sea and sun," I thought while I patted the goat whose cheese I was offered with bread and tea.

Someone had told me about a beach five kilometers north of Safaga, where tourists swam without much danger from sharks. Hitchhiking, my first ride let me out near a small port. Large and small rusty shipwrecks littered the small cove. As there were only a few people in sight, I decided to take a swim before finding a ride to my intended destination. I walked past a few small cement houses and into shallow water, becoming deeper as I swam among old ships that lay like corpses; modern junkyard sculptures, ghostly hulks harboring memories of ancient sea voyages.

Some young men were fishing on a long wooden dock jutting out into the sea on my left. As I swam past, they began yelling excitedly, jumped into the water and swam rapidly toward me. I swam away from the dock to the right toward a rusty ship. Another young man appeared on top of the ship and dove, hitting the water several yards from me. A semi-circle of the men began to close in on me. I hastily turned back toward shore.

There was something ominous about the way the boy-men glided silently toward me, their black eyes glaring brightly in the noonday sun. Sharp hungry eyes focused upon me like sharks upon their prey; adolescent human sharks hungry for white meat. I was reminded of a scene from a Tennessee William's play, "Suddenly Last Summer"; the part where some starving children devoured one of the main characters, a foreign white man.

Wondering what the youths would do with me if they caught me, I sensed that it would not be a friendly encounter. They might never have seen a foreign woman before. This was obviously a local swimming hole, not a place where tourists came.

Fortunately, I am a good swimmer. As the boys were almost able to grasp my heels, I made an extra effort. landed on shore and ran to my clothes near a cement house. An elderly man sat smoking a water pipe near the doorway. As the young men emerged from the water and strode toward me, eyes riveted on my body, I was fumbling with my dress, covering my bathing suit and body as rapidly as possible.

Seeing the elderly man speaking with me, the boys channeled their adolescent energy into a hail of questions. eating me with curiosity. I hastily excused myself and returned to the road. I had enough of these sharks of Safaga.

As soon as a public minibus came along, I jumped in. paying ten ersh (4 cents). The tourist beach was a pleasant wide sandy beach, curving around a bay. A few foreigners swam and fished. Feeling closer to civility and sanity, I began to relax, dozing beneath one of four scraggly palm trees.

The sound of feet scuffling sand nearby awakened me in late afternoon. A tall, very handsome Egyptian, probably in his mid-forties, asked if he could rest near the tree also. We conversed.

The man was an Admiral in the Egyptian navy, stationed in Safaga for a few months. His home was in Alexandria, where his ship was usually based. Life in Safaga was boring, he said. Most of the Egyptians there were uneducated, not very stimulating to a man of sharp intellect. He spent most of his free time swimming, fishing, and reading, going to sleep early. After all that I had gone through for the past few days, the company of this well-mannered, charming, sensitive man was a relief "Why don't we walk along the beach to Safaga now that it has cooled down," the Admiral suggested. "My friends call me Alex." We walked and chatted in the reddish-amber glow of the setting sun. Halfway to Safaga we came upon a seafood restaurant on the beach. Alex suggested that we stop and have dinner there, his treat. We dined luxuriously on crabmeat, swordfish, shrimp, clams, salads, and baked potatoes—a rarity in Egypt, accompanied by white wine.

A full moon was already glowing high above the sea when we left the restaurant. We strolled amiably along, feeling like old friends. I felt refreshed and young again. The light green of the soft cotton peasant dress that a farmer's wife in Fayid had given me, glowed phosphorescently under the moonlight. A soft breeze billowed the skirt. I felt like a sea priestess from a Dion Fortune book. Alex's gestures, smile and conversation were imbued with wisdom, intelligence, and compassion. The evening brimmed with magic. The gods and goddesses of the sea, moon and the night were casting their enchanted spells.

The near-death scene of the day before had faded into a bygone dream—confrontation with death followed by life as full as the moon above. We stopped to rest on a log. I felt invigorated by the caressing breeze and the energy of this alive and comforting man who responded to the mystery of the goddess. It felt as though we were alone in our own universe, in that vast desert-seascape. In the course of conversation, I revealed my past few days' adventures. A compassionate ear listened with concern. "My God, what an adventuress you are," Alex exclaimed. "We must see to it that you have a decent place to sleep tonight. There is no problem about money. Where would you like to sleep?" "I'd like to sleep on a boat moored out at sea." "Can I come and visit?" "Umm, maybe sometime.' "I'll check out the possibilities of boats tomorrow. Tonight you will sleep in a hotel" By this time, we were approaching the end of the strand of beach. An American chewing gum company had built a fence across the beach, into the sea, to prevent entry into the factory that sat on the beach, blight to the beauty of sea and strand. "What a lamentable spot for industry," I grimaced, as we walked over to the road. A sign saying, Oasis Hotel, was illuminated by the ugly orange glare of a fluorescent street lamp.

A young Egyptian manager sat alone behind the reception desk. He took me upstairs to see a room on the seaside. Inside the room were two double beds, a large closet, nightstands with lamps, a private bathroom, and sliding glass doors leading onto a terrace overlooking the sea. The only eyesore was the chewing gum factory to the left of the balcony. Comfort, at last! I returned to inform the Admiral that the room was more than sufficient. "Okay, I'll see you here tomorrow at six p.m. We can dine here and decide the next steps. I will try to find a boat tomorrow. In the meantime, relax and enjoy yourself. I'll bring you some books in English and a typewriter." Alex tucked some bills into my hand. "Please accept this to buy what you need. Your company has already been a great help to me."

After a delicious hot shower, I sank into the luxury of a double bed and space to myself. Sea breezes wafted in from the balcony through the open door. The light of the full moon flooded my bed. I felt so grateful for this gift of peace and my newfound friendship.

I spent the next day swimming and relaxing. At six p.m., sipping a bottle of lemon-lime tonic water in the restaurant, I waited for Alex.

Forty minutes went by. Feeling hungry, I ordered a light dinner. The young manager came over to talk to me, and then asked if I would like to share a bottle of wine with him on the terrace. He spoke English well. He said he was the son of the hotel owner. His company helped to ease my disappointment.

I went to bed wondering what to do. Alex had not given me a telephone number to call. I thought about his offer to live in his family's flat in Heliopolis, near Cairo, with his mother, where I would have a room to myself, videos, telephone, and all the comforts. In the morning, I decided to go to Hurgada to visit a German girl I had met at the Oxford Hotel in Cairo. She was belly dancing at a German resort for the summer.

Hurgada is a tourist town on the Red Sea, graced by some fine beaches. Most of the beach property is owned by big resort companies; German, French, American, Egyptian. The sherut taxi took about an hour to the door of the German beach resort. I asked for my friend Brigit at the reception. She was out. Rooms were expensive.

Walking along the beach, I found a camping area next to the resort. It only cost a pound to sleep in an old army tent. I swam and ate some food I had bought—apples, bananas, dates, cheese, and bread.

At dusk, a small group of tourists from various countries made a campfire on the beach. We cooked tea in a small aluminum cooking pot. I borrowed a blanket. Too sunburned to sleep well, I rolled around on the sand; little bugs nibbled on my tender flesh.

Brigit was surprised to see me when I found her the next morning. She invited me to a belly dance rehearsal with Egyptian musicians.

After dancing together for a couple of hours, I felt better. We ate lunch together and swam in the large hotel pool.

That evening we ate dinner in the hotel dining room; choosing a variety of foods from tables heaped with seafood, salads, vegetables, fruits of all kinds, deserts galore. I was invited to dance in the show that evening. Borrowing a costume from Brigit, I enjoyed being part of the variety show on the outdoor stage.

The next day I telephoned the Oasis Hotel to see if Alex had shown up. The manager told me that he had come the evening of the day I left. Alex told the manager that he had not awakened from a nap after work the night before. Disappointed to discover he had overslept, he still had hoped to see me the next evening. ""Please ask her to return to Safaga," he had told the manager.

In the meantime, I visited the large Hilton Hotel in Hurgada to inquire about the possibility of a singing job. They hired me to sing that evening for a special party. When I finished singing, some executives from Cairo invited me to their table for a drink. "Where are you from?" they wanted to know. "Cairo is my home base for now," I told them. "I am flying to Cairo in the morning in my private plane," one of the men said. "Would you like to come along?" I accepted this unexpected gift! I would soon be back in my room at the Oxford. It seemed more like years than days since I had begun my journey to Safaga.

SEVENTEEN

ecause I was traveling around with the dervishes much of the
time, I did not look for an apartment. Yet, I longed for a quiet
room without the hustle and bustle of a traveler's hotel. During my
fifth year in Egypt, I met two Sudanese brothers who told me they
had an extra room in a large flat in the district of al-Aguzah. On the
western side of the al-Bahr al-A'ma channel of the Nile River, across
from al-Gazirah (the Island), Aguza is a pleasant upper middle class
section of Cairo. The brothers' flat was on a quiet street, surrounded
by red and white flowered trees. The front door opened into a foyer. A
wide arch on the left of the foyer revealed a comfortable living room.
From the foyer, a small hall led to the kitchen and three bedrooms.
The brothers, Raoul and Hamid, offered me the largest bedroom
at the end of the hall. A balcony ran around the two exposed sides.
Birds sang in lush thick trees, the perfume of hibiscus and jasmine
scenting the air.

When I saw the large wooden closets and comfortable double bed,
I could barely wait to move in. I paid them one hundred and fifty
Egyptian pounds for my first month's rent. My clothes—hanging
luxuriously behind mirrored wooden doors—seemed as happy as I
was. They offered me the use of the kitchen, living room, bathroom
and telephone. Raoul and Hamid loved to cook, offering me delicious
meals, so I rarely cooked.

I had been negotiating with the BBC (British Broadcasting Corp.) about filming a documentary of my life with the Sufis. Now that I had a telephone, communication was simplified. I felt energetic and enthusiastic about feasible projects with western media, as well as Egyptian networks. In the pleasant living room, I could receive guests and hold interviews, serve tea and snacks, enjoy my role as hostess. An American newspaper reporter came to interview me. More interviews were planned.

I had lived in the apartment less than two weeks when—one warm summer evening, having just turned dark—from my bedroom I heard voices and sculling noises in the foyer. Fear permeated the atmosphere. I walked into the foyer to find police officers handcuffing Raoul and Hamid, forcing them to crouch on the floor. The policemen did not handcuff me; they told to sit against a wall on the floor. One policeman guarded us while the other two ransacked the apartment. I could hear them rummaging through everything, furniture banging around. After fifteen or twenty long minutes, they came out with a large bag filled with marijuana. We were ushered into a patrol car and taken to a police station in Rhoda.

Raoul and Hamid were like brothers to me. They shared their aspirations and their Sudanese culinary. Raoul wanted to be an actor. He was handsome and intelligent. Hamid wanted to own his own taxi. I had hoped to be able to help Raoul through connections I was making with theatre and film directors.

As we sat in the police station waiting to be questioned by the chief of police, Raoul told me that they had been selling some Sudanese marijuana in order to support themselves until they found jobs. To my dismay, I learned that most of the marijuana had been suspended over my balcony. I had never noticed it there. Perhaps they had placed it there that day while I was out.

The brothers were called into the Police Chief's office. I waited in the large dark room where we had been sitting. All I remember are the dark wooden benches upon which a few nervous people— including myself—sat. When Raoul and Hamid came back, they told me they had convinced the police that I had nothing to do with their illicit business. Two police officers took them away. I was sent back to the apartment to collect my things and get out. (Ten months later, I chanced to meet Raoul on a street in Cairo. He told me that Hamid and he had served six months in jail.)

It was midnight by the time I returned to the apartment. The Egyptian porter of the building was very upset. The chaos and confusion I found in the apartment was overwhelming. Everything I owned—in that part of the world—had been rifled through. Some red paint in a small jar had been spilled over many of my treasures. I did not know how to begin sorting through the mess. The porter finally agreed to let me stay there one more night so that I could organize and pack my things.

Already exhausted from the whole experience, l did not know where to take my things. Working as long as I could, I fell into an exhausted sleep at four a.m. By nine a.m., I had finished packing things into boxes. In the morning, the porter came to tell me that I must leave immediately. He let me leave some of my things in a storage room of his little house behind the flat, until I had another place to put them.

Two police officers came by to see if I was leaving. One of them wanted my little red radio, offering me five pounds. It was worth a lot more. Anxious to get out of Cairo, I let him have the radio. Physically and emotionally shattered, I took some clothes with me in a taxi to the sherut station behind the train station; there l wearily crawled into a crowded sherut to go to a mulid in the northern delta. The distance and energy of the mulid would restore me somewhat. This time, wandering, homeless, I felt ungrounded, not totally in my body. The idea crossed my mind that I might feel more comfortable in a tomb in one of the 'cities of the dead'.

When I returned to Cairo ten days later, I went to visit a Sufi sheikh and his wife who lived in a tomb-house near Sayyidah Nafisah. Most of their living space was outdoors; a wrought iron fence enclosed a small covered patio and a back yard with a few fruit trees and potted plants. A small cement room housed the tomb and kitchen. They slept in this room when it was too cold outdoors. They spent most of their time on the patio, where they cooked, ate, hosted visitors and slept. Many Egyptians lived in such tomb-homes. Some were large areas with shrubs, trees and flowers; sometimes the enclosed areas were large enough to house a family. The presence of t e stone tomb did not disturb these Egyptians.

I had already met the manager of these tomb-homes through his daughters, who I occasionally visited. These teen-age girls enjoyed demonstrating Egyptian beauty secrets, such as ripping hair off their legs, and other body parts, with a honey-lemon-flour mixture. We spent a couple of hours testing out various herbal hair rinses on this particular afternoon, while waiting for their father, Ahmed. I did not have enough hair on my legs to bother removing it.

These girls did not use kohl—the smoke-black made from burned almond shells and frankincense, plus antimony—used to line the eyes in ancient Egypt, sometimes still applied. I rarely saw modem Egyptians with kohl around their eyes; this custom was observed somewhat among more traditionally clad women. Among the dervishes, a few men sported black-rimmed eyes. El Arabi often used kohl during the last few nights of a mulid. He carried around a tiny flask of the black powder. Sometimes he applied it around, and inside, my eye rims. When he rubbed it onto the inside of my lower eye rims, it burned—perhaps from the metallic silver flecks of antimony. He said it would help me stay alert during the long nights of a festival; it did—if for no other reason than that my eyes felt like burning coals. I was also told that it was used to protect eyes from intense sunlight—diffusing the glare—in the desert. I often applied a milder form of kohl, instead of eyeliner or eye shadow.

Ahmed, the cemetery custodian, always carried around a huge metal ring filled with large iron keys. He seemed baffled when I asked him if I might rent a little vacant tomb. Ahmed knew I was a Sufi, but I was still a foreigner in his eyes, and a single woman. He hesitated, and then told me to follow him. As we walked through narrow dirt streets from his house to my prospective home, he glanced furtively around to see if anyone was noticing us. He made me walk several yards behind him, with a long shawl covering my face and head. At the little tomb-house, he quickly ushered me inside, lighting a candle. He told me that I could sleep there that night to see how I liked it. "Won't you be afraid to stay here alone," he asked in Arabic. I told him I needed solitude. He left, locking me inside. "For your own safety," he said.

Early in the morning, the holder of the keys returned to let me out. "I'm still doing yoga and meditation." He locked me in again.

This did not feel like a home; it felt more like a voluntary prison, not for me. When he returned I left.

The largest districts of tomb homes in Cairo are known as "The Cities of the Dead"; more than half a million—probably more than a million by now—Egyptians live in such cemeteries. It was at a large tomb-house in the vast area of Mamluk tombs, stretching for three kilometers north and south, on the east side of Shara Saleh Salim, that El Arabi had proposed marriage.

On the holiday of the Egyptian equivalent to our May Day, I wandered through the labyrinth of this settlement. Young girls dressed in their finest clothes joyfully carried flowers and food to family, friends and neighbors. Picnics abounded throughout the cemetery. Families gaily called to me to come and share their food. I stopped to eat with a large group in a spacious cool tomb, refreshing myself from the noonday heat outside. The entire cemetery was alive with color and festivity. A few shops and stalls sold food and other supplies.

Egyptians live in almost any structure that they can enter. If there is no shelter available, they will sleep on the streets on their straw mats, on rugs or cardboard, usually around a mosque. Even crumbling buildings, or unfinished buildings under construction, might be inhabited.

It was to a dilapidated building that El Arabi once led me to visit a Sufi woman friend. A wooden door opened to our knock, revealing one huge room behind the smiling face of our Sufi sister. The room was clean, pleasantly decorated with cloths hanging where the walls gaped. A television set was on. El Arabi spoke to her for a few minutes, gesturing at me. The woman opened a huge wooden closet and brought out an orange print silky dress. It looked too small for me, but since my bout with hepatitis, I was extremely thin. As I undressed to try on the dress, the woman gasped at my frail body and baggy ragged underwear. "Hiya masakin giddan," she exclaimed. ("She is very poor.") It seemed to pain El Arabi to look at me. He glanced at the TV, inquiring about the identity of a glamorous female singer. I felt like a poor urchin. The woman pulled the dress over my head and zipped up the back. It fit like a second skin, a little tight across the bust; however, with its flowing circular skirt, it was a dress for dancing. We thanked the woman, leaving behind my too-large white silk dress, perhaps better fitting my benefactor. How I loved to dance in that orange print dress; one evening at Sidi Ali, I danced vibrantly up and down the tile corridor between several saints' tombs, floating lightly like a feather.

Egyptians rarely met a poor foreigner; such as I was at that time. When I was healthy, I earned enough money to take care of myself. However, during and after illnesses I sometimes barely survived, unable to dance or sing for festivals or do shows or films.

The dervishes would sometimes explain to Egyptians who did not know me—baffled by my immersion in the dervish life-style, living with little money-that it was my love for Allah that kept me from seeking material comforts. Mesmerized by the dervish path, alternatives seemed superficial to me. Although I enjoyed singing and dancing engagements in folkloric shows, nightclubs and restaurants, the spiritual energy I found with the Sufis beckoned me more than money.

Sheikh Shahata (beggar sheikh) is an endearing example of the path of poverty. He lived humbly under his cloth tent roof near Sidi Ali. Sitting in the middle of several devotees while zikr music played on a boom box, wearing a fine robe, turban and jewelry—gifts from devotees—Sheikh Shahata radiated compassion and light. Visitors could help themselves from a large cauldron of beans or mulihiya that his wife cooked.

It was at the feet of Sheikh Shabala that I once lay in a dream-fantasy, in front of a myriad of candles, during a mulid at Sidi Ali. I had already visited several hidemas near the mosque. One hidema was tucked behind some trees, enclosed by high lattice screens. Good food and tea was offered. When I finished eating, one of the men, sitting with friends, offered me some white powder. I thought it was probably cocaine. Although I am naive about drugs, I did remember sniffing a tiny bit of cocaine once in Christiana, in Copenhagen, Denmark. It induced a relaxed pleasant feeling that lasted for fifteen minutes. I accepted a pinch of the white powder and sniffed it into my nostrils. Within a few minutes, I felt off balance, dizzy, uncomfortable. I sat in lotus posture and meditated for a while. My skin began to itch; scratching did not help. Great thirst sent me to the water faucet many times. I went out behind the hidema to vomit food and tea into some bushes. I felt uncomfortable among these strangers. Staggering two hundred yards up a dirt lane, I collapsed in front of Sheikh Shahata and his entourage.

Half asleep on the ground in front of him, I was aware of sandals over bare brown feet, and the flickering light of many small candles grouped together on a large flat rock, resembling a birthday cake. Colorful dreams and visions took my mind on journeys, the drone of men's voices comforting—my fathers, my brothers, my keepers.

More than an hour must have passed before I rose and thanked Sheikh Shahata for refuge and kindness, then reeled up the road toward Sheikh Mohammed's hidema. It was early morning, still dark. Alone on the road, I turned left. Halfway up the street, three young men came out of the shadows and began harassing me. I felt vulnerable. Like a knight in turbaned armor, El Arabi arrived by my side, staff in hand, guiding me to Sheikh Mohammed, depositing me into the safety of the warmly lit room; then he departed. This was before I knew El Arabi. Sheikh Mohammed and his comrades welcomed me. A water tap, over a large basin on one wall, beckoned me to quench my thirst, endlessly; drinking and drinking like a camel storing water for a long desert journey. A vomiting session followed each drinking. A woman placed a large bucket near the sink so I could drink and vomit in one place. The group was concerned, non judgmental. I felt accepted, protected. Sheikh Mohammed suggested that I sleep there. I longed for my own bed. I took a taxi back to the Oxford when I felt able, strengthened by compassion, without fuss or melodrama—a familial support group. Later I found out that I had unwittingly sniffed heroin. That drug was not for me.

Dreams of Egypt colored my nights for years—almost every night I was there, as well as after leaving the country. Most of the dreams were about Sufis, in environments where they gathered. In one dream—after I had left Egypt—I found myself searching for Sayyidah Nafisah. In a large city, I wandered through a labyrinth of asphalt streets. Cement buildings surrounded me. Occasionally I could see through openings at the ends of streets, or peer through skylines surrounding the city. As I got closer to where I thought Sayyidah Nafisah was, I waded through rubble and dust, feeling closer to the human warmth and sharing of Sufis. While structures crumbled to the ground, human caring continued.

In the dust, the jewel of the human heart still shines. Imbedded in the cement of modem life, the jewel is often lost. We are too busy plastering our lives with busyness and stress. Where Sufis congregate in Egypt, there is often dirt and rubble, stone disintegrating. In such an atmosphere, I found life. These were also spaces where my beloved might appear.

EIGHTEEN

"Wherever you are, whatever your condition is,
always try to be a lover."

(Rumi)*

*I*n late summer, I visited the poor section of Karmuz, in Alexandria—El Arabi's birthplace—for a mulid. Walking into a large well-lit tent, I spotted some musicians that I knew playing on the stage. When they stopped playing for a break they walked up to me smiling. "Mumkin enti renne schwaya," ("Maybe you will sing a little?"), the leader asked me. "Aiwa," (Yes!) the flute player exclaimed, leading me onto the stage, and then introducing me to the audience.

The usual preparatory ritual began: unzipping my hand-made, flower-decorated guitar case, tuning the guitar and tying my ankle bells on. I chanted fatah. Just when I was about to begin my first song, the large broad-raced sheikh of the hidema came to me smiling. 'The food is ready to be served. Could you wait and sing after the people eat? Come and eat backstage with us."

Before I could move, large trays of white rice, and white bread soaked in ratty mutton juice, dotted with chunks of mutton, began appearing on huge trays carried by young boys. As the steaming trays entered the room, the men began snatching and grasping at the food, clamoring over each other to reach their hands into the trays. I was appalled. Were they that hungry for greasy white rice and bread and a few pieces of fatty meat?

All those flailing arms stretched forward in my direction as the trays came out from behind the stage, where a little kitchen was set up. From my perch on the stage, I observed a scene reminiscent of an old Hollywood-style Babylonian movie. Unwashed hands dipped into the trays, stuffing globs of dripping food into eager mouths. Underlying this eating frenzy is the high value placed on mea which poor people could rarely—if ever—afford to buy.

Still, I did not want to seem rude, so I moved behind the stage; there I sat on a sack of potatoes, refusing to eat the prepared food, explaining that l preferred to eat scallions and raw vegetables. There were some carrots and radishes near me. Sitting there amidst the sacks of potatoes, rice and beans, I chewed on the vegetables, goat cheese, olives and farm bread. The clan members smiled at me humorously, realizing how shocked I had been by the mass-feeding scene.

I sang for a few more hidemas before the evening climaxed with a procession down the street past the mosque. By then, I was high above the street, in the mosque, looking out. I thought l saw a glimpse of El Arabi's turbaned head bobbing along in the crowd. I did not see him again that night.

A Sufi sheikh invited me to stay at his house in Karmuz. There his newly wed daughter and her husband offered me their red-draped bedroom to sleep in. They visited, talking and bringing me tea and sweets long after I expressed a need for solitude and sleep; they were so excited to have a foreign guest. Relatives and friends were already visiting downstairs when l awoke. One invitation led to another, so I began to know the residents of Karmuz. It was like a village within a city, as so many neighborhoods are, in Egypt. No matter where they live, Egyptians do not separate themselves into separate nuclear families. Not only are members of family spread throughout many dwellings, but also neighbors and friends form part of an extended family.

Ramadan was beginning. Candle-lit lanterns adorned the streets at night, when people were visiting one another in homes, watching extravaganzas on television, or taking walks along the Mediterranean Sea. Alexandria hosted musical concerts and plays in both outdoor and indoor theatres for Ramadan. The larger hotels featured all-night entertainment. usually folkloric music and dancing. During many of these nights, the dervishes in Karmuz were active.

I settled into a flat in Karmuz with an unmarried Egyptian woman who insisted that l stay with her, offering me the largest room. It turned out to be not just my room, but also the main living room, where her brothers, sisters and their families congregated. The woman would wake me up around four a.m. to eat the last meal before dawn. I began staying up most nights, kept awake by the buoyant energy in the streets and nearby apartments. In the early morning I went to bed with earplugs in my ears, a scarf tied around my eyes and a pillow over my head.

One day after I prayed in the mosque, a Sufi man led me down a little dirt path on the left side of the mosque. Beside a small creek running along the back of the mosque, we arrived at a door leading into the basement. Entering a clean white-carpeted room, we were greeted by eight Sufi men sitting along the four walls. After sharing prayers, conversation and tea, they took me through another doorway leading to the rest of the basement. A man was cooking over a gas stove in a large area that they used as a kitchen to prepare their meals. The cook invited me to stay for a delicious meal of rice and vegetables. By the time we finished our meal, I felt very comfortable with these Sufis. Two of them took me to a tiny room behind the kitchen, saying that I could sleep there if I wished. Most of them slept on the rug in the salon. When I accepted their offer, one man handed me a key to lock the door. No one came near me that night. It was the most peaceful place I ever slept in Alexandria. In addition, eight male servants of Allah guarded me. However, the room was tiny and dismal, so I returned to my lady friend's apartment to sleep for the duration of Ramadan.

I continued to visit my Sufi brothers, sharing prayer and spiritual discussions. One afternoon, when I walked into the saha room, I found El Arabi sitting amidst the circle of men, quietly rotating his prayer beads in his right hand. After a little small talk and silence, the sheikh of the group asked me if! wanted to marry El Arabi. Taken aback by the suddenness of this question, I was speechless. Since I had not seen El Arabi for a few months, I felt alienated from him. I gave a vague non-committal reply to this question.

El Arabi got up and walked to the door, glancing sideways at me, as if to say, "You blew it again," and left. As though I were holding an empty bag, I sat there feeling foolish, empty inside. When offered what I wanted, I was not able to seize the moment. Longing felt safe and comfortable, though unfulfilling.

The dervishes of Karmuz are enthusiastic practitioners of Rifai Sufism, a sect that employs self-infliction as part of their path. Most of the members have skewers and swords hanging on their walls, which they use to pierce their cheeks, throats, eyelids, and sometimes stomachs. An elderly Rifai Sufi sheikh showed me his assortment of rusty implements in his small house near the mosque. He had plenty of body-piercing experience. I had seen him in processions during festivals; a large skewer pierced through both cheeks, a small skewer pierced through each eyelid, and another skewer pierced through the skin below his chin.

A young Rifai Sufi man, who I sometimes visited, told me that he had pushed a sword into his abdomen. He felt fine, both during and after the procedure. It sounded like hari-kari to me. Yet, he appeared to be healthy and strong.

In Karmuz, and elsewhere in Alexandria, I attended Rifai gatherings. One hadra took place in a small graveyard near a roughly built shack that served as a family home. This raggedy group of dervishes presented a mystical scene on that windy cold night on a wasteland near the shack. A full moon shone through a lone scraggly tree. A bonfire, where we could warm our hands between zikr sets, glowed orange nearby. A few skewers jutting out from faces, silhouetted by the fire and moon created a perfect Halloween scene.

Many of these Sufis were almost toothless, because, for poor people who could not afford to pay dentists, the dentists sometimes pulled the teeth that had cavities, rather than fix them. Only wealthy Egyptians could afford fillings and orthodontic reconstruction. Some people even pulled their own teeth when a toothache became too painful.

A dentist in Karmuz worked on my teeth. His dental office consisted of a room attached to the right side of the mosque. It cost almost nothing for these services because the government or the mosque subsidized them. After he filled a couple of cavities, he told me that my teeth were all fixed. A few months later, in Switzerland, I found out that I had several cavities and needed two root canals. No wonder one sees so many missing teeth in Egypt.

One evening the Karmuz dervishes took me to a big Rifai festival at a mosque in another part of Alexandria. Skewers and swords were gleaming with polished luster, while the dervishes milled around in a large well-lit room, helping each other place the skewers in cheeks, necks, eyelids and throats. I was so caught up in the excitement that I found myself wanting to pierce my own face. Fortunately, the procession began before I manifested this inclination.

Drums beat out hypnotic rhythms as the dervishes danced through the mosque and into the streets, their skewers and swords bobbing out of various body parts. With pierced cheeks, some little boys entered into the ritual. One boy proudly showed me his cheek after he removed the skewer, revealing no trace of blood or holes. These Rifais were wild to behold! I sometimes felt as if they had emerged from deep within the earth. Their practices seemed to take them into deep regions of their psyche as well. Their color is black.

After leaving Karmuz, I decided to take a vacation in Aswan. I had been there a couple of times before, once by felucca (sailboat) from Luxor, and another time by train. The Nubians in Aswan, hailing from northern Sudan, are usually darker skinned than northern Egyptians. They seem happy and relaxed, enjoying a simple and tranquil life.

During this visit, I was invited to a Nubian wedding on one of the small islands clustered in the Nile River. I was hospitably received at an arched-roof stucco house. The semi-circular form of the long roof created arched doorways at each end. The interior of the house was remarkably cool. Dates, melons and tea were served as family and friends meandered in and out of the house before sunset. Later, beneath a moon and star-filled sky, the main festivities took place outdoors, where we were served sumptuous food. After eating, musicians and dancing girls entertained. This music had a slightly more African feeling than most Egyptian music; the region called Nubia extends from Aswan, Egypt to Khartoum in Sudan. That evening I danced into a timeless rapture, surprised how soon the sun arose in the morning.

While in Aswan, I met some dervishes I knew; they invited me to a series of small mulids in the area. In Aswan, there are small mosques in the Old Muslim Cemetery—on the southeastern side of Aswan town. These mosques are dedicated to some of the more famous saints, who are buried in northern regions, where the large mulids are held. These mosques host the names of such favorites as: Sayyidah Zaynab, Sidi Ibrahim al-Dasuqi, Sidi Abul Abbas al-Mursi, and others. Since many of the dervishes go north for the big mu lids, these birthdays are celebrated at a different time of year in Aswan.

These small memorial tomb-like mosques are set outside of Aswan in a desert landscape, some of them on top of hills or dunes. The sounds of flute and drums, plus the vividness of moon and stars, are clarified in the desert air, lending a romantic flavor to such gatherings. I felt very relaxed among these people and their land, to which they have a close connection.

The High Dam and Lake Nasser have flooded much of what was previously Nubian land; so many Nubian families have been relocated. Because of this forced removal, they have less space than accustomed to.

Nubians are aware of the fact that the High Dam has prevented the natural silting of the land, which occurred during the annual inundation of the Nile River, before the dam. Some of the elders reminisced about the natural flooding which created a rich deep loam, providing the organic fertilizer for agriculture along the Nile—from Aswan to Cairo, throughout the Delta, to the Mediterranean Sea. I have heard that chemical fertilizers have been introduced to replace nature's gift.

A tour guide in Aswan invited me to join his party of tourists for a visit to the Philae Temple on the island of Agilqiyyah, where the temple was moved after the construction of the High Dam. Its original site is submerged in water. It took more than ten years to move the Philae Temple to higher ground. The columned edifice was enthralling to behold as we approached the island by boat. As we wandered through the complex of temples and chapels, the tour guide explained the hieroglyphics on the temple walls. The largest and most important structure is the Temple of Isis, the main goddess of Egypt during pharaonic times.

While the tourists were still looking at the temple, I went into a small chapel to change into a bathing suit, so I could enjoy a refreshing swim around part of the island. The tourists were surprised to see me swimming as they boarded the host for departure. I climbed aboard in my wet bathing suit, covering myself in my clothes as we puttered back to Aswan.

Although the Temple of Isis looked lovely on the island, the building of the High Dam was disturbing. I had been told that the annual flooding of the Nile had flushed out salt from the river. Now the Mediterranean Sea is eroding the soil and infiltrating the delta—and perhaps farther south—with salt. Because the Nile River does not have its full force flowing out, the salt water can enter. I also learned that only four out of the twelve turbines of the hydroelectric power station were working at that time. Blackouts from power failure were frequent in Cairo.

With all that sun in Egypt, the whole country could be powered by solar energy. Human beings have a bad habit of turning to the earth for their needs when they could more easily—without pollution—harness energy from sun and wind. And let us not ignore the spiritual reward of receiving what is offered from above, instead of turning, churning, digging, ripping and sucking the life force from Mother Earth.

The sun is blazing out there, as if to say: "Here I am. You can use my energy without hurting the earth or any living creatures." Akhenaten, the Pharaoh who initiated sun worship in Egypt, recognized the power of the sun. We need not always search for fulfillment of our needs and desires from the earth. On both a spiritual and physical level, we can turn to the Great Spirit and the sun, finding illumination directly from Source.

NINETEEN

"If you want the truth, I'll tell you the truth.
Listen to the secret sound; the real sound,
which is inside you, the one no one speaks of.

(Kabir)

*A*ll health and difficulties plagued me through much of my last six months in Egypt. Looking back, I see that many of the problems came from not having my own quiet space, where I could center and restore myself. I was like an over-exposed film, capturing myriads of impressions, without a darkroom to develop the film. My guts often hurt. Microscopic parasites were eating my insides. Questions caused me to talk when I needed to be quiet. A great feeling of fatigue would overcome me from the attentions of people. I would feel they were psychically eating me. "Nas akul ana," (People eat me.) I once told El Arabi. If I closed my eyes, people would often nudge me and ask more questions. El Arabi would tell others that I was meditating.

It helped to define a meditative space by sitting on cushions with my back straight and my hands folded in my lap, or arms straight across the knees, with my hands in yoga mudra (pose). However, I was not always able to tune people out, especially when their focus was on me. Even when I was in Bahariya or the Sinai, I was plagued with the dramas and attentions of people. Part of this was due to my poverty, when I was unable to pay for a quiet space of my own. My face probably began to take on the tensions and fatigue one sees on homeless people. My exhaustion disturbed El Arabi. Able to rest almost anywhere, he probably could not understand it, although I have seen him exhausted also. People usually respected El Arabi's sleep in an area he would define with his staff, but they wanted me to entertain them indefinitely. For a wandering dervish, every nook and cranny could be a nest. This is where I failed as a dervish, at least in the eyes of those who could sleep in the midst of chaos.

El Arabi also cherished special places of solitude that he discovered. During a mulid at Sitta Fatma Nebawiya, he told me that he had found a wonderful tree in a little courtyard, beneath which he slept. Birdsong awakened him in the mornings.

My mother must have sensed my fatigue from my letters. She urged me to go home. By now, I could not visualize myself in a western society. Observing westerners rushing from place to place, looking at their watches, I clung to the timeless space that I cherished. I identified with the Egyptians. Like a mermaid or fish, I was caught in a net of love.

The Oxford Hotel was relatively quiet when I returned from Upper Egypt. My little room was occupied, so I moved into a large room with a Finnish girl. She was sick with the flu, lying in bed reading magazines. This mood helped me to relax for a couple of days.

Vajri was a big husky buxom blonde-haired young woman who loved to play with young Egyptian men. She would roam about the streets, and on trains and buses, in tight mini-skirts, to the dismay of her various boyfriends. I told her that such overt behavior embarrassed Egyptians, causing unnecessary attention. Even though overweigh she loved to flaunt herself. By doing this, she revealed a total lack of understanding of Egyptian decorum. However, I liked her wide Nordic smile, her boisterous verbal expressions.

One afternoon, I walked to the foyer to get us drinks from the cooler. Halfway back to the room—padding along in rubber sandals, a full bottle of 7UP in each hand—I felt and heard a squish, then a crunch under my right foot. I slipped, falling on the marble floor of the hallway as my right leg slipped out from under me. A blinding flash of pain shot through my right elbow as it hit the floor. It was not until my face met the cockroach on the floor that I knew what had caused me to slip. The cockroach was even larger than the usual ones in my room, which managed to eat, not only edible snacks in lidded jars, but devoured the filmy metallic-threaded polyester fabric that canopied my bed These cockroaches had crusty shells—perhaps the result of eating metallized polyester—encasing juicy bodies. This particular hallway dance could be described as "crunch, splat, and slide."

As I lay moaning, Mustafa came out of his little kitchen-nook where he prepared tea. "Aiwa, Tahra. Inti kwayis?" (Are you ok?) Mustafa grabbed my left arm to help me get up. My right arm dangled ominously, like a floppy puppet without a master.

I staggered down the hall to my room, Mustafa carrying the drinks. As I slumped into the room, Vajri eyed me lazily. "What happened Tara?" I told her that I had slipped on a cockroach in the hallway; her only change of expression was that her round pale eyes enlarged quizzically in her round plump face for a second, then she returned to her pulp magazine—undoubtedly more interesting than a loose hinged arm dangling above her head I plunked down on the thin-mattressed metal bed, the broken crisscrossed metal straps beneath creaking as they rubbed a few flakes of rust off each other.

I tried to read the book I had been reading before my fateful trip to the cooler. As shock subsided, the pain in my right elbow intensified. I began to realize that I might have more than a sprain or a bruise. The slightest movement sent waves of excruciating pain surging through my elbow. Even lying still, the throbbing pain prevented concentration on what I was reading. I remembered that a Sufi doctor I knew had told me that he would offer a free clinic near the Sayiddah Nafisah mosque during the mulid of Sayyidah Nafisah, which was just beginning. I found the scrap of paper with the address written down in Arabic. Vajri was still engrossed in her pulp magazine, occasionally heaving a sigh with her large bosom.

In a large scarf converted into a sling, I hung my limp arm, still thin from the bout with hepatitis. Struggling to get my left arm into a tight leather coat that a Sufi had given me, I then draped the rest of the coat over my shoulders. Gingerly, I walked down the hall to the elevator, surviving the bumpy ride down to hail a cab. The cab driver deposited me at the left side of Sayyidah Nafisah, as I requested. There was little sign of life. It was already nine p.m. The few people who had set up a tent or other hidema were either asleep or talking softly. I walked down the narrow dirt street next to the mosque. After finding the clinic number on one of the cement row houses, I knocked on the door.

A woman came to the door, ushering me into a room used for the hidema. She brought me a cup of tea while I sat on a cushion on the floor waiting to see the doctor. As soon as the doctor was free, he came out to greet me warmly, frowning at my limp arm. I followed him into his tiny examination room. "It might be broken", he pronounced after inspecting my elbow. "I do not have x-ray equipment here. You should go to a hospital to have it x-rayed for proper treatment." This was the arm that had strummed my guitar endlessly for almost five years in Egypt; now it was limp and throbbing with pain.

I walked in the cold night air until I could find a taxi. Exhaustion overtook me as I stepped into the taxi that pulled to the curb. A five minute drive took us to a very large old stone building. This was the hospital. The taxi driver deposited me at the emergency entrance. I waited in a drafty florescent-lit room until I was called into a doctor's examining room. After a brief examination, someone led me to a large dark room, behind some curtains, for x-rays.

Again, I was asked to wait. Sometime after midnight, I was informed that the largest bone in my right elbow was broken, that it needed to be operated on as soon as possible to prevent crippling. An attendant guided me upstairs in an elevator to a small waiting room for incoming hospital patients; there I waited for two hours, tired and cold, until a surgeon arrived to examine me. "It would be best if you stay overnight so we can operate first thing in the morning," the surgeon told me. Unfortunately, there is no bed available. If you do not mind, you could sleep on the floor of this room on cushions from the chairs. There will be a bed for you in the ward in the morning."

Lying there cold, with only one small blanket, I longed for my sleeping bag, which I had left on my bed at the Oxford Hotel. The first nurse on morning duty awoke me when I had barely dozed off. Too tired to talk, with nothing to read, yearning for solitude and sleep, I finally wandered into the women's ward. It was a huge room, with about five hundred people convalescing together. More than one person usually occupied each bed; some women were on mattresses or blankets on the floor, accompanied by their children. Small black and white television sets, brought by family and friends, faced many of the beds. Many of the women who were awake glued their eyes to the TV. They were not all tuned to the same channel, which, along with crying babies and moaning women, created a cacophony of irritating sound.

For a person like me, who likes her own sleeping space, this was lack of privacy at its peak. Most of the women had visitors coming and going. Various women hailed me to their beds to chat, curious about the foreign woman in their midst. A nurse offered me a little breakfast. The morning dragged on; no one came for me. I began to think that this was a sign for me to return to the Oxford, to sleep and reschedule the operation. I should have.

It was three p.m. when I followed a nurse to the operating room. It was a cold gray room with ugly fluorescent lighting. In the center of the room was a raised slab of concrete, with a bloody torn sheet on it; so much blood that it reminded me of a slaughtering block. My impulse was to flee. I protested, saying, "Perhaps I should wait for another time, maybe another place." As I was edging backwards toward the door where I had entered, two attendants lifted my body and placed it onto the bloody sheet on the concrete slab. Before I could protest, a large husky woman clamped a chloroform mask over my nose and mouth until I quickly lost consciousness.

When I awoke, I found myself lying on a thin pad on the floor of the women's ward, next to an occupied bed. Although groggy, I still found the voices, plus noise from televisions, irritating. When I mustered up enough strength to go to the toilet, I searched for a quiet spot to rest. I opened the door to a little room. It appeared to be an examination room, with a high narrow padded table, similar to a massage table. After gathering my blanket from my mattress, I moved into the little room, shutting the door behind me.

No one disturbed me that first night. A nurse even brought me breakfast there. The hospital staff seemed to recognize that this was my sanctuary until the room was needed. During the week that I stayed there, I had to vacate the room several times when doctors needed to use it to examine patients. The closed door helped to muffle noises. Still, the table never felt like a bed; sometimes I wondered if I would fall off while I slept.

Friday at the hospital was a mixture of gaiety and much noise; the Muslim holy day, as Sunday is for Christians. Large extended families came to visit patients, bringing tons of food. It was a glorious warm sunny day. Those who could leave their beds went to the balconies surrounding an inner courtyard where tall trees and smaller shrubbery and flowers grew. The balconies were packed with families gorging on quantities of food laid out on blankets, cloths or paper. Several families invited me to share their food. I ate a few bites here and there from this Egyptian smorgasbord. It is hard to resist such openness and hospitality, even though what I needed most was silence and peace.

My arm hurt at the elbow where the surgeon had operated. After a week or so, the itching beneath the cast became maddening, as I could not get to the itching area to scratch it. However, seeing so many sick people reminded me to count my blessings.

When I was released from the hospital, I returned to the Oxford Hotel. I had telephoned during my first night at the hospital to ask the manager to put my few belongings and sleeping bag in the storage room until I returned. Nevertheless, my sleeping bag—a welcome gift from a German woman—had been stolen. This sleeping bag was a source of comfort and security to me. It provided cleanliness and greater independence during my journeys with the dervishes. Now I would be obliged to rely on whatever blankets or covers were available in a situation.

The government officials of Mugama were still giving me the run around about renewing my visa. It would soon be five years since I had arrived in Egypt, which would make me eligible for resident status. A Swiss actress, who had befriended me, said that she advised against resident status because a resident was subject to the same laws as an Egyptian citizen. She said that the government tended to be more suspicious of residents and watched them more closely than tourists. A tourist was treated more leniently; problems were usually handled by the tourist's embassy. Tourists brought needed money into the country. In this respect, I was certainly not a valuable tourist. I had survived in Egypt with the blessing of Allah, my talents, and the love of the Egyptian people. Alhamdulillah!

Wrapped in mysticism, this adventure in an exotic land felt familiar; it also included many lessons in survival. To the Egyptian government—who, by now, probably had varied reports about my activities with the dervishes, not to mention the incident with the Sudanese brothers—I was neither a profitable tourist nor an economically deserving candidate for residency.

Sometimes I sang Islamic songs for the workers at Mugama, to their delight. However, the novelty may have worn thin when it appeared—to bureaucratic mentality—that I was not bringing much money into the country, had lived briefly in the house of drug dealers, and hung out with those 'weird dervishes'. Even more damning: I had been told that one of the police chiefs—who observed me spending so much time with the Sufis—had suggested to some of the elders that I was probably Jewish, perhaps even an Israeli spy. I speculated on this gossip when my visa was not renewed. At this time, I thought the process was only a delay.

TWENTY

*W*ith my arm in its cast, I attended a few more mulids, Unable to play guitar, I still enjoyed the music, ambiance and zickring. The plaster cast on my right arm accumulated numerous Sufi signatures in Arabic, along with sympathy and best wishes for speedy healing.

Back at the Oxford, I shared some time with my favorite residents. Six weeks passed before I returned to the hospital to have my cast removed. My released bare arm looked even more withered; the skinny long, skin-covered bone dangled limply; the elbow was still painful and vulnerable.

On the way back from the hospital, I stopped at Mugama to get my visa renewed, hoping for a better reception this time. I was wearing a long white wool, hooded cape, crocheted with rose metallic and rayon yarn. I had crocheted it together while convalescing; using a white wool blanket an English tourist at the Oxford Hotel gave me. There was a rather strong chilly wind coming off the Nile River that January morning. My throbbing arm felt so fragile. Walking down the hallway of the second floor on my way to the visa offices, I heard my name called out by a female voice, "Hi Tam."

I turned to see a small group of people led into a tiny cell-like room with round metal bars as a door. Then I noticed the small Turkish girl who had been staying at the Oxford Hotel for a while, standing behind the bars. I remembered that she had left the Oxford to travel with her German boyfriend to the Sinai. Before I could ask her what she was doing there, an official looking man in uniform asked me to follow him into a nearby office. I sensed heaviness in the air. Seeing the girl in the cell felt like a bad omen. The questioning that followed was tinged with suspicion. "Why have you stayed so long in Egypt," a tight-lipped Egyptian officer asked me. Raising my eyes from his medals and ribbons on the front shoulders of his navy wool jacket, I looked him straight in the eye and naively said: "Love; love of the people, love of Allah, love for a man." "He doesn't love you," the officer replied coldly, ignoring the other forms of love mentioned. "Oh yes he does. I can feel love." He glared at me icily. I felt I had betrayed my own heart by sharing such feelings with this man, who felt nothing but disdain for such foolishness. Did he know about El Arabi? Had I been spied upon?

He asked me to follow an attendant to another room. Again more questions. After three such strange interrogations by different officers, I was told to go with another man in uniform. I assumed that he was leading me to another visa office. The man ushered me down the wide stone stairs and out the door, holding my left arm.

A large van was parked on the cement plaza area, several yards from the door. The officer was leading me straight to it. When I saw the bars on the windows of the van and the Turkish girl and her group climbing into it, fear clutched me, mixed with anger. My attendant was now almost pushing me toward the van. Impulsively, I pulled my arm free and whirled around, the wind whipping my cape dramatically into a circle around me. "I am not going into that van," I exclaimed. "I have not done anything wrong." The attendant fiercely grabbed my right arm, wrenching the forearm behind my back, the still unhealed elbow crunching. Excruciating pain shot through the elbow like fire. He pushed me into the van, as another man in the van pulled me by the arms.

The group in the van consisted of foreigners; some of them with visa hassles, others with charges that are more serious. One Englishman had lived in Egypt for seventeen years, running his own business. He said that this was the first time that he had been arrested. He thought that they were trying to frighten him into leaving. "The Egyptian government goes through periods of paranoia, sometimes rounding up anyone who seems suspicious in any way, and either jails them, or makes sure they leave the the country. Yesterday, seventeen Egyptian lawyers were jailed, just because they have been voicing their ideas about laws, including changing some existing laws. They are in the same jail we are going to."

The Turkish girl, Mari, said that she had already been in jail several days. She and other foreigners in the jail were brought to Mugama to do paper work for their existing status in Egypt. Mari had been arrested with her German boyfriend in the Sinai when the police found a kilo of hash on him. She said she did not even know about it.

This whole scene was a bizarre movie to me, uncomfortable and scary. My feet were already cold in sandals before we entered the wet floor of the large building near Sidi Rifai mosque, which housed the jail. I had to wade through an inch or more of water to walk to the front receiving area. Had they just sloppily washed the floor,

I wondered? Was this jail experience a substitute for the skewers that the Rifai dervishes put through parts of their bodies? "I need to telephone the Swiss Embassy," I told the official behind the desk. "You can call them tomorrow morning," he replied, before a guard ushered the Turkish girl and me upstairs. The guard opened a metal door and locked us into a stone tomb-like room with three Egyptian women in traditional black caftans.

Mari immediately began chattering with her cellmates. They had established a rapport during her two-week internment. "I have learned so much Arabic during my stay here with these women; I'm enjoying our camaraderie. Still, I am worried about what charges might be used to indict me in connection with my boyfriend," Mari told me.

I was too tired for chatting voices, so conversed only a little with the women. I was still an outsider to this little club. I learned that the slender petite woman was there for dealing marijuana. This could be a long jail sentence for her. She looked sad. The other two women were in jail for minor thefts.

In the early evening, a guard opened the door to allow a couple of female relatives to pass in some cooked food they had brought from home. We all sat in a little circle sharing the food. Except for a bowl of mush, a piece of bread, and a cup of tea in the morning, I never saw much food supplied by the jail. The inmates seemed to rely on relatives for nutrition.

As evening descended, fatigue and depression overcame rue. The beds were just hard stone slabs along the sides of the room. After several entreaties, the guard brought me a thin blanket. Even with the addition of my cape over me, I felt cold all night. To darken my thoughts before falling asleep, I heard loud thuds and whacks, followed by screams and moans coming from a man's voice down the hallway. This went on for half an hour or so, until a tranquilizer I had bought across the counter of an Egyptian pharmacy knocked me out.

In the morning, we took turns taking hot showers in the bathing toilet area behind a curtain. This helped to revive us. When the guard brought tea and biscuits, I asked to phone the Swiss Embassy. At eleven a.m., the guard led me to a telephone. As soon as the secretary at the embassy understood my problem, she put the Consul General on the line. He tried to reassure me that he would be able to obtain my release if I had not done anything illegal. "I do not know how long it will take. Have patience, try not to worry too much," he reassured me in a fatherly voice.

Feeling more hopeful, I tried to enter into the spirit of camaraderie with the other women. Relatives arrived in the afternoon with roasted chicken, beans, falafel and salty tomato salad. Again, my cellmates invited me to partake.

After showering the next morning, followed by tea, I was pleasantly surprised when a guard came to inform me that the Swiss Consul was downstairs waiting to see me. A tall handsome man offered his handshake when I came down the stairs. He said that he had obtained my release for the afternoon, conditioned upon my return to the jail to sleep there that night. As we walked outside into the sunlight, he looked down at my feet in dirty worn sandals. "Perhaps we should go to a shoe store and buy you some new shoes," he suggested.

We walked down Talaat Harb Street, where there are enough shoe stores to shod most of the Egyptian population. There we wandered in and out of shoe stores until we could find a pair of shoes big enough for my size ten feet. Egyptian shoes never seemed to fit me. I have the same problem everywhere. I finally chose a pair of black sandals embossed with pharaonic faces in red and gold. Although they felt uncomfortable, I was hoping they would stretch with time. Besides, they were pretty. The offer of this gift cheered me.

As we wandered toward the Embassy, the Consul looked up at the dilapidated buildings. "This is really an unattractive city," he said, "so full of garbage, trash, crumbling buildings, noise, congested traffic." However, I could see that he found the place interesting—or at least exhilarating—from the twinkle in his eye. At the Embassy, I was served tea and Swiss cookies while we discussed my situation.

"I have not been told the reason you are jailed, since Egyptian government officials do not have to give a reason. However, you do need to leave the country. We can only obtain a two-week visa for you to gather your things and get out of Egypt. We can fly you to Switzerland; there you will have the help you need to get your life back together."

"Thank you. I really appreciate your help, but could I just go to Israel? I have friends there and job possibilities. Maybe I could return to Egypt with a renewed visa." I was having trouble letting go of my dervish identity and my emotional attachments. "Well, that's a possibility; certainly much less of an expense for the Swiss government."

One more cold fitful night was spent in the jail. The next morning I was released under the auspices of the Swiss Embassy; their responsibility was to make sure I left Egypt.

A bus reservation to Toi Aviv, leaving the following day, was made for me. I gathered my belongings from various homes and the Oxford Hotel, and then stored a small tent and other items in a large wooden box on the roof of the Swiss Embassy, following their suggestion. My intention was to return to Egypt after a short stay in Israel, where I felt confident that I could earn money singing and perhaps modeling again at the art school in Jerusalem.

The Swiss Consul accompanied me to the Oxford Hotel, where I planned to spend the night. "I do not like the feeling of this place," he remarked. "I think it is better if you spend the night at the embassy, in the garden social room. Miss Fischer, who you know at the embassy, will accompany you to the bus tomorrow morning." We carried the few small cloth sacks, containing my most essential belongings, and my guitar around the corner to the Embassy.

The social room was a separate building set in the charming landscaped garden. It was furnished with couches, comfortable chairs, and a few tables—one holding a coffee urn. A thick beige rug covered the floor. The Consul left me in the care of Miss Fischer as he wished me all the best, shaking my hand good-bye. By now, it was almost evening. Miss Fischer brought me a small take-out dinner. Intelligent and efficient, this attractive blond woman dressed smartly. She spoke fluent English. As I observed this example of social success—thinking how far those Swiss franc salaries stretched in Egypt, again I questioned my own life style.

The Egyptian djellabias, scarves and long dresses that I loved to wear, appeared shabby to me in the presence of modern Miss Fischer. Exhausted and ill, depleted by myriads of parasites in my body, and more or less penniless since the cockroach accident, I saw myself as an unsuccessful misfit in comparison with the prosperity and practicality of the Swiss Consular service employees.

My father had been one of these—a Chancellor and Vice Consul at consulates in Philadelphia, Los Angeles and San Francisco. As a child and teenager, I had enjoyed the Swiss celebrations and functions. Our home was a meeting place for interesting people from many parts of the world, as well as Switzerland. I loved that international atmosphere. hearing different languages spoken—especially French, as that was the language in which my American mother was most fluent, besides English. My Swiss father spoke five languages.

These Swiss dignitaries had not seen me in my element among the Sufis, where I was treated like a queen. If I had not been so tired, I would have encouraged the Consul and Miss Fischer to accompany me to a mulid that evening. Although the Consul had shown an interest in attending such a festivity, Miss Fischer said that I needed my sleep for the early morning departure. She would come to fetch me at 4 a.m. Miss Fischer commented on how my appearance had degenerated since my earlier visits to the embassy. "It is obviously time for you to get out of Egypt," she remarked. "You used to look beautiful and healthy. Now you are exhausted, without enough money to take care of yourself. Illness takes its toll." She looked weary, as if my fatigue was rubbing off on her.

We arranged the large couch cushions on the floor, where I preferred to sleep, and placed a small lamp near the head of my bed so I could read. It was a cool late January night. A small electric heater purred nearby to warm the room. Miss Fischer left. I could not seem to concentrate on the book I was reading. Though debilitated from lack of sleep, I was thinking about the festivities at the Sidi Ali Zayn al-Abidin mu lid, visualizing the lights, the people, the energy I so loved.

I walked outside into the garden and to the high wall that surrounded the grounds. There was no way to climb over it. I was locked in. What could have been a healing space became a prison. I finally dozed off for an hour or two before Miss Fischer arrived promptly at 4 a.m. She helped me put my bundles into the car and then drove me to the bus station.

A drowsy bunch of tourists rode in semi-silence—most people sleeping—to the Israeli border at Rafah. The bus stopped in front of a duty-free shop, the driver saying that we had fifteen minutes to shop before we boarded the bus and passed through customs. I had a few Egyptian pounds left and decided to look for a gift for a friend in Israel.

The bus had already driven over to the Israeli immigration checkpoint when I left the shop. I walked to the bus as the last person, except for me, was showing his passport to a young Israeli officer. My papers were in order. As the bus driver hailed me to get back on the bus, a young Israeli official came up to me, with my passport in his hand. "What were you doing in Egypt for five years?" "I was singing and dancing with the dervishes," I replied. He looked at me suspiciously. Further questioning made me think that he thought that I might be a spy for Egypt. He told me that I would have to return to Egypt. Feeling estranged, I walked across the pavement to the Egyptian border control. The officials were friendly, welcoming me back to Egypt. "Your temporary permit gives you two more weeks in Egypt before you need to leave or renew your visa," they told me.

A sherut taxi was filling up with Egyptians. I ran over to see where they were going. "Cairo," they called. The word "Cairo" sounded like honey to my ears. Cairo had been my main home for the past five years. I already missed the familiar friendly faces that greeted me everywhere I went in Cairo. With this ride, I could get to the last few hours of leila kebir at Sidi Ali. I swung my sacks onto the floor space beneath an empty seat and hopped in.

We were a tight fit in the taxi. Some of the Egyptians were going to the mulid. They were full of devotion for Allah and the saint whose birthday we would celebrate. I hoped to sleep, but could not. My body had already had enough driving for one day and now it had to endure another five hours of engine vibrations, sitting in a cramped position. It was after midnight when we finally arrived at the Cairo sherut station. Six of us shared a taxi to Sidi Ali, where the mulid was still in full swing. I was overjoyed to be in the bosom of my Sufi family again, although I only saw El Arabi beatifically asleep on a couch at Sheikh Mohammed's hidema.

After the sun rose, a young woman I faintly knew invited me to sleep at her family's tomb-home in the Sidi Ali graveyard. She offered me her clothes-piled bed, where I managed to catch a few hours of sleep entangled—almost strangled—in clothes, while serenaded by strong deep snoring from nearby beds.

Sunlight warmed the salon when I entered in early afternoon. Goat's cheese, bread, tahini and tea were offered. The goats were chewing hay in a raised pen at the back of the room, their faces peering over the wood rails as they watched us eat cheese from their milk. They were part of the family. I thanked them for such nourishment as I partook of my late breakfast.

That evening I intended to sleep early, but music coming from the nearby mosque beckoned me over for leila latima, where a great zickring session took place in front of the mosque. El Arabi was not there.

It was afternoon by the time I found a telephone on the street to call the Swiss Embassy to tell them I was back. "You are here in Cairo?" the secretary's amazed voice asked. "Well, you will need to come over here tomorrow morning to talk to the Consul. He is gone for the day."

The Consul's handsome face was wearing a slight frown when I entered his office the next morning. "What happened?' he asked. I sighed and told him the story. "We will just have to fly you to Switzerland," he responded after I told him about my aborted attempt to enter Israel. "I will begin making arrangements for you today. You will probably need to go to Graubunden, your place of family origin. That is how the system works in Switzerland, even though you were born in Bern. There is also a good hospital near St. Moritz; there you can get necessary medical attention. As soon as I find a home for you to live in, I will make a plane reservation. Miss Fischer will go with you now to find a place to stay in Cairo for your remaining days here. Good luck! Do not get into any trouble in the meantime."

TWENTY-ONE

*T*he next ten days were a dervish whirl of activity, plus confusion. I had convinced the Swiss Consul that I needed the next ten days of my visa to organize my belongings and say good-bye to friends.

Just a block down the street from the Oxford, I found a room in a quiet old hotel. Miss Fischer thought the hotel was quite charming, especially for its low price of five L.E. per night. The elevator did not work. I had to climb up five flights of stairs to get to my room. It was a large double room with two beds in it, a sink, a large hanging closet and a couple of chests of drawers. Down the hall was a bathroom; there was no hot water from the bathtub spigots, so I paid a servant fifty piasters to bring me a bucket of hot water to mix with the cold in the bathtub. The Swiss Embassy would have put me up in a more modern hotel but I wanted to nestle into as much Egyptian life style as possible for my remaining days. Only a few travelers were staying at this hotel. Most of the occupied rooms harbored single Egyptian businessmen.

The Egyptian man who lived in the room next to me spoke fluent English. He yearned for the good money he had earned while in Germany. ' Life was much easier there, more comfortable, except for my German wife. She made my life miserable. She will not even let me see my children now. Here in Egypt I have a low-paying job, living my bachelor life in this hotel. "You will be better off in Switzerland," he advised. When I told him that I was in love with an Egyptian dervish, he asked, "Why isn't he here with you," implying that I could bring him to my room. "Because I do not want any more hassles with the police," I replied.

In the meantime, I visited old dervish haunts. One afternoon El Arabi found me in the flat of a friend of ours near Sayyidah Zaynab. "There's nothing to do here," he said. "Let's go visit Iman in al Matariyyah." We hopped into a taxi and soon arrived at the dark two-room flat of Iman, his wife and baby daughter. Iman was glad to see El Arabi and I together. His wife was sweet and welcoming. We ate, and then bathed, pouring buckets of hot water over each other's head.

The next day we took a sherut to Zagazig to attend a small mulid. An attractive dervish woman offered us tea, flirting conspicuously with El Arabi. "Hiya helwa?" (She is beautiful?) El Arabi looked at me as if requesting my opinion. or to show me that there were attractive Egyptian women around, to help ease any longing he might have for me when l left.

Zagazig is the town where my first Egyptian boyfriend, Kamal, had grown up. I had heard that he had married an American woman who worked at the U.S. Embassy. Now he was earning good money in the United States, following his dream. He had been saving enough money to buy a piece of land in Zagazig. El Arabi wanted to take me to the mosque where Kamal's father was the Imam. "Ana hunak min kable," I responded. ("I have been there before.")

We continued our journey through the Delta to visit a Sufi farmer and his family near Dumyat. The men were warm and hospitable.

The women acted sweet at first, but when one of my favorite scarves disappeared, l became aware of a subtle jealousy.

One of the wildest dervishes I have ever met joined us at the house in Dumyat. Yusef claimed that he was not a Muslim. He said he was a Christian, but more than anything, he was a dervish. He would espouse his philosophy in a dialect of Arabic that was not always easy to understand, however the dramatic antics he used to illustrate what he was saying left no doubt about the message he was trying to convey. "I am dead to the world," he would exclaim, as he fell back onto the ground, supine.

Yusef had recently married a young girl; a marriage arranged by the parents of both families. He did not want to be married. "I did not consummate the marriage and I am not going back. They can find her another husband. I am already married to Allah," this ecstatic wandering ascetic exclaimed, his wild dark eyes dancing with light. "Ana dervish!" ("I am a dervish.")

While El Arabi conversed with the farmers, helping them sometimes, I took walks along the river near the house where we stayed, set into gently rolling terrain. The breeze and sweet music of the river softened the harshness of my present reality. One day El Arabi and I visited a family that lived right on the river. Walking down the dirt path to their hut, passing a delicate flowering tree, I thought it was a beautiful setting. As we turned a bend in the path, nearing the house, my illusion was shattered by the sight of heaps of trash and garbage in the reeds along the river bank next to the hut; plastic among the papyrus. I wondered why the family did not recycle. Perhaps they had no way, not even a donkey, to cart the rubbish away. Where would they take it?

Time was running out for me in Egypt, like the Nile River, which had almost reached the Mediterranean Sea where it would disappear into the larger body of water. El Arabi and I both felt tired and discouraged, wondering if there was a better way to resolve the situation, yet wanting to share this time together without hassles. Having sung for many politicians, I might have been able to pull a few strings through connections. I even had a letter from President Hosni Mubarak in response to a letter I had written him about my love of Egypt and its strong spiritual energy. However, there were too many choices, time-consuming undertakings that demanded my time. Perhaps my body was longing for a more comfortable environment and a chance to regain its health.

During our last evening at this little cottage, El Arabi propped me up on bolsters on the high bed to sing for the Sufi family. I combined almost every Sufi song I had composed into one long musical epic—a dervish symphony with many movements, including a sad Arabic love song, which expressed so much of my own feelings. I touched the source of human emotions—all the love, hope, joy, sorrow, compassion, longing and disappointment that I had experienced resounded through my voice.

When I finished singing, El Arabi looked up at me from his seat on the floor. His eyes were filled with love, acknowledgment and respect for the spirit that I channeled. We were connected to the well from which our love had sprung forth. No one spoke for a long time. We sat in the silent aftermath, allowing the energy to recede gently, gradually, basking in the stillness.

The next day Yusef accompanied El Arabi and me to Dumyat to find transportation to our respective destinations; El Arabi and I to find a sherut to Cairo, Yusef to return to his village to tell his family that he wanted out of the marriage.

Just as El Arabi and I were stepping into a sherut taxi, a policeman came up to us, asking us to accompany him to the police station. Perhaps he was suspicious about an Egyptian man accompanying a foreign woman. In a small town like Dumyat, such an alliance was questionable. Even in Cairo, I have heard police officers telling Egyptian men that they must have a tourist escort permit before they could accompany foreign female tourists. Neither of us was happy about the questioning, but we were not harassed. As soon as the Chief of Police looked at my passport and asked El Arabi a few questions, we were on our way.

During the drive back to Cairo, El Arabi slept most of the way. There was not much to say; I felt sad. In Cairo, El Arabi suggested that I meet him at Sheikh Shamubi's villa in the Delta in two days. Perhaps he wanted to consult the sheikh about our situation, maybe even have him marry us officially. El Arabi could see that I needed sleep and some quiet time while he went to a mulid in Fayyum. I indicated that I was not sure that I wanted to travel north again. The preparatory stages of the Sayyidah Zaynab mulid were beginning.

A few days later I was singing at a hidema at Sayyidah Zaynab when El Arabi entered, watching me lovingly. When I finished the song. he motioned me to follow him. He walked ahead, limping slightly as he leaned on his staff, giving the appearance of an old man. Occasionally he would tum his head to see if I was following behind. He led me into an old building, then up two flights of stairs. A sheikh friend opened the door when El Arabi knocked.

A few men and one woman were sitting in a circle, smoking a water pipe. Food was offered. El Arabi discussed my imminent departure from Egypt, seeking advice from the elders. They were mostly uneducated people, with little experience in such matters. The sheikh presented me with a few used cassettes, music of Om Khalsoum and Sufi munshidin. "We will miss you a lot, Tahra. You will probably come back soon."

No one knew how slow I am to leave a place, or how long it takes me to return. Once situated somewhere, I usually stay awhile. I seem to become absorbed into whichever culture or environment I am in, though never more so than in Egypt.

Why am I making such a big deal about this journey, I thought. I am just taking a three-hour plane ride to Switzerland. However, in my heart I knew differently. I wanted to have a strong reason to return to Egypt. I wanted El Arabi to confirm a deep love for me. I wanted to put that love in a box that I could hold up, so I could clearly see my direction. However, love cannot be encapsulated. Love, like water, flows in different directions with varied currents. Sometimes it glides smoothly along, it can be as peaceful as a still lake, at other times it rushes and cascades tumultuously with passion, or myriads of other rhythms and feelings.

El Arabi and I would glance at each other every now and then, as though trying to find the truth of our relationship, perhaps to even find fault with one another in order to make parting easier. I thought about how our sexual unions were often brief or hurried, even though El Arabi aroused great passion in me. He usually just took me when he wanted me, without precoital caresses—probably due to lack of private space or time. In some ways, this suited me just fine; no time to think, just respond to the passionate loving energy. "Inte mush araf hage bikhusus nisa," I proclaimed to El Arabi in front of the sheikh. ("You don't know anything about women.") El Arabi understood what I meant. At the same time, unspoken images of rapturous moments spent together engulfed me. I felt that El Arabi was also remembering such moments.

Our eyes met in that space of lovers' secret sharing. I recalled the night in Kafre al-Shibon, under the strands of twinkling colored lights after El Arabi had swept my naked praying body off the little prayer rug on the cold earthen floor and carried me to the large quilted warm bed. I thought about the New Year's Eve in a large tent behind Sayyidna El Hussein mosque, the night I was wearing my circular sequined ghawaz.ee skirt from Luxor. El Arabi had come close to me with his heart that night, telling me that I looked especially beautiful. The other Sufis in the tent were sleeping while we silently fondled, kissed and merged into rapturous union.

Now, on this rainy night, near Sayyidah Zaynab, El Arabi retorted, "Inti mush arif hage bikhusus flus." ("You don't understand anything about money.") Yet, in this state of mutual recollections we both softened, accusations abandoned in their trivia. The power of lovers took reign; our spirits fused, a treasure that we did not want to lose. Both of us were financially bereft and devoid of energy to rectify the present situation.

Perhaps for some seekers of spiritual truth, carnal encounters are considered debasing. I discovered that the sublime is experienced in moments when sensuality and spirituality fuse. Understanding in the mind is not always enough. When realizations take root in living experiences—within flesh, bones, womb, or in the deep rivers of the soul, I can best praise God.

Sitting in that dimly lit damp room, I thought back to the first spring mu lid in Tanta that El Arabi and I had shared. We were like teenagers; our love fresh, a new adventure, overjoyed with the delights of just being together. Walking hand-in-hand or looking into each other's eyes was enough to center us into our own universe. Everything that happened around us was simply a stage for our love story to unfold. The stage was colorful most of the time, with a background of music, zikr, and tribal unity. It felt as if an unseen force guided our love scenarios. We had the leading roles in this romance; the supporting cast was terrific.

Instead of taking the lead by inviting El Arabi to my hotel during those last few days, I followed him like a puppy dog to that dingy room each night, where we just talked and ate with a few elderly men. Perhaps we needed fatherly guidance. In the condition that I was in, these patriarchs probably saw little that I had to offer. I had never even cooked a meal for El Arabi. I never had a kitchen in Egypt. My mother used to say, "the way to a man's heart is through his stomach." She served her husband gourmet health-food meals.

One time in Tanta when I was tired of mushy vegetables cooked in tomato sauce, I asked my hostess if I could cook myself a potato. I was yearning for a baked potato with sour cream. Without an oven, I settled for a firm boiled potato, which I sliced lengthwise, inserting dabs of butter, salt, pepper, and a glob of yogurt—my substitution for sour cream—that I found in the icebox.

Taking the potato into the living room, I relished the moment I would bite into it. "Inte aize butata," ("Would you like some potato?") I asked El Arabi. "La!" ("No!") His face contorted with disgust. My culinary arts lost the one and only point they might have made in his eyes.

As I rose from a cross-legged position on that final night in Egypt, my left knee did not function properly. I arose slowly, awkwardly, trying to ease the unfamiliar pain. El Arabi regarded my feeble rising. I did not try to explain my dysfunctional knee. I was being torn up by the roots, wrenched out of the nourishing fertile soil; a plant accustomed to growing under brilliant sun, and the psychedelic lights and music of all-night festivals. A lotus had been born in my heart: in the wetlands of the Delta, along the long winding ribbon of the Nile River, and across the deserts. Now this fragile flower was being handled, inspected, criticized, and thrust out into cold mountainous regions of the north.

I already had glimpses of the western mind among Egyptians who embraced a materialistic western life-style. They did not want to be distracted from their view of progress by the illumination of spirituality. They wanted what I had rejected, while I embraced their old-fashioned customs, immersed in a traditional, ancient life-style. I could contrast modern western mentality by observing tourists caught in a time schedule that did not allow for spontaneity or the unexpected. They usually scheduled one or two weeks to ·see the sights'. Nor did they see the scenes behind the doors and windows, or touch the souls behind Egyptian eyes. They did not have time to let the moment unfold in its own rhythm.

Letting go of limitations, I abandoned myself to the present, delighting in the drama in which I was enfolded, leaving the direction to divine guidance. When the script became beset with difficulties, I lacked the energy or means to set limitations, to form a mold for the dream. The dream melted like warm Jell-O, running through the mosques, alleys and turf of Egypt, until it seeped through the asphalt cracks of Cairo and into the soil. Perhaps the compost of shared memories has fertilized some other hearts and souls; it has mine.

It was four in the morning when El Arabi and I got up to leave the sheikh's flat on that last night in Egypt; just enough time for me to pack my belongings before Miss Fischer would pick me up at the hotel to take me to the airport. On a small table in the sheikh's salon lay the large old iron hotel key—the key to my room. El Arabi picked it up, obviously wondering why we were not behind that door instead of where we were. He moaned wistfully, looking at me strangely, a question in his voice and eyes. We walked down the stairs and into the night without words.

The last I saw of El Arabi was his lanky figure loping off dismally in a light drizzle toward the mosque of Sayeda Zeinab. Tears distorted my vision as I rode off in a taxi to my hotel. For me, the light rain would soon be replaced by snow, but tears would continue to blur even spectacular vistas.

TWENTY-TWO

L is March now. The residents of St. Moritz are happy that snow has blanketed the countryside; this will bring the tourists. There was no snow until late February, on the day of my arrival in Switzerland, when it began snowing everywhere. Now there is more than enough powder for excellent skiing.

It was a lovely journey, glimpsed through tears and train windows; first the charming fairy tale buildings near the train station in Zurich, then whizzing by lakes, mountains and waterfalls, quaint villages, crossing bridges over deep gorges where water rushed and tumbled.

My right elbow is throbbing. The doctor in Sits says that it will always be painful. "Just take painkillers. If it gets too bad come over for an injection to kill the pain," he said. The doctor at the hospital in Samedan told me that the surgery performed on my elbow in Egypt was old fashioned. "They removed a piece of bone, which was totally unnecessary," he said. "There is not much we can do about it."

I decided there was something I could do about it; I began swimming a few times a week at the Heilenbad in St. Moritz, I also took advantage of other therapies offered there: hot mineral baths, mud-grass packs and massage.

In the hospital, my mind keeps returning to Egypt, to the Sufis, and most of all, to El Arabi. I usually go off to the rarely occupied reading room to cry and write my memoirs, which seems to help. Now I am supposed to wait in bed for a call to visit the psychiatrist; a new idea since some of the nurses and patients have been worried about my crying spells, which l cannot always control.

A nurse is briskly at my bedside, rousing me from my reverie. "Come with me now to see Dr. Gottingham." I follow her through the hall, down a flight of well-scrubbed stairs, and through some corridors. "Sit here," she points to a chair outside of a door. "The doctor will call you soon." A pleasant stocky man opens the door, smiles and beckons me into his large office. "Now Madame, what is the problem? The nurses have observed you crying a lot. They are concerned about you." I took a few photos out of a small envelope, placing them on his large desk. He spread them out and then stood looking at them. They were pictures of me dancing with the dervishes among tombs in graveyards, singing for festivals, and a photo of El Arabi and me taken on the evening that we first met at Sidi Ali. No one else had shown much interest in my photos; people often look ill at ease when I show them. Perhaps they do not want to be reminded of other realities, especially such strange ones.

The psychiatrist listened as I explained each photo and a bit about my life in Egypt. I was in his office less than twenty minutes. "Why, there is nothing wrong with you," he exclaimed. "You are just suffering from culture shock." "But I didn't feel any shock, or even feel strange in Egypt," I replied. "I felt completely at home." "That is the way it usually works," he said. "Culture shock is experienced when returning to one's homeland or a society that is similar to what one was used to before."

Later, when mulling this idea over, I thought that culture shock is perhaps, experienced when returning from a spontaneous playful society to a more serious organized society, where time and stress often play major roles.

The psychiatrist gave me a warm smile as he escorted me to the door. "It might take a few months for you to re-adapt, but you have nothing to worry about. This is a natural reaction. Hmm! Five years did you say? That is a long time to be in such an unusual society, especially in your case. It must have been an intense experience among those dervishes. Well, good luck!" Another encouraging smile as he shook my hand.

Monsieur Gaudense from the Swiss Social Services, beaming with his usual warm compassionate smile, was waiting by my bed when I returned. I felt that he somehow understood that the transition was not easy for me. I appreciated his kindness. "'Bonjour, Madame." He handed me an Elle magazine in English. "I thought you might enjoy looking at the fashions. There is also an article about some Balkan women singers who are becoming successful, which may be of interest to you." I later did submit a short article about my experience in Egypt, which Elle magazine published.

This kind man was acknowledging the singer in me. Many Swiss people did not consider singing to be a practical profession. Still smiling, Monsieur Gaudense handed me a chocolate ladybug wrapped in black polka-dotted red foil. Another person would hand me the same kind of chocolate ladybug, two years later, when I would leave Switzerland for my mountain home in northern California.

epilogue

*A*s I write this, the world is on fire with wars and weather. Unusual high temperatures—reaching into the 100s fahrenheit, pervade Northern California, where I live. We have also been besieged by wildfires induced by climate change. While these effects of global warming remind us that we need to replace the use of fossil fuels with alternative energy, the sun is screaming for attention: "I am here, free of charge, for you to harness my energy."

Having spent seven years of my life in the Middle East—five years in Egypt, more than a year in Israel, and several months in Morocco—I feel a deep psychic connection with that area of the world. This connection also includes human suffering.

Terror inflicted upon others is what breeds terrorism. We need only to look at the countries that have the most weapons—those that use military might to control others—to find the source of terrorism. Instead of demonizing others, especially those who dwell on top of oil reserves, we need to confront and root out our own demons. Blinded by greed, the 'powers that be' (soon to be replaced by more enlightened beings, Inshallah) have lost sight of the true value of cultures of various diversity. They have lost the ability to see the great offerings of history, science, and the arts. Many people in the United States do not even know that our numerical system is of

Arabic origin. These are the real treasures we should be exchanging, not armaments or gunfire. Our chiefs in Washington have said that they are going to "remake the Middle East." They have not even learned to understand the culture, the language, the essence of Islam, or the beauty and creativity that abound in that region of the world. If they would truly listen to beautiful Middle Eastern music, their souls could experience that place where we all come from. They have not been receptive enough to know what they are going to "'remake". What they seem to mean is: "We are going to control you. Once we destroy your culture, we will replace it with the American way of life: consumerism. You can shop in a Wall-Mart, while we take your oil."

If Iraq—as well as all countries that have been irrevocably damaged by wars and sanctions—are examples of "remaking", I cringe to think about the consequences of such occupations. Only ignorance and greed could provoke the destruction of the seat of civilization, Mesopotamia, where Iraq is situated.

We not only harm ourselves when we hurt others, we hurt all of nature. All forms of life are interconnected; even our breath becomes part of the air we share. Many alternative energy sources are available. The sun is shouting, "Collect my light, I won't even charge you." The wind offers herself freely to spin a wind turbine. Nature, like woman, does not need to be raped to capture her inner treasures. She offers herself willingly, when taken with respect and integrity, with knowledge, wisdom and love.

If man has the capability to make enough weapons to destroy the planet, he can certainly use his intelligence to create a better world, including the use of renewable energy, rather than destroy such a beautiful, bountiful planet, that offers us what we need as long as we use her resources wisely.

Instead of bombing the world into pieces, we need to open our eyes, our ears, our minds, and our hearts to the vast gifts that the Middle East has to offer, as well as those from all parts of the world. We may even learn to say "Marhaban!" ("Welcome!") Once we have learned to appreciate cultures—different from our own, we may find ourselves saying, "Shukran!" ('Thank You!'). Soon, we will form a chorus of voices raised, singing: "Salaam," "Shalom," "Peace"

ACKNOWLEDGEMENT

*M*ost of all, I am deeply grateful to the Sufis of Egypt for enfolding me into their society and mystical practices, plus teaching me their sacred music, which enabled me to contribute to spiritual expressions of devotion. They nourished me with food and love, encouraged my talents as a Munshid, singing sacred music in Arabic. Shukran! I am also grateful for their visitations in my dreams since I left Egypt, keeping our connection alive. I cannot find enough thanks for Sheikh Sayyid Mohammed Abd el-Rahman for introducing me to numerous fine Sufis, their families and clans in many parts of Egypt—particularly the Delta. His guidance was invaluable.

Thanks to my friend, Lilith Babbellon, an English witch, who I met the Oxford Hotel in Cairo, for encouraging me to write an article about my experiences with the Sufis in Egypt and submitting it to SHE Magazine in London. Having my work published, inspired me to continue writing.

I am grateful to the Swiss Consulate in Cairo, for aiding me during illnesses and problems in Egypt, and for sending me to Switzerland to recover. There I was kindly helped, especially in Sits, Grauubunden, in the Engadin—the village where my Swiss father and his lineage is from. A large Triumph typewriter was loaned to me when I received requests from European magazines for articles about my experiences in Egypt.

With affection, I extend my gratitude to Adelina Kuhn-Robbi and her family for inviting me into their home and encouraging me to work on my book manuscript while I was in Sits.

Thanks to all the wonderful people who take care of Salecina, the beautiful vacation center in the mountains of Maloja, Switzerland. Some of the happiest days of my life were spent there; it was a great place to work on my book and enjoy international camaraderie.

Special thanks to Martin Frishnecht, editor of Spuren magazine in Switzerland, who, after requesting the 'love story', invited me to his office outside of Zurich, where he gave me my first lessons on a computer (programmed in German), and offered me the use of his office to write the article for Spuren. He later introduced me to the editor of Tages Anzieger, which published a feature article I wrote, Tanz den Allah, in their weekly Magazine, Das Magazin.

Back in the United States, I extend thanks to Leslie Williams, owner of Orr Hot Springs, who believed in the value of my book project, offering me the use of his computer and office, including computer tutoring.

Dorotheya Dorman contributed her editing expertise., imbuing my manuscript with grammatical protocol.

If my wonderful artist friend, Ruth Frolich, had not invited me to visit her in Ein Hod, Israel, I might never have found myself so close to Egypt that I could not resist crossing over the border.

After reading my manuscript-of-the-moment, Hana Alisa Omer, a gifted artist and friend, who I met in Israel, contributed a beautiful painting, which I used for my first book cover. To see her other paintings, check her website: Hana Alisa Omer roz. Loeve.

Raul Parra Orizondo, who I met in Cuba a few years ago, has been a super energizer of my book and music projects, advising me in many ways. He has designed a beautiful website for me, as well as using his professional and knowledgeable skills to publicize my book, including Social Media. His website is: www.cordastutech.com.

Now, for this edition of my book, I discovered the photo shop talents of Deborah Hunter, to help redesign my book cover. Deborah Hunter also assisted me while recording the audio version of my book. More recently, she has been editing my audio book, which is now available. Deborah can be contacted through her website: www. deborahhunterart.net.

Also, thanks to Jacob Nasim for final Master editing of Audio Book.

*   *   *

ARABIC-ENGLISH GLOSSARY

afreet	— ghost, disembodied spirit that sometimes embodies or plays with people
agnebi (a)	— foreigner
aiwa	— yes
Alhamdullilah!	— Praise be to God!
Allah	— God
ana	— I
Asalamalaikum!	— Peace be with you! Used as a greeting, like 'hello'
baraka	— blessings
chador	— long dress and hair covering worn by orthodox Muslim women
djellabia	— long robe-dress worn by Middle Eastern men
enti or inti (fem.)	— thou, you
ersh	— Egyptian money (pennies)
ettawil	— tall
fakir	— poor person (sometimes a mendicant)
felafel	— a popular Middle Eastern food; pita filled with deep-fried chick pea balls, lettuce, tomato, tahini and humus
fellahin	— peasant, farmer
ful	— beans

gagir	— watercress
gidden	— very
gowa	— inside
hadra	— to be present, to practice zikr at Sufi gathering
haram	— forbidden
helwa	— beautiful
hidema	— place where a Sufi clan gathers at a festival
hiya	— she
howa	— wind
howaria	— wandering like the wind
hunack	— there
huwa	— he
imam	— a prayer leader in a mosque; a spiritual guide
inshallah	— if it pleases God, hopefully
inte (masc.)	— thou, you
jinn	— ghost, apparition
kaman	— also
kebir	— great, big
ketir	— much, very
kushary	— macaroni dish with lentils, tomatoes, crisp fried onions on top
kwaiyis	— fine, ok
leila	— evening
ma'assil or tempek	— tobacco mixed with molasses for water pipes
macam	— sanctuary, place of pilgrimage
magreb	— first meal of the day after fasting (right after sunset)
marhaban (pl.)	— welcome, greetings
masking	— poor
Masr, Misr	— Egypt, also a popular name for Cairo
midan	— square, plaza

mish	— not
mulid	— annual festival commemorating the birthday of a dead saint or sheikh
mulihiya	— a slimy green leaf vegetable
mumkin	— maybe, possibly
munshid	— singer of sacred music, such as Sufi ballads and odes in praise of Allah and the Prophet Mohammed
mussein	— person who calls people to prayer (usually from the top of a mosque)
nur	— light
ragabiya	— small mulid, 6 months from the large mulid
Ramadan	— month of fasting
renne	— sing
saha	— meeting place for Sufis, it is the space for a group of spiritual practitioners
saiidi	— person from Upper Egypt
sawa	— together
schwaya	— a little, small
seisha	— water pipe
sheikh	— spiritual teacher and leader
sherut	— collective taxi
shukran (pl.)	— thank you
summe	— fast, abstinence
sura	— verse
tarika	— path
tul	— length
tul illail	— throughout the night
Yella!	— Go on! Let's go!
Zikr	— Sufi chanting, usually with movements, often with music

For information about the author, photos, CDs of her music, Egyptian Dervish Dance workshop, book readings and signings, plus other events, visit Tara's website at: www.tarasufiana.com

www.ingramcontent.com/pod-product-compliance
Lightning Source LLC
Chambersburg PA
CBHW020436130626
46549CB00001B/173

*9 7 8 1 9 6 6 6 5 2 4 0 3 *